Fathers and Mothers

by Aldo Naouri

First published by Odile Jacob 2003

Published in the United Kingdom 2005
by Free Association Books
London

© Aldo Naouri 2003

French-English translation by Graham Robert Edwards 2005

All rights reserved, no part of this publication
may be reproduced, stored in a retrieval system,
or transmitted, in any form or by any means,
without the prior permission in writing
of the publisher.

This book is sold subject to the condition
that it shall not, by way of trade or otherwise,
be lent, resold, hired out or otherwise circulated
without the publisher's prior consent in any form
other than that supplied by the publisher.

British Library Cataloguing in Publication Data
A catalogue record for this book is available from the British Library

Produced by Bookchase, London
Printed and bound in the EU

ISBN 1 853437697

For my grandchildren

By The Same Author

Published By Odile Jacob (Paris)

De l'inceste, with Françoise Héritier and Boris Cyrulnik, 'Opus', 1994, 2001

Le Couple et l'enfant, 1995

Les Filles et leurs mères, 1998

Questions d'enfants, with Brigitte Thévenot, 1999

Réponses de pédiatre, 2000

Published by Éditions du Seuil (Paris)

L'Enfant porté, 1982 and collection 'Points-Seuil-Essais', 2002

Une Place pour le père, 1985 and collection 'Points-Seuil-Essais', 1992

Parier sur l'enfant, 1988, and 'Poches Odile Jacob', 2001

L'Enfant bien portant, 1993, republished 1997 and 1999; new edition 2004.

CONTENTS

Ackowledgements		i
Foreword		iii
Chapter 1	Histories And History	1
Chapter 2	Once Upon A Time	19
Chapter 3	The Gift Of The Father	46
Chapter 4	Solid Mothers Versus Nebulous Fathers	87
Chapter 5	Children At Stake	142
Chapter 6	Restoring The Child To Time	178

ACKNOWLEDGEMENTS

This book would never have seen the light of day without assistance from a host of other books that I read in order to make this one as useful as possible. My initial training, the prejudices acquired during the writing of earlier books and - though it seems indecorous to admit it - a degree of laziness have decided me against quoting chapter and verse for all my sources. All the same, I feel that I must express here my enormous gratitude to all the women and men who, transcending the custom of communicating with peers alone, have published their work and made it accessible to the greater number.

Equally I owe a particular debt of gratitude to four people who, without fully realizing it, became my constant and ongoing conversation partners. They were, in alphabetical order: Françoise Héritier, Marc-Alain Ouaknin, Ginette Raimbault, and Heinz Wismann. In giving their names, I do not in any way presume upon their endorsement, support, or willingness to underwrite my views - far from it, since none of them knew anything about this book prior to its publication. I wish simply to thank them for the friendship that they have honoured me with, and to signal to them how important they are to me. They have been my companions, in no order of preference, during some marvellous moments - moments that they enabled me to experience, like those whose virtues Montaigne famously extolled within the definition of 'conversations'.

I should also like to express here my immense gratitude to my publisher, Odile Jacob, for the trust that she has always shown in me and for the unfailing support that she gave me throughout the writing of this book. I am bound to say that without her none of this would have been possible.

Finally, I am keen to express my thanks to my wife, Jeanne, for the patience and understanding she showed while I was writing this. I am grateful to her for, once again, agreeing to be my first reader and for the frankness, grounded in the length and closeness of our relationship, of the reactions she shared with me.

FOREWORD

Our children are infinitely better off than those of just a few decades ago. Yet although their physical health has considerably improved, they present problems that give increasing cause for concern. I have seen this for myself over the forty years in which I have been in paediatric practice.

We cannot go on ignoring the contribution of parental weakness to this situation, especially in those areas where there is a need to prohibit or thwart certain behaviours or to exercise authority in general. The paternal void, which has recently become such a vogue issue, is no chance effect. It is the result of a long process which has been active over several centuries and which has intensified in recent times.

Things being as they are, the child, having been hoisted to the tip of the pyramid of societal values, has become a domestic tyrant whose exploits are now the subject of park-bench and dinner-party conversations alike.

It is not my aim at this stage to attempt any more detailed analysis than is fairly apparent to anyone who is alert to what is going on around them. What I want to do quite simply is to explore the conditions of existence of the sort of family that is now labelled 'traditional' in an attempt to discover what provides its essence and to see whether this can be integrated into our modern ways of life and outlook. After all, it may be that, having rejected a whole bundle of arrangements considered globally outmoded, we have lost something without which nothing further can be embarked upon, still less built.

This book deals with the mother, the father, and the child. My modest hope is that it may help towards a better understanding of that trio, which is the very essence of life.

Chapter 1
Histories And History

Greta

Greta. No sooner had she sat down than the name lodged in my head with the association that returns to me now - that of Garbo, the famous, icy heroine of the interwar period. This Greta had the same beauty, the same carved features, carriage of the head, reserve.

She had come a long way to see me with her little Cécile. Cécile hadn't slept a single night during her sixteen months of life. As she sat straight-backed in her chair, Greta related to me the medical merry-go-round, the projected diagnoses, the various pieces of advice lavished upon her, and the treatments tried without the least effect. I listened to her as she went over the details of her daughter's draining symptoms. The more she said, the stronger grew the diagnostic hypothesis that was entering my head. So much so that, without even examining her child, I wrote and handed her a referral, saying that I was convinced that an oesophageal and gastric fibroscopy would reveal an oesophagitis. She seemed surprised. I didn't like to tell her how sorry I was that no-one had previously mentioned this diagnosis, despite the fact that it was so blatantly obvious. I slowly went back through what she had told me to show how it was consistent with the step I suggested. She left, seemingly unconvinced and undoubtedly somewhat vexed.

As chance would have it, the next day I was on a visit when my colleague called me to say that she had little Cécile in front of her. She had just left the surgery of the specialist I had recommended - I had never imagined that she would be seen so quickly. The results of the fibroscopy indicated an oesophagitis with an advanced ulcer, and this had prompted the mother to return to our practice immediately without further notice. My colleague asked me what sort of treatment I envisaged. I gave her the details and requested that she tell Cécile's mother to bring her daughter back to me for a further consultation in three or four weeks' time.

I didn't need to wait that long. The following day, Greta telephoned me, declaring that the medicines had worked wonders - I ought to mention that I had prescribed the strongest ones straight away - and she said that the very same evening Cécile had slept through the night for the first time in her life. Then she added: 'Even so I need to see you myself. As soon as possible, please.'

I didn't know what she had to tell me, and I couldn't see what bearing it might have on the diagnosis I'd made. I generally take such requests seriously, but I had no suspicion that our next meeting would be the first of a series extending over several months.

I very soon learned what lay at the heart of the drama Greta wanted to talk about. She told me of the existence of a first, second, and then third lover in her life. Her mental torment came from the fact that she didn't know which of the four men with whom she was having sexual relations was the father of her child. She had racked her brains and done all the relevant calculations without being able to come to a final judgement. She had got round to thinking that Cécile was the daughter of the man with whom she shared her life, but she had major regrets about her inability to be totally certain. Beginning there - and without any active prompting from me - our meetings gradually went back over her life until she disclosed the memory of an incestuous attempt on her by her father when she was about ten years old. The attempt failed when someone else came into the room where, in a drunken state after a meal, her father had cornered her. He had said to her: 'Forget you're my daughter. If you aren't, you won't mind doing what I ask.'

Her story left me wondering whether her sexual behaviour was an unconscious desire to preserve Cécile from the eventuality of an incestuous act. Or, to put it another way, was it a highly ambivalent attempt to free her from having a solid link to her father? Be that as it may, once the child was there, Greta had felt bad about condemning her daughter to that sort of uncertainty.

A Transacted Life

Their son was only five months old. But the ferocity of their conflict over him had reached unbearable heights.

They had known each other for many years. She was a senior executive in a large industrial group and he was head of department in a subcontracting group; they had frequently done business together. Despite meeting regularly at luncheons, seminars and other training sessions, they had kept their distance, and continued to address each other by the formal French second person singular, vous. I was somewhat thrown by this when I first heard them talking together. Until, that is, they told me their full story.

One day, during a routine business luncheon, the two had got round to talking about their lives. His personal drama was that, though married for over twenty-five years to a woman he loved, he had not been able to have children with her, despite recourse to the panoply of remedies afforded by medicine for this type of problem. She was so moved by his distress that she immediately asked herself how she might help him. She herself understood the joys of parenthood: she had a daughter of 15 with whom she was so delighted that she had been able to resign herself to having no more children when her husband became sterile after a prostate operation. She admitted to her luncheon companion that she could easily imagine the pain she herself and her husband might have gone through, had she been unable to have children.

When they parted, they felt a little closer to each other, having each imparted to the other a small detail of their personal lives.

Fathers and Mothers

It was she who, some time later, during another of their luncheon dates, brought the subject up again. She said she had found the ideal solution to her colleague's problem. She had even discussed the idea with her husband, who thought it made sense and had unreservedly backed it. In effect she was offering herself as a potential surrogate mother who, of course, was disinterested. Children were so wonderful, so full of promise, and so much a part of life, that no one should be deprived of them or ever stop having them. Things would be easy. He would acknowledge paternity during the pregnancy, and she would give birth anonymously. The child would immediately be his responsibility as the father and definitively the couple's, once the wife had gone through a legal adoption procedure. After the shock of surprise - not quite so easy, after all! - champagne was drunk and an understanding arrived at worthy of an agreement between industrial groups. The wife was initially dumbfounded by the report of what was proposed, but ended up concurring fairly enthusiastically. So much so, that ensuing episodes involved downing further bottles of champagne, albeit in the privacy of a hotel room, where the endeavours to effect the solution took place.

Since the transactions were well-intentioned and the protagonists honest, there were no further sexual relations once pregnancy was achieved. The plan was executed to the letter: the father acknowledged his paternity before the birth, the non-biological parties kept out of the arrangements, and the mother gave birth anonymously. After five days, the baby boy was handed over to the father, who took him home to his own and his wife's great joy.

The complications began when the prescribed legal deadline arrived for the generous surrogate to confirm her surrender of her child. This she refused, insisting that the child be returned to her, on the ground that he was hers entirely.

Relations became acrimonious, and the matter became litigious. The court, unaccustomed to dealing with so unusual a case, reduced it to one of reconstituted families and treated it as such. Which was formally pertinent, save that no family had been deconstituted or reconstituted prior to the child's birth. And just as in a previous era the child would have been deemed the fruit of adultery twice over, so the judicial ruling on his status did nothing to resolve the symbolic dimension of the relationships that each of the four parental figures had established with him. The natural mother denied the father's wife any status in regard to him, and reduced the father himself to his mere reproductive functionality, reckoning that her own husband was amply capable of fulfilling the remainder of the task. The natural father would have preferred to make his own wife - much less cruel and perverse in his eyes than the natural mother - the mother of his child, thereby denying the other man, who was called to the rescue, the least role or function.

The Virgin With The Spoon

Disturbing. Touching. Astonishing. More than that even, for their industry, goodwill, modesty, and awkwardness all moved me deeply. He above all seemed not to know where to put himself. With his pleasant face, reminiscent of a rust-coloured bulldog, and his large, sulky moustache, he was trying to check his merest movement, lest he should do any damage with the large hands and massive body which, clearly, had always troubled him. She was small and hunched up, shifting between a blissful smile and a look of real terror, which gave her face and eyes a disturbing mobility. Apparently haunted by the fear of dropping the imposing package that she clutched to her bosom, she continually experimented with ways of holding it. It was a baby, a four-month-old daughter, Marie. She quickly told me that they had obtained her from an organization dealing in international adoptions. Raising the question of their sterility in order to understand its nature and gauge in advance how their experience of it might be affecting their ongoing relationship, I had the impression that I was increasing their uneasiness. Once I explained the sense behind my questioning, he blushed, lowered his head and, fidgeting on his chair, told me that they did not really know whether they were sterile or not. And as he realized that I didn't entirely understand what he was trying to tell me, he went on to say that in twenty years of marriage they had never consummated their union, owing to a complementarity of phobias that they each scrupulously respected. As I doubtless failed to master my surprise, he thought to add, blushing further and rocking slightly on his chair, that this nevertheless did not stop them pleasuring each other.

The consultation continued. I answered their questions about the medium- and long-term effects of adoption, and examined their child, who was doing fine. As they didn't live in the district, I gave them the name of a colleague close to where they lived, provided them with a letter addressed to the colleague, and agreed they would contact me again if and when they felt the need. They went away apparently satisfied. I saw them again occasionally.

One day they came back to announce to me ... a pregnancy! I was delighted with their news, and did not hesitate to congratulate them. I even went so far as to cry up the miraculous effects produced by a first experience of parenthood. I told them how amazingly often in my career I had seen the trial-run offered by adoption trigger pregnancy in couples supposed to be sterile. I was about to tell myself that their so aptly named Marie had had the additional merit of making it possible for them to confront and overcome deep-seated inhibitions. But, as though tapping into my train of thought, the father was concerned to explain to me that they had not altered their normal practices. Anxious to convince me by giving chapter and verse, he spelled out that they had simply looked round for a do-it-yourself solution appropriate to their situation: they had used a teaspoon. 'And it worked first time,' he added, puffing out his chest and giving a cheerful, triumphant look.

I saw them again. This time, with their baby, born of a virgin mother. A boy. They had given him the forenames Victor, Constant, Prudent. It occurred to me that they could not have chosen a finer formula to sum up their project and destiny. They were in seventh heaven. Even so, this did not stop them firing some inevitable questions at me - after all they hadn't come to me to talk about the weather. What could they look forward to? What would be the status and future of siblings where one was adopted and one born naturally? What should they, as parents, do to prevent drawing attention to the children's differences? How ought they to modify their behaviour towards each of them? How should they manage the inevitable jealousy that one child might feel towards the other? How could they achieve an appropriate position of neutrality when needing to arbitrate? As meticulously as they no doubt managed their finances together, they had drawn up a long list of questions, which they ticked off as I gave them answers.

After that I saw only the father, alone. Several months later. His wife, he said, no longer wanted anything to do with him. He was very depressed. She had thrown him out. She had begun by forcing him out of the conjugal bed as soon as she knew she was pregnant. 'Even before, as soon as Marie was there, our moments of intimacy and pleasure became rarer and rarer. They finished altogether once she fell pregnant. She couldn't understand what I was moaning about; she called me a savage.' The situation had then got worse and worse, until she decided to demand a divorce and ordered him to leave immediately. It was now a court case.

It seemed to me that, on top of his frustration as an ejected father, his reason for coming to me was to tell me of another source of distress, that of being unable for quite some time to find another partner with whom to share his phobias and the solutions that he had found.

The Wreck And The Builder

I began by wondering what pretext that the venerably aged couple before me had alleged in order to obtain an appointment from my secretary. I'd have assumed them to be grandparents of one of my little patients, had the sheet in front of me not been blank. What could their visit be about? What could they want of me? What could justify their presence in a paediatrician's consulting room?

She slouched on her chair, ill-kempt, badly dressed, not all that clean. Which was all the more striking, inasmuch as he was bright-eyed, well turned out, upright, and seemed overflowing with energy.

It was nevertheless on account of a child that they had come. 'For our child,' he said. 'My child,' she interrupted, rising out of her torpor. He nodded in my direction, by way of conciliation, as one does in the presence of mad people or ungovernable children, so as not to revive conflict and to have, for a moment at least, some peace.

Even though I as yet knew nothing, his whole person appeared to call me to witness. His misted eyes looked continually at her, then me, then back again. With great patience and in an effort never to use words that might reflect back on him - some escaped, all the same, among them a few rather unkind words - he began telling me their story. They had lived together for more than fifteen years, having met on a holiday beach. He had never had children, had never married, and lived with his ageing mother, who, incidentally, was still alive. She, the woman with him, was divorced, had had four children from two separate households, and was a grandmother several times over. They shared a family life during the early years of their union, followed by a time on their own once the two last children left home. At that point, she fell gravely ill. 'Was that my fault?' she interrupted, accusing him of labouring the coincidence. 'No, of course not,' he hastened to reassure, attempting to grasp a hand that she speedily withdrew. Severe health worries came along one after another, necessitating various surgical operations and amputations, including in the genital area. 'No shortage of complications,' I thought, as I awaited the appearance of the famous child they had both supposedly come about. He'd always been there, he continued, reckoning that the least he could do for her was to be there, and allow her 'at least one hand to hold, as and when she wanted.' That seemed definitely to be the way he handled things, I thought, a pattern inherited from the past if not the expression of a fixation. She hadn't worked for ages, and he was sorry he couldn't give her anything any more or spoil her. 'I didn't ask you for anything!' she interjected, as he carried on trying to explain to me that he had put at her disposal all the proceeds of his small building firm. One day when he had launched into this sort of reckoning up, beseeching her to tell him what more he could do for her, she had seized the opportunity to confess, in tears, that what she needed the most was not money or luxury, but a small child to bring up, that would be really hers, that would give meaning to a life that she felt had become empty. As she seemed transfigured merely by the evocation, he took serious note of what she had said. One evening he came in carrying a thick file. It had cost him a great deal of time, energy, and money, but he came to give her what she asked for: a little boy, three months old, to fetch from Ceylon (Sri Lanka). At first, she didn't believe him. Then, the joy she showed was so great that he had the feeling that he had at last 'really built for [them] both a solid building that could withstand ordeals and time.' 'You can't stop people dreaming,' she murmured, continuing wearily and almost inaudibly, 'but you aren't responsible for their dreams.'

Given his work responsibilities, and his concern about how much everything had cost, including the journey, he suggested to her that she went out alone to pick up their baby.

Which she did.

'When I saw her arrive, with the basket in her hand, I wanted to shout for joy. She finally had what she wanted. And I'd given it to her! But when I saw our little Christophe, my feelings were almost stronger. I sensed that, without realizing it, I too had waited for him, all my life. I felt overwhelmed with gratitude towards her for enabling me to know what I was experiencing for the very first time. Thanks to this woman, and to the idea she had had, which all our friends and acquaintances had regarded as a whim, I at last felt a father.'

This feeling grew stronger as the days passed. So much so that by the time the usual legal procedures for adoption reached the confirmation stage, he presented himself as the father, or at least as the candidate for paternity of the child. It was impressed upon him - such was the legal position then - that he could not be the father as he wasn't married to the adoptive mother. Thinking that this was an easy obstacle to surmount, he addressed himself to his partner of so many years' standing and in an emotional yet simultaneously amused and grandiose fashion asked her to marry him. When she refused, he believed she was joking. But it didn't take him long to perceive that she was entirely serious. He couldn't get used to the idea that he could be sidelined in that way. He went back over the whole story, emphasizing the fact that he was the one who had taken the initiatives. 'You owed me at least that,' she answered, 'after all the time you've lived in my house rent-free!' He repeatedly mentioned the money he had spent in all sorts of circumstances, only to receive the retort that 'money doesn't create parenthood; anyone can buy a child!' She then went on and on about how she had gone in person, and deplorably alone, to fetch the child. He got out his diary and his accounts page to show how much work he had had and the state of his finances at the time, and she then hammered him a bit more by reproaching him for not thinking about taking out a loan. As for the work that was under way, that was just it - 'men are never able to look to higher things and detach themselves from the material side of their existence.'

Several days later, she used registered mail to request him to vacate the premises and never return.

Could I help them ..., he asked - '... help you, perhaps,' she said, cutting him off; 'I never asked for anything, and I don't need any help now.' - to understand how they could manage this situation and share the adventure of parenthood?

'Happy people have no history.' Such has always been the assertion of common sense, and one often overhears this maxim used.

Happy people have no history. You could almost say that the rest drag theirs after them their whole lives long, allowing their actions to consist in passively carrying out a programme imparted to them by their history. In truth those who consciously try to control their life's course do so most often with such ferocity that the result they achieve is scarcely better than the one they sought to avoid. It is also not hard to see how the irony and sadness of such personal blind alleys may have been at the root of the notion of fate (*fatum*), against whose effects the peoples of Antiquity maintained it was vain to struggle.

Such a prospect would be an occasion for despair, were it not open to everyone to acknowledge their limits and to entrust to the next generation the responsibility of righting the helm. Children, conceived in this perspective, have from time immemorial been reckoned to have the wherewithal, thanks to their brand-new energy, determination, and the love put at their disposal, to reverse a contrary lot. They each clearly have no option other than to seize with both hands the history that falls to them; though they do not choose their history, it remains indispensable to them, since it is the foundation of their existence. Whatever it is and whatever this inherited history contains, the child will be there, loyal and enthusiastic, to receive it, renew it, even tussle with it in his or her turn some day. This is what children have always done. It is indeed what establishes and justifies their status.

It is always possible to object to the idea that such an ostensibly dismal logic underlies every act of procreation. One may suspect it of deference to some dark ideology. Or protest against so excessively cynical a description of the cruel fate it appears to deal the child. Or even reject it. It makes no difference. The lot of the child will go on being what it always has been. That is why no individual can be held any more responsible for his or her history than for the unconscious within which it is written.

To have three lovers in addition to one's life-partner may seem reprehensible to many. To spend twenty years of marriage indulging simply in heavy petting and then use an everyday utensil may seem pitiful. To conceive a child on the pretence that it is for someone else may be judged villainous. To take possession of a baby in order to survive, or to enjoy its charms, while priding oneself on having simply intended it as a gift, may be interpreted as acts of exemplary selfishness. All that may be so. Yet none of the protagonists in these histories had, or could have had, any choice other than the one imposed on them by their life equation. The same may equally be said of all those women and men, those fathers and mothers, in more or less ill-assorted couplings or indeed alone, who have taken advantage of the increasingly lenient outlook of recent decades to try to invent new relationships with one another as well as new patterns of parenthood.

It is perhaps gratifying that in our own day means have been found of offering people caught in their own private torments places and techniques capable of providing, if not ready-made solutions, at least a degree of clarity to help them manage their situations. We may rejoice that such approaches, taking account of the ways in which their past may have collided with their present, can sometimes open up a future to them and, more especially, protect children who otherwise would have had to shoulder the burden of their history alone. In earlier times, individuals endowed with similar determinants might have found the course of their existence blocked, even if they did not go mad themselves or pass on a history liable to generate madness. It is their sort of problems, the most frequent today, that societal structures as a whole strive so hard to resolve. Indeed, you might be forgiven for inferring that the only histories thought worth perpetuating were those carefree enough or well-ordered enough not to 'create history'!

But is such perfection practically possible? Is it even theoretically conceivable? A history that is beautiful and has no defects? Some hope! Some illusion. If human beings were satisfied with their fate, if they did not have a desire to change its course, would they continue to procreate? Not necessarily. If it is true that to have a child is a way for people to console themselves for their mortal status, then the desire for a child is never immune from the projects people entertain in regard to their own destinies. This was less obvious years ago, because people simply accepted the large numbers of children that were born then. But nowadays it is the only reason why people procreate. They procreate in order to take revenge on a contrary lot, convinced that they can preserve their children from the error of which they consider themselves to have been victim. In effect they are giving the business the benefit of their experience. They focus on the very area from which they have been set up to believe that the notorious error will come, but they fatally commit another, or others, coming from a different direction, from which the child in turn will want to safeguard his or her own children, and so on, and so on. In short, this is redolent of the strategy employed by prison authorities when dealing with long-term prisoners. They encourage the prisoners to think about their release, however improbable, so as to stop them from committing worse things still. To allow every generation the hope that they will do better than the one before may be a factor of social peace and survival that is integral to the human condition.

Even though it has become more obvious these days, this dynamic has long existed, and there is no shortage of treatises, some of them extremely ancient, showing the concern that our predecessors always had regarding the destiny of the child, and giving advice and recommendations about it. Looking merely at the Roman period, we see that alongside his prerogatives over his children, the Roman father had duties towards them, one of which was that of maintaining their freedom, i.e., safeguarding them from slavery, a duty that the Latin language itself enshrined in the Latin word for children, *liberi* ('free ones'). Since that period, and surely even before that, it seemed important to place the child at the heart of the family, constituted and defined as it was by the cohabitation of a man and a woman, whose relationship was deemed to be necessarily lifelong. Humanity as we know it has experienced tens of centuries of containment exercised by the societal context around the couples that formed within it. It was expected, indeed it was sometimes compulsory, until fairly recent times for individuals who had procreated together to stifle their dissensions, sacrifice their own aspirations and comforts, and remain united on behalf of their child(ren). They moreover made an effort to do so, even if they did not always succeed. This containment, with the associated, clearly differentiated roles and prerogatives of the partners, created for the children the environment in which they developed their personalities.

There is no question any more of all that today. Societies, our western societies in particular, have changed too much, though the current generation may not even be aware how comparatively recent the changes are. Who remembers the difficulties of particular famous couples to gain official recognition of their union, because one or the other or both were already married and they could not undo their earlier ties because divorce was forbidden in their country? It seems incredible, as if surely dating from very long ago indeed, and yet the facts I allude to are less than forty years old. How is it that they have vanished from popular memory? The simple explanation is that the evolution in mentalities has considerably speeded up, and our memories, overburdened with the succession of daily events of which we are over-informed, cannot afford to clutter themselves up with facts that no longer have current relevance.

Things being what they are, the only acceptable, unanimously agreed dimension now is individualism, and every one is encouraged to sacrifice nothing of his or her individual and immediate happiness. It is not at all rare to see young couples quickly form, break up at the first altercation, then re-form and break up again, as though their notion of love could not ride the slightest hitch. Where they have had the desire or the time to procreate, one sees them, years later, with their grown-up children - I have even seen some with their grandchildren - and they then have remarkable observations to make about the damage caused by the long-standing cherishing of illusions. Contrary to what might have been expected, the report they give of their experience is not a proud or positive one. Perhaps it is time to bring back into fashion the notion that parents have a duty towards the children they bring into the world, and that their first duty is to reflect seriously before deciding to separate.

The very idea seems at first sight crazy. Yet it was raised recently by social workers in America, who concluded, on the basis (as ever) of plentiful statistics, that the children whose parents stayed together despite their disagreements did better than those whose parents separated. The evidence seems to argue that couples should be encouraged to treat themselves and use the therapies that have been developed for relationship difficulties. After all, there is no more shame in doing that than in seeking treatment for the skin, the heart, or the stomach. The reason the advice is so little followed is that couples continue to be enthralled by the fantasy - and a toxic one it is at that - of romantic love.

Are we to infer, then, that the nuclear or extended family, supposedly on its last legs, might still have something to say to us or have a future before it? Work that centres on children is starting to suggest answers to this question.

Observation shows that children, especially very young children, are prodigiously sensitive to all that manifests itself in the world above their heads in terms of balance and harmony. So much so indeed that any deterioration, however small, in that balance and harmony is going to produce either lively confrontations on the level of interparental relations - something true of the conflicts in three of the case histories described earlier

- or symptomology, like that exemplified by little Cécile's oesophageal ulcer.

Insofar as we may be able to admit such a precondition, we are precluded from wholesale rejection of the attempts, going right back in time, of societies that were precursors to our own. Instead, we would do well to examine and question the project they each tried to implement according to the means at their disposal. It is only in the light of the answers obtained that we shall be in a position to review how our contemporary societies, over some decades now, have dealt with the issues, and imagine the sort of solutions that today's children sorely need.

If, in our own times, more and more people have more and more history and are therefore less likely to be 'happy people', it is worth asking how precisely the new arrangements that have been adopted, the toleration acquired, and the open attitudes that we have made every effort to cultivate may affect the development of today's children and those of generations to come. Will future generations, by eliminating the last vestige of constraint, mitigate the lot of the children they have? Or will they, on the contrary, leave their children to battle alone with the anxiety that children have always known and which lies at the very basis of the constitution of their symptoms?

We must not lose sight of the new, ever-growing difficulties being registered by parents and teachers - both groups that deserve sympathy - or by the therapists whose numbers have expanded exponentially in what looks to be a mushrooming market. There is neither shame nor embarrassment in recognizing that, whilst our children are infinitely fitter physically than fifty years ago, they present more and more surprisingly worrying behavioural problems. I can attest to this from my own career in treating children, as well as from the experience of plenty of my colleagues, who share my concerns. How has this come about?

A whole host of disparate factors may be cited as underlying this development, not least the highly toxic ideology of consumption. Yet at the same time we cannot ignore the failing state of parental options, particularly where saying 'no', imposing constraints, and authority in general are concerned. The father-shaped vacuum - now back in vogue and the subject of a phoney academic line absolutely bent upon making the father the active agent of boundaries - has not come about by chance. It results from a long process that is already several centuries old and that has simply entered a new and more radical phase in recent years.

As I remarked in the foreword, things are now as they are, and consequently the child, having been hoisted to the very top of the pyramid of societal values, has become a domestic tyrant whose exploits are the subject of park-bench and dinner-party conversations alike. Now, is that situation simply to be deplored and accepted? Or should it be reflected upon in order to find a response to the challenge it presents?

My immediate purpose is not to provide any more advanced analysis than that which is available to anyone looking around and observing what is going on in their immediate surroundings. I simply want to look at the existential conditions of the family we now dub 'traditional' - which is a semantic way of signifying its current obsolescence and rejection, even though it does still exist - in an attempt to discover the factor that provides its essence and to see whether this can be integrated into our modern ways of life and outlook. After all, as I said in my foreword, it may be that, having rejected a whole bundle of arrangements considered globally outmoded, we have lost something without which nothing further can be embarked upon, still less built.

It was through embracing these vast horizons and asking such questions, among others, that I ended up writing this book. I began the project with the thought that however excellent an individual's memory may be, it rarely goes back more than two or three or, in the case of those who live the longest, four generations. That is fair enough, given the human life-span, but it leaves us particularly vulnerable to the persistence of watchwords whose true value (if any) is not clear. I therefore decided rather to explore what lay further back, indeed much further back in the past, and to investigate whether in the journey back in time there lay hidden something that might be decisively important for us.

For in essence we ourselves are no more than passing actors in an adventure that began so very long ago that we know neither how it has propelled us into our own times nor what messages it has placed in us - messages which we can no longer decipher and whose possible decisiveness for our own daily lives we do not know.

Do we have access to the content of these messages? Can we access them? Nothing, of course, is more uncertain. Yet the accumulated work of palaeontologists, ethnologists, and anthropologists over the last half century represents a mine of fascinating information that offers a possible source of insights into the motivations underlying the recent transformation in which we are all either spectators or participants.

No reader should be surprised, therefore, to discover that the next chapter moves into fields that might seem foreign to a paediatrician's purpose. And yet they seemed to offer the only means possible to convey a full awareness of the adaptive constraints of our species. It is truly staggering to see the extent to which we have continuously had to adapt, whatever the cost; and not just socially, i.e., in relation to our environment, but above all in response to the conditions imposed upon us by the history we inherited. By tracing this adventure step by step, as edifying as it is fascinating, my aim has been to convey how the parental figures, forever caught in the silent struggle that has never stopped placing them in opposition to each other, slowly developed their personalities to become what they are now while nevertheless remaining essentially the same. You could say that whatever cultural veneer they acquired, they were no more able to jettison certain reflexes than they could ignore the biology that ordered many of their behaviours. It is thus possible to appreciate the extent of the miracles that they have accomplished, each in his or her way, to maintain the species, to enable it to make progress and to conquer the surface of the globe. It is all the easier, too, to weigh the importance of the changes in the social environment that have so profoundly altered the relationships of mothers and fathers, of the men and women that they have always been and continue to be - even if the change, of which we are witnesses, leaves us dumbfounded by its employment of a logic that is turning out to be as stubborn as it is unstoppable.

We shall need to admit, therefore, that for all our impressive intelligence we cannot remove in a flash what has been written in us so deeply and for so long, especially as we find it difficult to acquire even the accent of a foreign language or become accustomed to other lifestyles than our own.

This realization of what we have inherited should help us to understand the vehemence of the conflicts we experience today, especially with our partners, and to confront the despair generated by the limits to a communication that, though ostensibly ever in the forefront of our existence, has never been more difficult than it is today. This same recognition of our inheritance should also, where the dynamics of relationships between parents and children are concerned, help us to better identify the timeless features inherent in such links and draw the necessary lessons. For, if we want to avoid compromising the development of generations to come, we cannot stand idly by and naively applaud solutions which individuals have invented for their own personal convenience, and which cannot be assumed to cement society.

Chapter 2
Once Upon A Time

It is well known, because the awe-inspiring fact is so oft-repeated, that the Big Bang that gave birth to the universe occurred about fifteen thousand million years ago. What is perhaps less well known is that life probably began to evolve about three and a half thousand million years ago. Compared with these dates, the appearance of the first hominids clearly distinguishable from their primate cousins - with whom, according to differing sources, they share between 98% and 99.7% of their genes - is relatively recent, since it most likely occurred a mere eight million years ago.

Until recently it was believed that this development occurred in East Africa, following a major geological event, which established the necessary conditions leading to what was dubbed the 'East Side Story'. Although recent research has cast doubt upon the geographical precision of this hypothesis, it has not challenged its dating. Even so, it was to take another two million years - i.e., about six million years before the present - for the selection of modern man's primary ancestor, the so-called Millennium Ancestor, to occur. The Millennium Ancestor thus constitutes the trunk of our genealogical tree, most of whose branches apart from our own - for the development of the species was not linear, as was long believed, but multiplex - led nowhere.

This development seems to have involved an inexhaustible series of trials and errors, which ensured the survival of the species over a time-period that is hard for us to visualize, comprising, as it must have done, several hundred thousand generations, whereas living memory is barely capable of tracking back four. How indeed is one to conceive of a span of time equivalent in length to several thousand times the era in which we live, which itself seems to us already to have lasted a very long time? But does that matter? Yes, though we need to take the trouble to track right back through that long history. In spite of the advent of the Millennium Ancestor, the reality is that it was to take millions more years, till only some two hundred thousand years ago to be precise, for the selection to occur of our most immediate ancestor, *Homo sapiens*, who would set about conquering the world and experience a final transformation, just thirty-five thousand years ago, into *Homo sapiens sapiens*. This last *Homo* settled down to a sedentary life and gave birth to our modern cultures a mere seven and a half thousand years ago - in historical terms, practically the day before yesterday!

It transpires that this lengthy evolution - we might almost call it a gestation - obeyed a selection mechanism that persisted down the generations, i.e., individuals whose characteristics did not permit adaptation to the prevailing environmental conditions disappeared, while those who survived passed on to their descendants the very characteristics that enabled them to survive. This evolutionary process was marked by any number of important events, including physical modifications without which nothing would have been possible.

Bipedality, the capacity to stand upright, was acquired some 1.6 million years ago by the human ancestor thus called *Homo erectus*. This new feature enabled him to look further into the distance, and thereby obtain better sight of his prey and orientate himself within his environment. At the same time, it considerably modified the body he had inherited.

The first thing to change shape appears to have been the pelvis. This became both narrower and more opened out, thereby providing a container for the viscera that was better adapted for moving about and running. But this particular modification entailed another radical transformation, which was much more important still in view of its murderous implications for the mass of gestating females. All those that were capable of carrying their gestation to term, producing mature babies possibly able to walk, died in childbirth and were therefore eliminated. The only females to survive were those genetically predisposed to produce large prematures, who were smaller and lighter, born after nine months of pregnancy.

The head, which took on an increasingly upright posture, saw its volume grow considerably. This allowed further development of the brain. The dentition also evolved as a result of the ongoing interaction with the environment. One day, doubtless much later on, in response to the need to communicate with other group members - as has been demonstrated by mathematical modelling comparing animal sound production to that of articulated human language - the laryngeal pathway dropped. This allowed the expression of a sleeping gene favourable to the birth of speech. If the specialists are to be believed, speech long remained rudimentary; the ancestral language from which all subsequent languages developed dates to barely 100,000 years ago.

Once the hand was no longer needed for locomotion, its capacities increased. In particular, it perfected its contacts first with objects and then with the tools that *Homo habilis habilis* learned to use.

Henceforth, the exploration of the many shapes found in the environment became recordable in an ever-expanding brain. Fundamental were the connections between the neurones, which had gone on being established down the ages; these constituted, if not a genetic baggage for future generations to inherit, then at least an epigenetic support for traceable knowledge, potentially transmissible as such and capable in its own right of creating an infinite number of new connections.[1] This led eventually, down through the many slow millennia of evolution, to *Homo sapiens sapiens*: the *Homo* who, knowing that he was knowing, would undertake as much to expand and transmit his knowledge as to teach it to his fellows and offspring.

SOME KEY STAGES

Being essentially preoccupied with his own survival and the preservation of his species within a hostile environment that forced him to struggle all the time to keep alive, *Homo*[2] continued to accumulate adaptive capacities,

---

[1] It has been estimated that if a modern man's brain connections were counted at the rate of one per second it would take thirty-two million years to count them all.

[2] The simple term is used here so as to avoid going into the detail of the various branches or running the risk of making serious errors over their particular characteristics and capacities. These branches, which are enumerated in literature elsewhere, were effectively alien to one another, though they sometimes experienced parallel developments.

resolved his alimentary difficulties, and foiled threats against him by developing the most ordinary defence mechanism, the most commonly available to all animal species, namely escape. Frantic flight turned him into an eternal migrant. By moving from one place to another either alone or in groups of varying sizes, *Homo* ended up colonizing the entire world, though it was never a deliberate strategy. What he took with him was his energy, tenacity, knowledge, technical acquirements - the domestication of fire is 400,000 years old! - and his tools.

Hordes would settle here and there, for limited periods, in particular in territories that they would then defend against the possibility of invasion, while others would go in search of subsistence or settlement elsewhere. Given space and time, together with ecological and climatic conditions - for there were plenty of glacial and warm periods - populations developed whose evolutionary details created diversity among groups. The fact that today's humankind comprises populations of differing physical type does not cast doubt upon the common origin of these populations. As molecular biology has demonstrated, these are simply the result of ad hoc adaptations to different environments.

These differences, present among human groups since prehistoric times, go to explain both the curiosity and animosity that were to characterize the mutual relations between groups. Although plenty of cross-breeding must have occurred, thereby enlarging the range of ethnic diversity, there must also have been confrontations and wars, leading to regroupings by affinity, to the formation of societies and even of territories. Such tendencies are familiar to us, too.

THE EMERGENCE OF THINKING

There is much proof to show that by the time *Homo* reached the *sapiens sapiens* stage, he had already turned his back on his original animality, and had begun to reflect upon his destiny, his reason for existence, and his place in the world. This again is close to our experience, that is if it is not indeed the same as ours behind the indications for it, which would seem to point merely to a difference of expression. Either we ourselves are still very primitive, or else these humans, whom we regard as primitive, were more modern than we might at first sight believe!

It is probable that even before he reached the *erectus* stage, and possibly even at the outset of the 'East Side Story', *Homo* had become sensitive to those clues in the environment that not only related categories of like things and beings, but also revealed their contrasts. Thus was established the notion of difference, a concept that *Homo* was able to wield as a highly reliable tool. This notion, fundamental to the elaboration and development of thought, was crucially important in the most intimate part of the construction of our species. For it alone gave rise, during human evolution, to all that must have obtained in terms of morality, law, and rules of exchange among groups and individuals. Given that we, today, are still unfortunately having to do battle with racism, with rejection of the Other and, more generally, the different, we have to acknowledge that we have not greatly progressed. Considering the temporal distance that separates us from our distant ancestors, we may be inclined to wonder to what extent our endeavours are an improvement upon their efforts and good will!

Contingent differences must therefore have been laboriously observed and collected, not least the daylight returning after night. People surely long feared that the night would not end: 'It'll be light again in the morning' is something we still spontaneously tell our children to comfort them in their night terrors. Then, possibly, it will have been noted that the sun illumined the day and the moon certain nights. Again - though the order matters little - the blue sky, the rain, hot and cold, dry and wet, hard and soft, moving and motionless, animals that were fierce and those that were not; later on, nights with and without moonlight, the cycle of the seasons, and so on.

It is likely that the interest in category differences followed on from the one primary and half-articulated question relating to the primordial, sexual difference observed equally among the animals. This difference underpinned the irrepressible behaviour that sent each individual off in urgent search of a partner who would be suitable because different. The benefit that *Homo* derived from this essential motor to the perpetuation of the species will undoubtedly have induced him to be no longer satisfied with experiencing it as an urgent instinct but will have led him to question this too in order better to control it and indefinitely increase it.

Let us therefore keep in mind this guiding schema, and we shall see whether it produced effects, however distant. I would sum it up thus: the sexual instinct constituted a central motor; the quest to improve the performance of this motor, having prompted an awareness of all kinds of differences beginning with that between the sexes, gave rise to the beginnings of reflection; this in turn reinforced commitment to the notion of difference, thereby making it the bedrock of all thought and keystone of all behaviour.

A CHANCE MISHAP

Until I set about writing this book, I can honestly say I had personally never felt the need to find out more about the vast and mysterious area of mankind's beginnings. I made do with the crude notions that, like most people, I had gathered from what I had read. I knew, and accepted like everyone else, that the Law of the Species was the Law against incest, and that this entailed exogamic matrimonial choices which were facilitated by the establishment of particular arrangements consisting in the exchange of women. I did not know - and did not take the trouble to find out - when precisely these arrangements had been instituted. I imagined that they were sufficiently ancient to allow me to forgo further investigation. However, recent reading, together with further research that I have undertaken in this field, has made me realize just how fragile the various proofs on the subject are; there is, moreover, an absence of convergence on points of detail within the various scenarios advanced honestly as hypotheses, none of which pretend to tell the whole truth.

Faced with this information alongside my own observations of the mother–child dyad, the nuclear family, the extended family and, last of all, broken and reconstituted families, I was induced to venture, not without some hesitation, onto this territory, reflecting on my gleanings in an effort to bring them together in a convergent and coherent way. I noticed, first of all, that anthropological hypotheses, developed on the basis of palaeological datings, did not attribute any date, however approximate, to the establishment of the Law against incest and the universal practice of exchange of women which might have given rise to it, be contemporary with it, or result from it. The only date I could come across, and which therefore drew my attention, was that of the first hominid burials, which took place, according to the sources, between 150,000 and 80,000 years before present. I therefore asked myself what could have happened to make human beings one day start burying their dead.

I must confess how delighted I was to be raising that particular question. First, because, in contrast with the distant 'East Side Story', the albeit imprecise date of the earliest burials was apparently so recent, and related to a practice that presupposed a profound and considerable maturation in thinking processes. Secondly, it predated indications of artistic or religious preoccupations, if not the rise of mythologies. Thirdly, it encouraged me to think inductively, tracking back from my own observations to the event itself.

Forty years of medical practice, and more especially of paediatric medicine, years in which I have listened to the stories and conversations of mothers, fathers, women, men, girls and boys, and adolescents, on their own or in groups, have led me to conclude that the main question to trouble all the individuals whom I have met is that of death. What I am saying is that all humans, whatever their sex, age, condition, culture, learning, language, geographical residence, nationality, beliefs or religion, are plagued with anxiety about its coming. It is a preoccupation that is part and parcel of being human, though clearly it does not prevent living itself.

Fear of death inhabits our conscious mind and, more than any other feature of our species, renders us uniformly identical with one another. It is fundamental to our structures and all our behaviours, as it is also to our exchanges with others.

I cannot let the matter rest there, however, not least because the possible misunderstandings on the subject are legion. When I speak of fear of death, I mean the muffled fear that we feel at the thought that, whatever we do, we shall die one day or another. This has absolutely nothing to do with what is covered by the vague notion of a death instinct. That notion refers to the fact that we are programmed on an instinctual level to delay the arrival of our death, as, for example, when we manage to stop short in the road so as not to be mown down by a maniac at the wheel, or when we know that we are in dangerous circumstances and must exercise prudence. Instinctual behaviour of that sort is mechanistic and purely animal in essence; it is geared to self-preservation, and has nothing to do with the sort of fear I am talking about.

Fear of death is also entirely different from the so-called death drive. This is an unconscious force that tends in a sense to draw living beings towards the organic state from which they issued. It works on us without our knowledge, and governs to a considerable extent the relationship that we have with life, our own and the life of others. The death drive amounts to the foundation of the life drive, which builds incessantly upon it. We cannot escape it: when we sink into sleep or when we bury ourselves in silence and solitude, unwittingly we are following the death drive. Yet sleep rests us, and we are thereby made fitter for our daytime activities. Similarly, we better enjoy conversation and company after a period of withdrawal. It is as if we were advancing up a very steep slope and, though inevitably drawn toward slipping, we managed to find, here and there, a supportive ledge. Points of support on the slope allow us either to rest awhile before moving off again in the opposite direction or to progress further up through the help they give us. Some of us, who are described as having been taken over by the death drive, may allow ourselves simply to slide down the slope. This is what happens in melancholia or in serious episodes of depression. Or it may take the form with others, as for instance criminals or the notorious suicide bombers who have in recent years become such a diabolical commonplace of our day-to-day life, that, as they pass, they destroy the anchorage points of others and draw them into their own death.

The death instinct, death drive, and fear of death are obviously closely linked in the psyche, though the death drive, when operative, clearly diminishes the intensity of the other two: if I am taken over, or allow myself to be taken over, by the death drive inhabiting me, I have no use for my death instinct, which I will shrug off; I will also laugh at my fear of death, which in fact will have deserted me. This last point shows, incidentally, how necessary it is to the maintenance of life, when it stays within reasonable limits.

The imagery used here, that of a slope, footholds, climbing, is familiar to everyone, owing to its frequent appearance in action and suspense movies. The process it illustrates concerns us all without exception, to the extent that even if we have experience of the chains of events it implies, none of us has prior knowledge of when such a scenario may strike us personally.

What clearly distinguishes the fear of death from the death instinct and death drive is the underlying conscious awareness, be it acute or more or less violently fought against, of our mortal state. In other words, fear of death presupposes a mental process integrating that state against the backdrop of a general process integrative of any number of other phenomena; it is a process that could never have come about, had we not been equipped with instruments of reflection and awareness of ourselves and of the world about us as we perceive it. This is what leads me to infer that *Homo erectus*, or *Homo habilis*, for instance, down all the hundreds of thousands of years of their evolution, during which time they based their capacity for reflection upon the primary notion of difference, would certainly have been, like the animals, devoid of the fear of death. They would have seen their fellow creatures die around them: from accidents, exhaustion, or sometimes because they killed them themselves. But what they felt about it would have ended there. They would most likely have been incapable of thinking or imagining that the same could happen to them, being content to relate the modification in the state of their dead fellows to the simple notion of difference between life and death, according to the model they had long used to register existence in the animal kingdom.

All of this leads me to suggest that fear of death became established in mankind at the precise moment when one member of the human race buried the body of another. But what would have prompted someone to do such a thing? It seems to me that the question has never been put in such a form.

I do not subscribe to the hypothesis that the earliest burials were stores of food: that *Homo*, a longterm consumer of carrion and a cannibal, was inspired to use burial as a place for storing food that he would be sure to find again. This hypothesis does not seem to be capable of explaining the rise of funerary rituals that became established and went on to become general. Nor do I think that this early burial came about by chance.

But why did this particular corpse, the first ever to be buried, cause the gravedigger, who certainly would not have known that he was innovating, to inaugurate a practice that had not been envisaged during the previous millions of years of the species's evolution? There had always been dead bodies, all over the globe! The answer that I postulate to this question is that the first human dead body to be buried must have inspired fear - an immense and considerable fear such as had never been experienced before, a fear so great that the originator of the act of interment reacted by a powerfully defensive gesture without knowing in the least what he was doing. The only explanation that I can envisage for the act is that the gravedigger suddenly feared that the dead man was going to get up, hurt him, and destroy him.[3] It was as though the strength, awful power, and perhaps prestige of the individual on the ground had not been touched and still lived on in him, even dead. Struggling violently with the strange and unknown fear that he sensed rising within him, the protagonist wanted to totally neutralize the dead man and reduce him concretely and definitively to powerlessness. He therefore hurriedly rolled over him one or more heavy rocks. Then he covered that with all he could find, a heap of stones, branches, earth, simple pebbles. He would not have stopped - before fleeing, only to return subsequently, I would suppose - until he was satisfied with his work and had definitively removed the menacing cadaver from his sight.

The scene is not difficult to envisage. But such a scenario, if accepted, compels us to infer that the protagonist's fear, that the corpse might get up and take revenge, was, like his ensuing burial of it, not an effect of chance. It testifies to the sudden hatching of a conscious process of anticipation thitherto probably unknown and radically different from all other effects deriving from the simple instinct for survival, the death instinct, which had reigned alone until that moment.

Clearly, there would have existed before then a process that passed for anticipation in the strict sense of the term. But it would have been automatic, a reflex. To get away from a fierce animal or flee from a potential enemy: such have always been a part of the instinctual mechanisms of all animals. The stimulus to this sort of process has always come from movement, either from a moving object (falling stones, a torrent, waterfall,

---

[3] This type of fear, which still haunts us, contributed to the success of George A. Romero's celebrated 1968 film, The Night of the Living Dead.

etc.), or a living creature, i.e., one also moving. Movement has always excited prudence, if not flight. The cadaver, recognized as such, should not in itself have excited such a reaction. In order to gauge the truth of this, it is enough to contemplate how a vulture approaches its prey. Dominated by mistrust, it proceeds by a circular movement in a spiral that gradually brings it closer to the outstretched body while nonetheless enabling it to stay on the watch for the least movement. Once it has measured the immobility of the object enough to judge it definitive, it leaps upon it at an opportune moment.

Homo must have always behaved like that. Except that this time, the corpse he identified as a corpse frightened him. He feared that something might come from it. We can infer that, if he was induced to experience fear, it was because he had every good reason. It is as if that fear, which must have been present for a long time before the establishment of burial, did not merely persist in the company of the cadaver, but suddenly swelled to an unbearable intensity. The soon-to-be gravedigger's non-instinctual, conscious anticipation, which amounted to thinking about the sort of risk he was running - death - at a moment that had not yet arrived, surely presaged in him a realization of his own condition, i.e., that of a mortal clinging to life. Furthermore to become aware of his mortal state was equally to establish the embryo of another realization, that of the existence of time and of its passing. Something was perceived before it happened, within the immediate proximity of sudden fear and at the very moment when the present reality forced itself upon the onlooker's attention: all of that in succession, like an assault, intermingled, in some sort of order yet thoroughly uncontrollable. It was probably the first and most violent traumatic episode in the history of the species. It may be envisaged in the way in which images are offered in certain horror films, i.e., the reality evoked a frightening *flashback*, which immediately gave way to a *flashforward*, which itself, in turn, overlaid the objective reality, the sequences remorselessly disjoining, intermingling, and superposing one another in all directions and at breakneck speed. The violence that resulted from the experience would not simply have been recorded at the level of the neuronic connections that it created and installed, but doubtless would also have exceeded this register by entailing a massive secretion of stress-like molecules that would be bound to flood the mass of the cerebral structures and perhaps modify the connections, if not the relationships. Probably what resulted was an irreversible modification of the individual's sensitivity and condition, and his animality, changed and overtaken by the incident, would necessarily have experienced itself as invaded by what is understood nowadays as belonging to the register of complex emotions. What were being laid down here were the first markers of a new stage of humanization.

Many more violent experiences of this sort would need to occur over hundreds of subsequent generations for them to be noted, dissected, demystified, integrated, and organized enough to constitute a register of feelings and make possible a realization of the existence of time and its passing. This would also open the way to a realization of the fact of being alive and, subsequently, to the perception of self as being subject to the laws of the strange dimension to which the self was assigned - which is perhaps the best way to characterize the condition of being mortal. The process took millennia, if not tens of millennia to install itself fully. Whether it occurred through the transmission of an experience, natural selection, or a form of inherited acquisition is certainly an important question on a speculative or scientific level. But as far as each one of us is concerned, it is easier to think in terms of a period of evolution from the time when our distant ancestors first split flints down to the speculative and technological achievements of our contemporaries.

All this has been passed down to us so efficiently that the emergence of anxiety is detectable today in babies. It happens in the third quarter of the first year of life, reaching its culmination towards the end of that third quarter in a phase known as 'the anxiety of the ninth month'. This is when the baby suddenly perceives that it is an independent being, totally separate from the mother; until then it has believed itself to be simply a part of her. In risking such a parallel, I am not saying that for *Homo* all of what was experienced would have been analyzed and clearly perceived straight off,, far from it. I am merely saying that a violent process took place, and that it was probably responsible for organizing new connections in the brain - just as it also would have triggered a sharpening of perception in a cascade that similarly would have taken millennia to achieve a settled form. It is even possible to venture that such a process of formation - involving us - is still ongoing.

We still need to ask why that first buried corpse aroused such fear. I would suggest, from the outset, that it must have resulted from a murder. Hence the necessity to make sure that the body really was dead, something that must have made the feeling it evoked all the more strange. For to kill others would have been an ordinary, rather than extraordinary, event, and not something that a perpetrator would normally regard as particularly important. This murder, however, was probably the fruit of lengthy premeditation, i.e., what we today would describe as an assassination.

In all likelihood, as I have hinted, the murdered person was an especially frightening individual, as much because of his status as of his strength, violence, irascibility, or cruelty. In such circumstances, one can easily imagine several individuals being involved in committing his murder; moreover, the burial that ensued was also probably a collective undertaking. I can almost see frustrated young males conspiring to kill the dominant male of the horde to put an end to both his tyranny and his exclusive enjoyment of the horde's females.

The fear of reprisals that the assassins experienced undoubtedly culminated in the odd anxiety that came down upon them. Its intensity and shared character would have put the seal among them on what they had just invented: the embryo of a common history and of a substantive social bond, both based on an equally commonly shared undertaking, not one simply intended to satisfy the immediate and circumstantial needs of anonymous individuals.

Once buried, the corpse was removed from the food chain and could not be eaten by vultures. Nothing prevents us from imagining that it would long have been the subject of nightmares - the capacity to dream probably existed at that stage of development, just as it exists in babies - and that those nightmares renewed, even reinforced, the fear it had aroused. With a view to ending their fear, the perpetrators may have experimented by burying anonymous corpses in order to check repeatedly that the procedure made them powerless. They may also have returned periodically to the first corpse to check that it still lay under the mound under which they had buried it. They may even have added to their original effort, thereby anticipating the later practice of maintaining tombs, their repeated actions gradually helping to diminish their dread. All of that probably had a role in gradually generalizing the practice, and gingerly opened the way, urged by this new-found anxiety, to questions about the afterlife and to a ritualization that would slowly spread, establishing the relationships that we continue to have with the dead.

THE LAW OF THE SPECIES

The scenario that I have just constructed out of nothing apart from the dating of the earliest burials is of course - for those who know it and will have recognized it - closely related to the one that Freud himself constructed, in his book *Totem and Taboo*, published in 1913.

Freud postulated that, at a hazardous stage in its development, the human species probably abandoned its humanoid status and became humanity; this occurred following a pivotal event which introduced a compelling order sufficiently different from what had gone before to radicalize the separation that humankind had begun to operate between itself and the animal kingdom. He hypothesized that one day, frustrated young men within a particular horde had ganged up against the horde's dominant male, killed him, and set the seal on their complicity by sharing his cadaver in a cannibalistic meal. From this murder, which he describes as a founding event, and which he was to revisit several times, emphasizing its importance in particular in his *Moses and Monotheism* (1938), Freud dated the imposition of the Law against incest as the fundamental Law of the new species. He explained, indeed spelt out, that the 'brothers', tortured with remorse, would have punished themselves by denying themselves the benefit of their 'father's' females and, in so doing, would have established and then decreed the Law.

The extreme similarity between my imagined scenario and Freud's is certainly no accident. By citing Freud, I show that I have read him. That is why I have not hesitated to discern a collective murder behind the invention of burial, though I do not know whether Freud himself could technically have considered burial. Whilst I should have welcomed the possibility of my scenario's constituting an intermediate stage in the trajectory sketched by

Freud, which goes from the murder to the Law, nothing is less certain: where he speaks of a cannibalistic meal I postulate burial, and where he speaks of remorse I postulate the emergent fear of death. Above all else, it is impossible to know whether it is not premature, at such an evolutionary stage, to employ categories as clearly defined as 'father' or 'son'.

Here again, I find myself confronted by an absence of dates at the core of the palaeoanthropological sources, a fact that appears to rule out any likelihood of settling the debate. For, if the first burial followed the establishment of the Law against incest, then total credence can be given to Freud, there need be no objection to the plain use of 'father' and 'son', and, while not ignoring the possible emergence of the fear of death, we do not have to accord it the same importance in the psychic and affective economy of beings. On the other hand, if the first burial occurred before the Law was established, it becomes as impossible for me as it would have needed to be for Freud to use terms like 'father' and 'son': for the genitor would not as yet be remotely aware of the bond linking him to his progeniture; nor would the young males ganging up against him be aware of his contribution to their existence. In the latter case, nothing would prevent the first burial being the key event in a thought process leading to the slow yet inevitable establishment of the Law of the Species, while the relationship envisaged by Freud between the founding murder and the Greek tragedy of Oedipus, which he was to make the touchstone of his theory, would remain in abeyance.

What is certain, at least, is that the event described can have supervened only at a precise stage in the evolution of the relationships existing between individuals in hordes whose configuration has been outlined. What we can say, in sum, about that configuration is that where reproduction was concerned, it consisted of beings who were guided solely by instinct, made do with the conditions prevailing around them, and therefore continued to be definable in exclusively biological terms. Thus while genetrixes went on fulfilling their time-honoured role as mothers, they were faced by a mere sire who was profoundly selfish and violent, and no more aware of his role in procreation than an ape is today. It is, moreover, easy to imagine that his concern for his progeny would not have gone very far beyond that exhibited by some primate sires, i.e., a readiness to kill them if they interfered with his primordial activity, that of sex.

It is no less certain that the murder described in either of the aforementioned scenarios was going to profoundly change the species's evolution. While Freud articulated the change as taking the form of a an immediate consequence, namely, the establishment of the Law of the Species, insofar as the guilt of the 'sons' drove them to abandon the enjoyment of sexual relations with their 'father's' females, I personally am inclined to think that the Law's establishment would have taken infinitely longer. It seems to me that Freud's scenario introduces a sudden, quasi-miraculous transformation about which a degree of caution is required. When one thinks of the way in which today's torturers and other authors of crimes against humanity resist all challenges to their behaviour, it is hard to imagine how individuals infinitely coarser than they, uninitiated in any of the moral discourses that would come only tens of thousands of years later, could undergo such a radical reversal in their natural tendencies.

What I regard as more likely is that, having invented the notion of complicity and seen how efficient the union of small forces against one big one could be, the murderers would have taken advantage of the immediate benefits their crime brought them. I think that, in the most classic criminal fashion, they would have seen their project right through - and this is all the likelier, if they had undergone the new, and highly unpleasant, experience of the fear of death. They would probably have shared out the newly available females in a way that was necessarily inequitable. For it is likely that the group had a hierarchy, based on the relative physical strength of unequally endowed individuals, and that this hierarchy persisted. The strongest among them would have made the most advantageous choices, taking the most attractive females, and would have left the remainder to their fellows who were less blessed by nature, and, though they might regard themselves as thwarted, would simply have had to make do. The agreement sealed both by the murder and its consequences would thus be the foundation of a new order and of new relationships without the involvement as yet of any law governing the species. The group's profile would simply have changed from that of a horde with a dominant male who kept all the women for himself to that of a group within which an early form of conjugality had been established. The arrangement would doubtless have immediately satisfied each man, since he would have been the exclusive owner - and above all recognized as such by his peers - of one female, enjoyment of whom was guaranteed by the implicit pact.

It can by no means be excluded that the founding murder was closely associated with such motivation, and that a link gradually took shape associating sex with death. It would not have been the sort of link we would understand today, i.e., the realization that sexual reproduction could only have come about in the evolution of the living world as a way of compensating for deaths. Rather, this link would not have gone beyond the level of the protagonists' violence, associating the sexual drive with the drive to kill. The former drive, possibly supported by the latter, would have managed to satisfy an objective that was soon to become central to the species's behavioural logic, namely the use of coition to ease stress occasioned by the fear of death. I should add that this concerned the male, and him alone. For, if the founding murder can have concerned the females to any degree, it must have been in some other way. They had obviously provided the trigger, but they were, and kept themselves, totally apart from it. The murder may have provided an opportunity for them to take formal note of the male drive to kill; they may have been thereby led to fear it, for both their own and their offspring's sakes, and to experience, like the males - by a probable effect of contagion likely to have taken millennia - the fear of death. But their more extensive relationship with death, like their awareness of time, was doubtless not affected in the same way as that of their partners. We may go so far as to imagine that they had long had a deeper experience of life than their males. They had had to live through the death of their offspring: it is possible to envisage their reaction as akin to the truly shattering descriptions primatologists give of the behaviour of apes with the bodies of their dead infants. Although these ape mothers are aware, by the fact that it no longer clings, that the infant is dead, they continue to carry it around for days on end and try to feed it and continually smell it; finally, they scent its decomposition and abandon it in order to rejoin the group, yet not without looking back several times, as if tormented to the very end by a mad hope. Let us imagine, then, these humanoid women, for millions of years, living through such experiences. The life experience that they passed on to their offspring would differ totally from what their offspring would receive later from the males in general and from their progenitor in particular. No doubt they saw to it that their daughters imitated and repeated their behaviour - as in so many cultures still today - whilst contenting themselves with giving their sons the bare essentials, in the knowledge that they were destined to join the male clan. The differential relationship of the sexes towards time, and consequently towards death, is something that has given rise to a maximum of misunderstandings, and it remains, even today, an area where it is strictly impossible to establish common ground.

It probably took several tens of thousands of years for the intuition of the sex–death relationship to be of practical use to explain the beginnings and ends of life, when the question arose of developing stock-rearing, followed by field-cultivation. For all that, the ongoing situation - the chain of events and the succession of the generations after the founding act - would throw up its own problems. The initial pact having guaranteed only the form and not the basis of relationships, security must have long appeared precarious; fears that order might be overthrown can certainly not have been easy to dispel. It is not hard to imagine how jealously each male would have watched over his exclusive ownership of his female.[4] One can also imagine how slowly and with what difficulties the initial horde, together with the relational logic that characterized it, assumed the outlines of what would consolidate slowly through the evolutive fog to take the form of a society, the first ever, which would grow as it tried to find its bearings and, even so, became a model to follow. No, the initial pact among accomplices and the inequitable share-out that followed certainly did not put an end to problems.

What happened, and in what way, possibly, did things evolve as the generations passed? The situation cannot have been straightforward. To get some idea of it, it is enough for us to bear in mind the lability of our own historical memory. With only a very feeble trace of what he had experienced, each accomplice must have got by as best he could in bringing up his descendants - unless there were interruptions in the form of regulatory ritual visits to the grave (a precursor of later cults of the dead), or upkeep of an episodic narrative of the crime (another precursor, this, that of the myth).

---

[4] A type of behaviour still very much alive today, as is attested by Othellos of all kinds! There is still a long way to go before men will be successfully convinced that a sexual relationship with a woman does not automatically make her strictly his property.

While there may have been males who were immediately amenable to giving up their desire for exclusive sexual possession of the females of their own group, i.e., of their daughters, there will certainly have been others who must have lapsed into a repetition of the sort of past against which they themselves had revolted. Such variation in behaviour is not surprising. One only needs to recall how often, in modern times, spirited and generous revolutionaries have in their turn become the worst dictators once they attain power. Events must have occurred amidst the greatest disorder with, in some places no doubt, the profound echo of the step that had been taken historically, namely the union of weak forces against a stronger force, a mechanism that in our own day continues to be illustrated from time to time and all over the world.

No doubt there were plenty of other murders to come, during the innumerable succeeding generations. No doubt other brothers conspired to kill the dominant male of a different horde from theirs and confiscate his females. There is nothing to prevent our imagining that subordinate young males in a foreign horde might have offered their alliance against a share in such booty or that, conversely, they might have ganged up in turn to defend the females close at hand against such a foreign invasion. No doubt most of the contours that alliances could conceivably take were discovered. In the end something will have happened to reveal the close link between the violence generated by frustration and the enjoyment of sexual partners which that violence was intended to achieve. Every male would eventually start to ask himself whether it was better to live in a horde with frustration unless prepared to risk death, or whether he should try his luck,[5] join another horde, and make alliances with them. It is therefore possible to imagine that after several millennia, or several tens of millennia, a more consistent notion of belonging to a group may have emerged, one that conferred to each of its members the idea of links with others, and doubtless helped to lower stress related to the fear of death.

Even so, the human world continued without fathers or father's sons

---

5 This would have required the sort of adapted physical means still typifying the shape of today's adolescents: a short torso and long legs enabling the young male to run fast and confront danger in the quest for a partner, while the pubescent female became covered in a layer of fat intended to preserve an unborn child through a period of famine.

and daughters categorized as such. Essentially what obtained was understandings among males about the possession of females. No doubt the as yet distant - very distant - notion, supported by funerary practice, of some sort of sharing that provided protection against violence slowly made headway within a particular territory or within a few hordes, and with it the concept of the couple. In all likelihood couples were formally constituted and mutually recognized one another within a framework that provided something approaching what could be envisaged as some sort of legitimacy: an island of individuals recognizing one another in the midst of a disparate human environment! Within the different couples, each male, provided with the particular female that fell to him, would seek the assurance of possible alliances to defend his property against other males, single or not, belonging to or foreign to the group. The social bond, inaugurated long ago at the time of the famous murder of the dominant male of the first horde, would in effect have found its first application, with a form of more or less clearly enacted convention giving it still greater solidity or even indeed formalization.

Several millennia probably passed before all of this settled down, and the model of the horde became less common. The maturing of progeny must in every generation have revived the question of the horde model, coming as something of a jolt, a sort of 're-emergence of repressed material'. It is impossible to see by what miracle the male genitor succeeded everywhere in declining his female progeniture when they reached maturity, nor how young males stricken with hormonal upsurges, might spontaneously have given up copulating with their sisters or mother.

But it was then, probably, that it became obviously necessary to categorize and name the links between individuals. The genitor did not need to be aware that he had a role in procreation; that was probably not clearly perceived until agriculture and stock-rearing came along.[6] But he would have been credited as having a specific link with his female's progeny. A sketchy outline of the categories of father, sons, and daughters, as opposed to a mother who had always been recognized as such, would begin to settle

---

[6] His precise role was destined to be mysterious for a long time yet: the spermatozoid was not recognized until 1670, after the invention of the microscope; the first fertilization was observed only in 1875!

into place. A new convention would probably make a necessary appearance, extending the first one and making it simpler to regulate the relationships within society for the individual protection of all the members of the species living in the environment. According to its provisions, mating could only take place between individuals that were fundamentally foreign to each other. But in order for such a convention to be unanimously adopted and, above all, practically effective, it would have been essential to secure it by a Law, one that forbade incest, which would only then become the specific Law of the Species, and which would once and for all prohibit matings and couplings between close relations.

At long last, an order based on language had imposed itself on one based on instinct. One might equally say that male order received at this time its first formalization, imposing itself on women who, lacking the physical means to opt out, probably contented themselves with not belonging to it, thereby inaugurating the form of struggle that they were destined to carry on for all time as best they could against the oppressive sex. Whatever its rights and wrong, this order constituted an adaptation that would favour the undeniable progress of a species destined thereafter to be totally different from what it had been until then.

At the same time, it is not farfetched to infer that mankind's progress was facilitated by a biological evolution that was undetected and undetectable until the last few years. Recently geneticians have been able to demonstrate that the Y chromosome, invented by evolution some three hundred million years ago and conferring on the male his specificity, has lost a considerable amount of its material over time. Originally made up of some fifteen hundred genes, it now contains barely fifty, and at this rate will disappear totally in some ten million years' time. The process has been slow, but it is not unlikely that several hundred thousand years ago it entailed, among other phenomena, a noticeable drop in testicular testosterone production, the substance which we know is responsible for addiction to sexual activity, as well as for the aggression correlated with it.

Something else is possible, too: the quasi-consensual order established by the Law of the Species, while doing little to diminish the fear of death now integral to *Homo*, must nonetheless have made it more 'livable with', since individuals no longer had to fear losing their life as soon as the need to copulate forced them to risk it. I would draw a parallel here with the regular successes I have recorded in my own practice whenever I have taken on children who have reached that age when, tortured by the idea of death, they express their anxiety through refusing to be separated from their parents, be on their own in a room, or close the door to the lavatory, and perhaps have terrifying nightmares and untimely nocturnal wakings. After listening to them telling me their worries, my practice has been to say to them that they are not alone, since everyone has at one time or another asked themselves the questions they ask. Then I have gone on to speak of the evolution of longevity down the ages, ending up by telling them that they have every chance of reaching nearly a century of life - which indeed is the truth. I have noticed how this reassurance (given moreover by a doctor) has tended to stir up instant relief within them and can, on its own, cause their symptoms to disappear.

I do not consider that, leaving aside the moot question of historical stages, there is any need for argument between proponents of the Freudian hypothesis, those of the anthropological exegesis, and the personal scenario that I have had the audacity to put together. That the various stages in the process should have given rise to differing hypotheses about them is not in itself of such great importance, since the outcome is the same: a Law enacted and interiorized, not the effect of an instinctual avoidance as observable in certain animal species.

Twentieth-century anthropology delved much into the background to these questions; its response was to trace the coming of the Law against incest back to the rule concerning the exchange of women - of which I have tried to give a rapid account here - as being the most effective solution and the one dictated by necessity.[7] When the anthropological investigator asks the primitive man why he has taken his wife from outside his group rather than marry his sister, he laughs and replies that if he had married his sister, he would not have a brother-in-law to take hunting with him.

---

[7] Such exchanges came to involve varying accommodations that were dictated by environmental conditions; such accommodations are basic to the different kinship systems observable across the world.

A POWERFUL AUXILIARY MOTOR OF EVOLUTION

The sense behind these exchanges is still not wholly clear. Why did men subject women and dispose of them as they did, swapping them between each other without any concern for the women's consent? I mentioned earlier the male's greater physical strength. But is it credible that that alone was enough? Women had always held all the trumps, including undoubted strength, great resistance, and great stamina, enabling them and their progeny to survive in complete self-sufficiency. What other factor might have intervened to explain how the male sex, which, in spite of its ratio to the female sex of 104:100, is not far from being considered by ethologists as a parasitic sex, was able to maintain itself as it did?

As I am daring to do so much hypothesizing, let me venture to suggest that this factor relates to the threshold of sexual excitability, which has always been very different between the two sexes.

However great the extent of our evolution, we have never stopped being animals subject to the laws of biology. As if to assure better development, oestrus or 'heat' - the period of sexual availability found in female animals - vanished from our species at the beginning of the 'East Side Story'. Unlike the females of other species, who are sexually available only during short periods of the year, those of the species *Homo* immediately became so continuously. It is worth emphasizing the notion of availability, inasmuch as males in other species, faced with unavailable females remain uninterested, whereas they relentlessly attempt to mate with them, even fight to the death for possession of them, as soon as the ambient atmosphere signals the triggering of the oestrus, as if they were themselves conditioned by the chemical signal issuing from the bodies of their females. The availability of the two sexes being in phase and directly linked to the release of the oestrus, the female animals obey the laws governing the perpetuation of the species, receive the winner or whatever male is around without the least scruples, and become infertile once again as soon as they have been fertilized.

The disappearance of oestrus within the human species enhanced the status of another factor, one that does exist in other species and which explains why the relations we observe in them assume the direction they do, namely, it is always the males that battle for the females and not vice versa. The factor at work here relates directly to the particularities of sexual anatomy and physiology, and is nothing other than the threshold of sexual excitability.

In all species, including humankind, the sexual excitability threshold is always much lower in the male than in the female. 'Men only think of one thing' is a comment women often make, and in a sense, biologically, things have to be that way. After all, is it possible to envisage a female initiating coitus with a male in a flaccid condition? On the other hand, it is always possible for a male to initiate coitus with an uninterested female, even in the face of opposition, through rape. Work with couples experiencing problems reveals, moreover, that male impotence causes far more difficulties than female frigidity. Some may wish to refute observations like these as merely effects of time-honoured male chauvinism and the no less time-honoured mistreatment of women. Such an approach, however, would be partisan, because it ignores a host of collateral factors inherent in the difference between the sexes and their specific dynamics.

This natural mechanism was neither unimportant nor an effect of chance. It was of fundamental service to the perpetuation of the species. In all animal species, the males parade and display their possible advantages in order to be chosen by the female, while the female, being programmed to provide her descendants with the best possible genetic material, will try somehow to take her time to pick out the male with the best qualities. If such strategies no longer seem either so blatant or important today in our species, it is nonetheless possible to discern equivalents in the way in which in many societies matrimonial dowries are organized. While in some societies men 'buy' their wives by paying the bride's father a compensatory amount, the exchange is sometimes done in reverse, and the bride's father has to pay a sum to his future son-in-law if the marriage represents, for the daughter, her family, and therefore her descendants, a rise in social status.

It has therefore always been the case that the difference in sexual excitability thresholds has guided relationships, accounting for both their direction and the form of hierarchy they have taken, and entailing a flagrant asymmetry in the conditions of life of the protagonists. The males, once their sexual needs were satisfied, were free to go hunting or gathering to feed themselves. Their females, occupied with looking after their offspring, were in a different boat. They nevertheless got something out their submission to male initiatives. Like the female primates, they had orgasms - orgasms that were certainly more intense than the male orgasm, though not until the later twentieth century did the work of Masters and Johnson confirm what had been affirmed since Antiquity in opinions attributed to Tiresias.[8] The relationship in either sex between the height of the excitability threshold and the intensity of the pleasure experienced in the sexual act would appear to be a constant one. In opposition to the seemingly unmethodical inconsequentiality of males concerned simply to repeat the act to regain a dazzling pleasure that was both quick and difficult to renew forthwith, stood the less spontaneous sexual arousal of females, which was nonetheless balanced by pleasure that was more ample, intense, much more prolonged, and easily renewable. The purpose of this substantial pleasure premium was probably not simply to re-establish a form of equity, compensating lower frequency by higher quality. It no doubt also enabled women to better assume the tasks demanded of them by their offspring, for whom they were solely and heavily responsible, and to whom they were, as in the rest of the animal kingdom, viscerally attached. In the remote period about which we are talking - though it prevailed in an equivalent guise until a comparatively recent period and arguably exists still - their submission to the male severely compromised their freedom of action, stopped them from accessing an autonomous food supply through hunting or gathering (of which they were clearly capable), and compelled them to rely on the unpredictable allocations of their male companions, that is, when these did not simply consist of the surplus or leftovers from his meals.

Whatever novel may be said about female physiology today, it remains essentially the same phenomenon. Although it seems inescapably to have been drawn into a debate with new repercussions, this is simply because the relatively recent transformation in the condition of women raises again the question of the nature of femaleness, whose mystery remains what it was when Freud spoke of it as a 'dark continent'. One might add this parallel, for the record, that while women, in addition to deriving solid pleasure from the

---

[8] William H. Masters and Virginia E. Johnson, Human Sexual Response (London and Boston, 1966).

care they lavished on their offspring, enabled the species to survive, it was probably the addiction of men to their sexual pleasure that led them to become explorers and conquerors of territory. Whether this conquest took place on foot over millions of years, or one day availed itself of an armada of galleons to find a new route to the Indies, whether it took the form of sporting records, the creation of businesses, financial operations, or the launch of rockets into space, its motor, taking the avenue we call sublimation, similarly remained resolutely the same.

Apart from revealing the cardinal importance of the fear of death, this reading of the immense distance in time travelled by humanity shows how the social bond was established together with its earliest manifestations, namely, the group, the subgroup, the sub-subgroup, and so on. Enabled, as it were, by this reassuring inclusivity, the couple was then able to establish itself. Finally, much later on, the notion of family intervened, with the sort of sociological dimension we are familiar with today.

What this history also points out to us, as if we needed it, is how important mothers were down the ages, and how central the place they occupied was from one end to the other of the evolutionary chain. Huddled in her feminine condition and identity, which became ever more marked as evolution went on, the human female, like most vertebrates and especially mammals, assumed alone the gestation and extended care demanded by a progeny of immatures. Because her assumption of these tasks went uncontested, she developed in regard to this progeny a ferocious attachment produced by pleasure that was authentic and had doubtless always existed.

Meanwhile, for the other partner in procreation, the one universally referred to today as 'the father', things were fundamentally different. It is already clear that from one end to the other of his slow evolution, practically the only thing that powered him, as in the animal kingdom, was his sexual desire, in whose self-referring service he placed his strength, energy, and determination. In the beginning, he was a mere genitor, and did not even realize that he was that. Later, he became a partner in a couple, which introduced him to his place as social father; the environment now accorded him, first, exclusivity over his female partner and her progeny, and, subsequently, recognition as the one who conferred identity on a progeniture whose members were intended to cross with the progenitures of others. It was very much later, i.e., at a comparatively recent date on the historical scale, that he assumed such ornaments of fatherhood as seem to us essential to his definition, yet even these now seem obsolescent to no few of our contemporaries, while others are seeing them once again as crucially important.

In order to understand how all of this has brought us to the point where we find ourselves now, we must go on patiently unravelling the history of humanity as it developed into a time nearer to us.

Chapter 3
The Gift Of The Father

THE DAWN OF CULTURE

Homo patiently allowed to knit together the brain connections that he had inherited down the ages since his distant ancestors first had the idea of standing upright. Over time, he underwent some ferocious selections and numerous mutations, which ended up giving him a reactive organism very similar to our own. He succeeded, finally, in managing more or less satisfactorily the violence generated by his sexual needs. Now, suddenly, he found himself one day having to grapple with the long-lasting effects of the crucial experience he had just been through, i.e., the sudden appearance, at the time of the first burial, of the fear of death, which entered him with all its emotional cortège, totally disrupting his condition.

This realization caused him to attribute a status to this death. It led him to see it not only as something that could be given and received, but also as something inescapable, something that could not but concern him, which he could do nothing about and could know nothing about. Are we, in this respect, so different from him? What do we know of death? Not much, it has to be said. We have scarcely even a vague idea about the deaths of others. They move us, even if regrettably less and less as the media make us only too familiar with the terrorist outrages and the other horrors that happen so often in some places. They sadden us, and sometimes distress us when they are of those we know; when those closest to us are concerned, our relationship to the world may be significantly and lastingly affected. But what do we know of our own death? Nothing. And is it by chance that our unconscious knows nothing of it? Truly, nothing. Save that we strive, all of us without exception, not to believe it possible, lest we should find ourselves incapable of doing anything but take cover and await it.

This notion, which, having become an obsession, *Homo* never thereafter succeeding in throwing off, will certainly have marked his psyche with early questionings about his condition as a living being and about the sense of his place in the world. He will have tried to ease the pressure, initiating the famous process that would one day be dubbed 'repression'; but all he will have gained from his efforts will have been to witness burgeoning within him a strange, new phenomenon assimilable to the conscious memory. Doubtless he had long been equipped with an embryonic memory of a sort, and without any doubt at all he had for tens of thousands of years been capable of recalling the places he had been through, the plants and animals he had come across, and the traps he had set. But nothing entitles us to imagine that before he experienced that emotional cataclysm at the time of the first burial, he could have had a memory of emotions, be they ever so simple and infrequent. But once that had happened, his behaviour and gestures would have been sufficiently affected to explain how he could pass on to his descendants, however distant, if not the explicit content of what he had experienced, then at least the indelible trace it had left; knowledge of precise details would not be needed for the effects to persist. We understand from our own times the ravages caused by what we obstinately try to hide and what people as if by chance describe as a 'skeleton in the cupboard' or 'body in the closet', though to substitute 'the corpse in the first burial' would be to trace the phenomenon back to its origins. This new emotional recall facility will have produced some curious phenomena. Strange visions will have recurred in *Homo*'s mind, assailing him irrespective of his wishes - visions that will have disturbed him, because he cannot have failed to recognize a host of details that one day would end up being called 'memories'. We do not know how many days, months, centuries or millennia it took before, accepting their existence, he would take pleasure in conjuring them up at will, organizing them as he chose and combining them in all different ways, placing a particular detail now here now there, before or after some other, to realize that that this activity did not produce a new effect. At some time or other he will have become sufficiently adroit at the exercise to do the same with mental screens for things he would like to be able to forget. At some time he will have played with them and integrated them in such a way as to extract from them a desire, a fantasy, or even a form of project. Did this take place in an age far distant from us or more recently? No one can say with certainty. Yet there had to be a time when what we know of our mental mechanisms settled into place.[9] That can only have occurred on the basis of acquisition of the process we call memory.

The effects of the acquisition of memory however go much wider than we imagine. Memory implicitly witnesses to our place in time, as well as to the impossibility of removing us from it. What I remember, that which passes through my memory, lies in my past experience. I know it as I cannot fail to know it, because it is from my present that I am able to make that incursion into the past. But just as I cannot fail to recognize that my present was once my past's future, I shall sooner or later have to agree that my present will quickly become a past and that it has itself a future, and that this will necessarily come to pass, whatever I do, and however much I may deplore the fact that my view of the future is less efficient than the view I think I have of my past. I live, therefore, in time. I am subject to it; it rules me, works me, makes me. Not only do I have no hold over it, I cannot even hope to gain a hold over it one day.[10] While it may be possible for me to summon at will the memory of my past, I have absolutely no way of returning to it or changing its course; equally, though I may make plans for my future, I cannot make an incursion into it to assure myself that what I envision will come to pass.

Homo will slowly, though surely and ineluctably, have gone through the process I have described. As he moved from being assailed by memories to being able to summon them at will, he must have come to see his existence as one that unfolded: one in which the time he inhabited was vectorized, i.e., took its onward direction, from a past that was over and gone (even if accessible to memory) toward an uncertain future of which he had no knowledge - apart from the inevitability of its end, since he was no more than the object and plaything of that villain time, and death sooner or later would

---

[9] It is not impossible to imagine already at this stage the establishment of what psychoanalysis would in time unveil as the unconscious: the atopical part of the mental processes that is forged over time by each individual and intended to manage the drives via a collection of complex mechanisms in perpetual interaction with the physical and societal environment.

[10] Hence the popularity of films that make use of machines that time-travel or enable people to time-travel at will.

get the better of him. Such a perception will fatally have drawn him onto the slippery slope of metaphysics, constraining him to respond to his many questions on his place in the world with answers influenced by his environment, which he could not fail to hold, seeing what comparative peace they brought him. In the end, even *Homo*'s decreeing of the Law of the Species was implicated in the time issue, as a way of allowing him to deal with his mortal condition.

At the same time, *Homo*'s growing intelligence will finally have given him, at the very centre of that fundamental discussion of his, an acute awareness of his many needs and of the onus on him to organize satisfaction of them. This doubtless will have launched him into strategies of exchange which will have led him to identity the individual agents likely to favour his plans, as also those likely to be hostile or indifferent. Alliances will thus have come into being in response to circumstances, and these may sometimes have endured with the usual logic governing this sort of activity. Embryonic social relationships, foreshadowed already for tens of thousands if not hundreds of thousands of years, must then progressively have taken shape, leading to models of group living whose modalities cannot have been very different from those we are still familiar with today. While the existence of the Other was by now identifiable, it will have been only as pertaining to an individual or individuals who were at first sight hostile or threatening, but who might become useful if an attempt to profit by them were made. Basic self-interest surely presided over these exchanges, in which notions of sacrifice would have been unknown, not to say indecent. Nevertheless lines of force and alliances would finally be taking shape, sometimes opening the way to forms of fidelity or attachment in which the parties concerned ministered to the most petty of mutual interests. Swelling the organization of these contingent exchanges, there were probably others, whether within groups or between groups, that would inform the beginnings of the myths that would anchor the opinions and beliefs of the moment.

It goes without saying that this evolution was probably long confined to only a very few groups, and that these did not necessarily start out by being the most populous. With their fewer confrontations and wars, they must easily have prospered compared to the groups that had not opted for the relational model they had instituted. It may be that they then acted as unintentional proselytes or their model infected other populations. But the millennia which went by will certainly not have allowed even the most patent progress to spread homogeneously; nor will identical results have occurred among societies that evolved independently within environments hermetically sealed from others of the same type by distance. Such disparity is easily inferred from the records of explorers from the last few centuries or, more simply still, from our own anthropologists and documentary television writers. After all, the Papuans of the Sepik, the Amerindians of Amazonia, the pygmy tribes, and the Mongol horsemen have never before had such huge audiences!.

THE NOMADIC AND THE SEDENTARY

Within this slow, complex, multidirectional evolution, one fact seems nonetheless well established: that around twenty to thirty thousand years ago, part of this collection of populations started to become sedentary. This development marked a crucial stage in the species's progress, and established for those concerned a relationship with the environment whose effects have not as yet, even today, run their full course. This is not to say that nomadism did not long prevail; after all, we witness its continuity into our own time.

But what are nomads, and what is it that pushes them into nomadism? They are individuals who, at a particular time, abandon a place that no longer suits them or seems hostile; they go off in search of, and sometimes find, a place that suits them better, until in time that new place no longer answers their needs, and the process repeats itself. It could be said of nomads that as the result of an accumulation of probably unpleasant experiences, all of which will have served as lessons that the same things could recur, they have definitively given up the attempt to modify their environment. They will, for example, have learned that when a well dries up, it is no good waiting around for the water to return. Given the knowledge we possess today, we can only congratulate them on their wisdom. But things that we today can subject to logic will long have been for them an occasion of catastrophic experiences, from which, if they survived, they will have drawn lessons to pass on to their descendants. The same will have been true in regard to the immediate neighbourhood, the surrounding fauna, the pasturelands, or the paths to take.

Modern history contains an edifying illustration of this phenomenon. The conquest of the territory of North America by the Europeans was greatly facilitated by the natives' lengthy failure to react due to their deeply nomadic temperament. When invaded by populations who were determined, owing to their culture of origin, to settle the space they took over, the Indians did not offer resistance; they probably viewed the invasion as an unexpected yet unremarkable impact upon their habitual environment. For a long time, therefore, they simply moved hunting-ground, just as they had always done when game became scarcer. It was only when the room to migrate became extremely small that they at last reacted. But it was too late: by then the conquerors, with their long sedentary tradition, had taken advantage of circumstances to settle and directly change the environment through techniques they had brought with them. We know what massacres resolved that question.

Contrary to the behaviour of the nomadic groups, a number of *Homo* groups at some point happened upon rich territories that suited them. There they settled, ceased once and for all roaming about, and became sedentary, probably for the first time in the history of the species. Confident that the land was inexhaustible, they will certainly have begun by simply idly enjoying their good fortune. Any why not, when the fruit weighing down the trees begged only to be picked and the abundant game was so easy to catch? With nature so generously renewing the miracle as the seasons went round, they were doubtless long spared any worry about how they, or their descendants, would manage. Especially as, once they saw their resources in danger of running out, they had only to manage and exploit them to achieve brilliant results. They became emotionally attached to their environment, and now took the initiative to act upon it so as to adapt it to their needs; over several millennia they progressed from the single hut to the village through various intermediate stages, which comprised rudimentary houses, disparate groups of huts and houses and, subsequently, hamlets. Possibly through a process of habituation, which recorded *Homo*'s activities in a form of experience that was itself transmissible from generation to generation, this sedentary lifestyle brought, first, a better understanding of the context of life, before opening the way to its tangible exploitation through stock-raising about ten thousand years ago, followed by field-cultivation some centuries (or perhaps a millennium) later.

It does not matter a great deal whether these developments took place in scattered zones (though it is believed to have occurred in the so-called 'Fertile Crescent', today's Middle East), or whether they came sooner in some places than others. What does matter, however, is that the sedentary way of life implied that *Homo* now had a more harmonious relationship with an environment whose profile seemed less hostile because it was managed and provided reliable subsistence. This in turn made it possible for humans to spend some of the energy devoted to simple survival on taking care of the environment and investing in it. In other words, they set about making a definitive physical and emotional investment in geographical space - an investment whose intensity and scope would probably be responsible for the social conventions that would lead on to the subsequent building of states and empires. It was probably in this way, around ten thousand years ago, that in some places the earliest cultures were born whose echoes have even managed to reverberate to us.

THE NOMADIC, THE SEDENTARY, AND THE RELIGIOUS

During the tens of thousands of years that followed his shock discovery that death was inevitable, *Homo* was able to develop all kinds of procedures for easing the pressure of anxiety that realization had caused. To these may be added diversionary, nullifying, or rather consolatory tactics - all of which, incidentally, continue today - intended literally to reject death's irreversibility. Funerary rituals, just like numerous cave paintings, testify to the rise of questionings, as well as early beliefs about the existence of some sort of afterlife beyond the common term. It is a type of preoccupation that has indeed never fallen away, and indeed it continues to stir up the most extreme passions. What good, for example, has it done these last few years to heap scorn upon the convictions held by Islamist suicide bombers that after their death they will be welcomed into paradise as heroes, awaited by seventy virgins prepared to submit to their desires?

The urgency of questioning around the fear of death is certainly what has lain since long, long ago at the root of the many religions designed to offer answers to those questions. Yet these religions seem to present remarkable variations according as they relate to either sedentary or nomadic populations. It is clear that the conditions of existence, working closely with the effects of immediate relationships, eventually created a state of mind specific to each of the two conditions.

Sedentarization must have encouraged its followers to believe that everything was their due and to behave somewhat like spoilt children. Finding themselves in a generous environment, from which they believed they had good reason to expect all things, they invested in it emotionally. This was all the easier inasmuch as such happiness was to each one an echo of what it had been to live in maternal space - first, the uterus, followed by the bosom - before confronting the harsher realities of existence. Hence the tendency over a long period to honour the eternally providing mother through the creation of female cults and, later, investment in idols. It is possible to understand the idol in this context as the equivalent of our small children's comfort blanket or 'teddy' - what since Winnicott we have come to call a 'transitional object', meaning that it represents the mother. The mother represented here was devoted, generous, enveloping; she was above all else a comfort in all circumstances, reassuring on every subject, the fear of death being by no means the least among them. This is hardly surprising in the light of what was alluded to earlier, namely that the women, having taken no part in the founding murder that led to the earliest burial, effused a connection to time, death, and the fear of death that was remarkably different from that of the men. It is thus possible to establish a close connection between a favourable environment, a devoted mother, and idolatry, since these three factors all contribute to the same function.

The fact that all of this could subsequently become more complex, giving rise to a multitude of objects and authorities of more or less weight, to the extent of creating pantheons, does not alter things. The object of the exercise was still the same: to block the ill effects of excessive anxiety through the intervention of a representation of maternal power.

Fathers and Mothers

It was just like that - to take an example familiar to all - in the religion of ancient Egypt. Five thousand years ago, the Egyptian religion was already highly developed and complex, having long since elaborated a coherent mythology replacing the common idols of cruder religions with objects of adoration endowed with strongly symbolic potential. The numerous divinities on offer ranged from the sun to cats; they included the Nile itself, bulls, owls, and crocodiles. Although each of these was endowed with a specific power, all served to protect their worshippers. Against what? Against uncertainty, evil spells, ill fortune, adversity - in short, against everything near at hand or remote that could pose a threat to the enjoyment of life, i.e., everything that more or less spoke of hateful death. Nor did things stop there, for the Egyptian religion left traces behind it; its assertion that there was an existence after death went so far as to profess that the essential began in reality only after this current stage, and that it was important for everyone, during this life, to make preparation for the 'great journey'. We know what this could involve: the embalming, the mummies, the provisions for the journey, the pyramids, and the rest. The idea was a judicious one - mother, with her multiplicity of representations, was going to defeat even death! It was enough simply to think it: why worry about the end of your life as a living being, when you were given to understand that it was only a change of state? Death was not the end, but the beginning. All that was needed was to proclaim it - and of course believe it - and that in principle ought to suffice. And it did suffice for some three millennia. It sufficed for the building of a structured, prosperous, powerful, and relatively pacific society.

We could do a round-up of all the variations on this theme from this period, including the Canaanite and Mesopotamian versions whose traces have come to us either directly or through the borrowings that later religions made from them. Yet the results would be broadly similar, consisting in an original invention conforming to an environmental given, expressly comforting and appeasing in that it conjoined the effects of a reassuring geographical space with essentially maternal provisions that were at once tender and subtly negating.

When we get to the religion of the Greeks - which was subsequently adopted by the Romans and adapted for their empire - the strategy changed entirely. Yet the result aimed at was still the same. A mythology constructed out of the primitive chaos - like most of the religions round about - gave birth to a pantheon of gods whose peculiarity consisted in their being remarkably like humans, save that they were not subject to death. It could be said that the Greek arrangement sought to alleviate the enduring fear of death by sending the message that people simply must not allow themselves to be invaded or crushed by the fear of death, because the immortal gods, who direct the world and mankind, behave in exactly the same way as humans, with the same hierarchical relationships, alliances, and dissensions, and yet they are similarly confronted by apparently insoluble problems, conjugal setbacks, whims, and moodswings. Why worry about the inevitability of death when protection from it is no help in dealing with everyday life? Moreover, the Greeks still had their remarkable universe of Hades, entirely devoted to lodging the dead and where everything, time excepted, went on in perfect symmetry with earthly life, permitting both continuity of thought and reunion with close family - was this perhaps another version of the Egyptian 'great journey'? Given the brilliance of Greek civilization and the contribution it continues to make to the modern world, one can only salute the extraordinary effectiveness of its invention.

Despite their number and the influence they acquired over the world's surface, these various models were not always successful in winning over to their logic the nomad populations that remained stubbornly resistant to it. Over time the nomadic option, too, had to fashion and model - as it doubtless continues to do - a cognitive arrangement correlating with a particular state of mind resulting from the tens of millennia of migration during which the ancestral *Homo* set about conquering the planet. The nomad had no cause to invest in his environment, since he endlessly changed location, sometimes experienced difficulties in finding anywhere really suitable, and lacked confidence in the environment's capacity to provide his descendants with the resources they needed. He therefore did not invest emotionally in the geographical space through which he journeyed; on occasions, he even distrusted it. One might almost suggest that he will have been familiar with conditions that constantly negated the promises implicit in the maternal outlook, persuading him, if not to demystify it, at least to keep it at arm's length. Perceiving his existential journey as subject to uncertainties about whether his descendants would survive, he will have taken the measure of the risky nature and elusiveness of time, thereby obtaining an even more acute awareness of it; this will have compelled him to take account of his need to flee and to manage his own lifespan - both things that will have prepared him somewhat to acquiesce in his mortal condition.

When, much later on, the nomad began to conceive of religion as both an answer to the search for meaning in his life and the most effective way to parry the pressure caused by the fear of death, he invented the first monotheistic religion. This was well before the flowering of Greek civilization (8th to 3rd centuries BC). The Hebrews, who were the inventors of this monotheism, were a nomadic tribe in Mesopotamia whose actual name meant "those that pass". After 270 years in Egypt, they produced a text, the Torah, which narrated the facts and foretold the future of the tribe's history, whilst at the same time recording the body of its beliefs. The Torah, which is more familiarly known under such names as the Pentateuch or Old Testament, and which can probably be read as recent mythology compared to the rest of what we have been discussing, was supplemented over time with a voluminous corpus of commentaries known collectively as the Talmud, intended to sharpen up the content of the message that the Torah was supposed to deliver. Commentators long ago noted how, although the first book of the Torahic text ascribes important roles to strong maternal figures - the matriarchs Sarah, Rebecca, Leah, and Rachel - and recounts in detail their interventions, they are thereafter ignored, and the very word 'mother' drops out of the text after the receiving of the Ten Commandments. It is as if the whole enterprise were designed to thwart the manoeuvres of maternal authority and to limit its power in favour of the establishment - an original development in this period - of a society of fathers. To carry out their enterprise, the Hebrews relied upon the famous One-god whom they gave themselves and whom speakers of other languages have striven to give a name, resorting to such pronunciations as Yahweh, Yohveh, Jehovah, and the like. In fact, the written form YHVH is strictly speaking unpronounceable and functions as a sort of logo, condensing into four letters the three modalities, intertwined in no order, of the being's insertion in time: has been, is, is to be.[11] This shows how monotheism, the option adopted by a nomadic people, was founded above all else upon the injunction given to its followers to be conscious of their insertion in time.

MOTHER, FATHER, SPACE, TIME, AND DEATH

The special relationship that the sedentary had with their geographical space - which as I have said, bore some resemblance to a relationship with a mother - undoubtedly represented huge advantages for them, as has been appreciated since Freud, because it promoted self-confidence as well as an enterprising and technical mentality, things long neglected by the nomadic, who had opted for a different solution. At the same time it is possible to substantiate the truth of this by examining the way in which the monotheistic religions have dispersed throughout the world in recent history.

It is well known that Judaism never had a proselytizing tendency and has always rather discouraged conversion. The people described as 'the elect' must have found the modalities of their chosen status rather too burdensome to get others to share it. Though chosen, they stated that they had regrets about that fact, and that they were only chosen so as to accomplish the course that they had been ordered to take - a course which, once achieved, would make them an example to lead all humanity to their faith in the One-god. It was a vast, not to say impossible task, demanding strict asceticism and infinite patience, in which time remained the main ingredient.

Unlike Judaism, its offshoot Christianity opted for a proselytizing

---

[11] The logo's particularity is that it speaks to the eye alone, rather like the arrows and diamond shapes on the road or the stylized lion on a brand of automobiles. However, this mode of 'speaking' is remarkably efficient; the retention and memorization of its message are infinitely superior to those of all other means of communication - hence the fortune spent by the marketing sections of large firms in finding an effective logo. It should be pointed out that the third person singular in Hebrew, as in other Semitic languages, including Arabic ('has been, is, is to be') additionally fulfils the naming role that the infinitive has in languages like French and English ('to have been, to be, to be in the future') - cf. Latin, where the first person singular has acquired this function, as may be seen in any Latin dictionary.

approach, which was directed to the salvation of all humankind; this approach began as mild enough, but became less so later, when it became mixed up in politics. Its fundamental teaching introduced a mother, Mary the mother of Christ, and Christianity spread readily through the western temperate zone with its abundant resources and longterm sedentary populations; the inclusion of an important maternal symbol helped to supplant the traditional idol/transitional object where this was still current, as in the cults of the Greco-Roman pantheon.[12] On the other hand, Christianity met with far greater difficulties in the regions where nomadism, ever distrustful of essentially maternal promises, still prevailed owing to geomorphology and unreliability of resources.

When Islam in turn built upon the contributions of Judaism and Christianity with a proselytizing determination that even now seems undiminished and an unstoppable focus upon eternity, it spread readily through nomadic regions right into the Far East. Yet it stopped at the gates of Vienna, where it failed to convert populations that were already Christianized - and we know to what extent their history, including the crusades, had rooted in them the notion that they were defending the one true faith.

Of course, it would be naive, given all the many variables, to reduce to so skeletal a schema the aims and contributions of religions that together share - sadly not without tension - a large portion of the globe. It would be equally naive for me to give the impression that I could sum up in a few sentences notions as vast and complex as those of space and time. My more limited aim is to go on pursuing my idea that management of the fear of death has never ceased to preoccupy humanity in every area. All religions without exception have attempted to control it by bringing to bear their own particular answers. Almost all of them, even the monotheistic ones, have intimated, even when they have not declared so openly, that there is a life

---

[12] The power and efficacy of Mary as a maternal figure contributed to the successful relaunch of western Christianity in the early Middle Ages, at a time when it had begun to lose energy; it was this period that saw the abundant growth in iconography of the Virgin With Child theme. The symbol of Mary was again made use of in similar circumstances in the mid nineteenth century in the guise of the dogma of the Immaculate Conception. France of course very early on claimed the status of eldest daughter of the Church and placed itself under the emblematic protection of the Virgin Mary: modelling its pyramidal structure on the Church, it was to forge a strongly centralized state unique in Europe which the Jacobine revolutionary constitution left untouched.

after death.

All the same, it is not sufficiently well known that the essential message of Judaism - a religion poorly understood even by Jews - boils down to an order given to the Jews, the strange formulation of which is: 'I have set before you life and death: choose life!' It is this message that organized the mainsprings of Judaic society as well as the way in which it envisaged its connection to the world. However paradoxical it may seem - 'I'm letting you choose this or that: choose this' - it nonetheless underlines the fact that the Torah makes no explicit mention of what happens after death. Nor is there anything else that mentions it during the six to eight centuries that the kingdom of Israel lasted. Although subsequent commentators have interpreted various phrases as implying the belief that the soul was immortal, it is not until the period between the early second century BC and the late second century AD - and then doubtless under the influence of neighbouring religions still inured to proselytizing zeal - that we come across a reference to the resurrection of the dead and the afterlife. Without ever entering into detail about the abode of the deceased, SHeHoL, the texts of the period nonetheless make mention of it. A text about how individual prayer can count on a blessing from God to restore life to the dead is a late addition possibly dating from around the BC/AD boundary.

Christianity, availing itself of the resurrection of Jesus, to which it endlessly bore witness, experienced its own peculiar rise. It continued to hold forth about the afterlife, about paradise, hell, purgatory, and even invented, in the eleventh century, the realm of limbo, destined for babies dying without baptism. It quickly used its notion of the afterlife to ground its political sway, being prepared to make use of its power of intercession to sell interventions of grace, a feature that eventually provoked the Protestant schism.

Where Islam is concerned, today's media, having in recent years had to report on so many events involving some of its adherents, have widely publicized that religion's views on the subject. They are more radical, and in particular more evocative and still more vivid than those of Christianity. The Koran is studded with references including any number of subtleties about the afterlife. Since, moreover, the Koran ascribes to God absolute power to which the human being has no choice but to submit (the word 'Muslim' literally means 'submitted'), its references to the afterlife acquire all the greater force. It is understandable, therefore, how misreading of the Koran's message could feed through into Islamist suicide bombing, a phenomenon which itself is reminiscent of the human sacrifices of the religions of idols, especially those of the cult of Baal, which Islam has always violently opposed.

Buddhism, and the other Far-Eastern religions that we have hitherto ignored, resolved the matter in an even more original manner, by regarding the body as simply the dwelling place of a soul whose vocation was to be constantly reincarnated until it reached perfection. It was an outlook that made it possible to neglect the body, which might be indifferently burned, placed in the river (in the Hindu variant), or fed to vultures (as in Tibet).

The religious enterprise has therefore always been important, and the passions it continues to raise today are evidence of that fact. This is because it attempts to achieve some resolution of an inherently tragic destiny. Even if religion is no more than an option on particular beliefs that people can decide to hold or not, there is still a human need to find a way to combat the pressure caused by fear of death, so as to invest in life and check the forces of self-destruction that beset everyone, as well as the society to which they belong. That fear is so strong and can often be so disabling that, in order to defend themselves from it and lighten the load it represents, people will clutch at the solution offered them by the beliefs, religion, or faith within which they entered the world, adhering to the same and being ready to defend, with their lives if necessary, the relevance and truth of that framework.

The truth of this is even clearer since the end of communism, which has seen a revival of the very religions from which the people were previously deemed to have been set free. It goes to show how superior to the promises of materialism the protective recourse that these religions are perceived to afford still appears to be. The point was aptly summed up by André Malraux, when he said famously: 'The twenty-first century will either be religious or it will not be.' Despite its prophetic overtones, Malraux's opinion was in reality based simply on the observations that he, as a great traveller, had made of the different worlds he had passed through. Surely the horrific wars and massacres of the twentieth century, combined with unprecedented media saturation of a world suddenly reduced to the scale of a village, has steeped our human fellows as never before in a fear of death whose pressure seems to have reached a level that is at the limits of the tolerable?

BACK TO THE LAW

Looking closely at this situation, we can see that there are basic resemblances to reactions after the first burial. However huge and effective that first boulder rolled over the frightening corpse may have seemed, it failed to lessen the alarm that had been kindled. It needed another boulder, then another, then branches, earth, and whatever was to hand. Yet all this was not greatly effective, since the fear, far from disappearing, turned into an irremovable anxiety. In effect, all the previously mentioned religions add up to so many new boulders intended to dispel the effects of that anxiety, whereas the Law of the Species that was established (or had already been established, depending on the standpoint one adopts), ought in principle to have sufficed on its own.

For what did that Law, which outwardly prohibited unions between close relations in order to advance the exchange of women, promote if not the delineation of a succession of generations in an irreversible process that, conforming to the unfolding of time and its onward direction, ought long since to have anchored human beings in time and caused them to accept its logic? Not that that would have been the conscious aim of the Law's promoters. It was pointed out earlier that whatever historic scenario we opt for, the primary object of the Law's adoption was to establish the terms and conditions whereby women were exchanged. But as with any number of other rules in life, its consequences and meta-message would have imprinted themselves upon human beings. To be placed in an arrangement and give acceptance to it always ultimately entails adhesion to the arrangement's content - an adhesion that involves the body as well as mental attitudes. From the Actors Studio we have learned that actors called upon to play particular roles will only give a truthful performance if they can make an effort to feel the emotions of the character, which is something that the text and the situations acted will certainly assist. But it has been shown also that just mimicking the emotions played will in turn profoundly modify the actor's own inner world.

Be that as it may, it is common knowledge that the Law of the Species was not universally easy to impose. It was a tall order: something major and totally new. The anthropologist Frazer humorously enquired why humanity had needed to make such a law, when nobody had ever felt the need to invent one to stop people putting their hands in fire. That was a subtle way of indicating that we are all, without exception, so attracted by incest, that humanity needed and continues to need a Law to stop us succumbing to it. Saying that is not to prejudge the effectiveness of that Law, since every society undertook to strengthen it with no end of legal arrangements.

As for the factors making such arrangements necessary, these clearly related, first, to the relationship that every male believed he could have with his mother, and secondly, by extension, to his relationship with all that was close to him. If one recalls that women were not consulted when treated as an object of exchange among men, it becomes easier to understand their natural inclination not to discourage insistent interest directed towards them by their children. They were indeed disposed to welcome such overtures. There were reasons for this. If we take literally the anthropological definition of incest, namely, 'to make the same with that of oneself', it is conceivable that mothers might be drawn to it for more than one reason. Besides the opportunity it afforded to protest against the Law and put brakes on its execution, it offered them the chance to believe that they could reproduce as if by cloning, or, at the very least, that a mother could abduct her children and make them hers alone with the view possibly of bestowing them upon the history into which she herself was written. That children borne by her and durably marked by her should wish to return 'inside' her is by no means extraordinary. Women who have had several children often say, when questioned about the arrival of a new baby, that their earlier-born regresses, seeks the breast, feeding-bottle, or napkin, and may even voice a desire to go back into mummy's tummy. This is all understandable, if one bears in mind the fact that the child does not want to grow up, for he knows already that life comes to an end. Now, without the intervention of mothers themselves to make clear the Law, there is virtually no chance of obtaining the submission of the children to it. When mothers fail to do this, they lock their children into longterm problem areas that can be both harmful to them and capable of transmission across generations. The following clinical vignette is an edifying lesson on this theme.

You Must Always Have A Ready Answer

It was a charming, seven-year-old cherub, with blond, curly hair, and bright eyes, that I had before me that day. His lively presence made quite a contrast with his mother, who seemed both drained and desperate on account of the problem she had come to consult me about. For some years already and despite recourse to various specialists, the cherub, the fourth of her seven children, was encopretic, i.e., he could not retain his stools and soiled his pants. When the symptom was discussed, it seemed not to bother him; in fact, he rewarded me with a smile that was almost divine. Taken aback by this attitude, I ventured to ask him what he thought of the problem. His instant reply was: 'The only thing I think about, the only thing I care about is marrying my mummy.' More than surprised, I was rendered literally speechless. Because the Law generally bears down in spite of everything with such weight and power, such sentiments get voiced only occasionally, and then at best have to be heard between the words - or call for acute listening skills after many sessions of commentary on drawings. It is hardly ever trumpeted, particularly not to a third party who is virtually a complete stranger. I felt I ought to answer this cherubic imp with some firm, well-structured words. But he parried my every remark with a disarming reply. What about his father? Oh, he was going to die one day. And supposing it was a long wait? Oh, he'd wait. Wouldn't she be old by then? He'd still love her. Might she be ugly? No, she'd never be ugly. And so on. The next time I saw him, some two weeks later, his mother was in an even more collapsed state, while he treated me to the same cherubic smile and similar sentiments spontaneously expressed: 'Nothing's different for me; I still want to marry Mummy.' It was as if

he was pleased to have found a confidant, and could forget about his incontinence. Once again I took the unfortunate route of appealing to him logically on the subject, only to discover that he was as implacable and impervious to argument as ever, even though I was if anything more persuasive. Telling him to stop doing it was no good, and he was unafraid of sanctions. That might work with others, but in his case his love was so great that he was prepared to brave everything. At the following session, I was so struck by the mother's total absence of reaction to her child's repeated declarations, that I recalled another mother, who one day had complained to me about similar declarations that her own son constantly pursued her with. I remembered, too, that when I asked her how she had reacted, she had told me that she had quite correctly answered the boy, 'But (sic) there's your father!' Having heard this, it was easy for me to demonstrate to her that such a formula, especially starting with that 'But', was bound to maintain the child in his dead end. I related to the mother of the cherub the story of this earlier child, and she was sufficiently impressed by it to tell her boy on the spot that the project he had in mind for their future life together was of no interest to her, that she had a husband whom she loved, who was the father of all her children, including him, and that she didn't want any other, that he was her son and would remain so for ever, and plenty of variations on the same theme.
The cherub's symptoms disappeared that very evening.

As long as he was not disabused, this cherub remained intimately persuaded that he had every right to feel as he did. It required his mother to reject clearly and unswervingly the content of his message for him to finally abandon the illusion he cherished. That kind of thing is typical of scenarios of unhappy love, and often the fear of causing pain to a wooer, male or female, can lead to a falsely based relationship and indefinitely prolong the torture engendered by misunderstanding.

The situation was thus taken in hand and resolved by the mother's clear-cut attitude. What would have happened if she had not taken that stance? Various factors would have eventually caused the encopresis to disappear; the boy's desire to marry his mother would eventually have been buried. But while the disappearance of the encopresis would have had no further effect upon the development of the defecatory mechanisms, the repression of the desire would have left the psyche with a trace that would have availed itself of the first opportunity to re-express itself with the same energy. Another clinical vignette may be cited to illustrate this point.

The Extremities of Love's Pretensions

I had already detected how very nervous the couple were. On the father's initiative, they had had lots of consultations about their daughter, a baby of just a few months, yet had never questioned their own anxiety, which they both considered legitimate and which they put down to their inexperience. One day, at nightfall, the child had profuse diarrhoea, although she had been seen to be in perfect health by my colleague during an afternoon consultation that very day. There followed a dash to the hospital and a wait at Accident and Emergency, with the most being made of alarmist remarks by a young duty intern. The upshot was a scene in my clinic the following day, with the father putting us in the dock. He could not accept that it was possible for his daughter to fall ill just a few hours after being examined and declared fit. I had enormous difficulty calming him down, but eventually succeeded. I then took him back to the secretary's office to make the appointment he was requesting for me to check that his daughter was cured. When we arrived there, and as if better to apologize, particularly to the secretary, to whom he had been hostile earlier, he burst out in irrepressible passion concerning his little girl, 'Please understand. I love her. I love her. I love her. I love her to distraction. I'm mad about her. I love her so much that I'll never let any man come near her. And there'd better not be any that try. It's quite simple: when she grows up, I'll marry her!' My secretary burst out laughing, and the wife, dumbfounded, opened her eyes wide. For my part, I said to myself: I must remember to get this man to talk about his mother at our next consultation.

It occurred to me that if I was not mistaken, this young father, 'mad with love' as he himself said, had taken us into a vision of the world that illustrated to perfection the genesis of an incestuous dynamic likely one day, if left unchecked, to be acted out. It can always be suggested that such words as were used by this young father were quite harmless and were never more a jest. That is a good excuse. Like others relating to activities that are trivialized and regarded as harmless, like those of fathers who for years take baths with their daughters, pretexting that it will familiarize them with the opposite sex and prevent the sort of foolish inhibitions that could give rise to repression, prudery, and ignorance - that indeed is the commentary that accompanies such behaviour. But whether it proceeds from a whim or a pseudo-desire for emancipation, and however stigmatizable it would be for anyone other than the incriminated father who sees nothing wrong in it, such behaviour always protests the love that promotes it and justifies its practice.

The questions raised by such love are as follows: What is its nature and visible content? What does it carry within it? What future can it have? What is its source, and what are the currents that maintain it? It is difficult to give a simple reply to questions as extensive as these. But it seems to me that the best way forward may be to reverse the problem-solving dynamic, i.e., to begin not with the symptom produced, but with the conditions that led to it.

My primary point is that father–daughter incest does not happen by accident; it does not come about in a haphazard way, nor does it occur in just any circumstances. It is prepared over a long period by small, yet perfectly traceable, deviations from the Law in the behaviour of earlier generations. In fact it is never anything more or less than the incestuous act that the small boy (the later father) believes that he was called upon to consummate with his mother, and which multiple factors will have prevented him from carrying out.

I would go so far as to say that if the father who in my second vignette declared that he wanted later to marry his daughter harboured the germination of an incestuous impulse, it was only the resumption of an impulse identical to that of the cherub in the first vignette, i.e., it was an impulse that the father had had as a boy. I would also advance that the initial impulse, having been repressed as such, was not due to the existence or hatching of perverse dispositions within him, but occurred only because he, too, had been the special target of strong impulses coming from his mother. That would explain why the Law of the Species has provoked, and continues to provoke, so many problems. It is because maternal attitudes towards time and the fear of death have always been, and perhaps were even before the first burial, radically different from male attitudes. This is not to say - far from it - that mothers are solely and entirely responsible for difficulties encountered in the Law's application. Their propensity conveys any number of strengths that no child can do without to have a fulfilling life. But this propensity needs to be boundaried, so that the child can interiorize time and in turn make it the essential ingredient of his own person. Incest, as an issue, is therefore intimately bound up with that other issue, time. But for the assumption of time, there would be no humanity, only animality - or perhaps we should say only animality in humanity. For, even though incest avoidance behaviours have increasingly been identified in primates and birds, avoidance is all they are about. In human beings, on the other hand, the Law of the Species has been decreed and been communicated through language - as illustrated by the exchanges between my cherub and his mother - and through an awareness of its implications: submission to the logic of the passing of time, and account being taken of the ineluctability of death, which is its consequence. Incest deliberately ignores the succession, even the existence, of the generations, and needs to be read both as an attempt to fix or reverse the passage of time and as a presumptuous (and preeminently 'murderous') drift of thinking that believes it can ignore such laws and successfully block them.

Most probably in order to make the Law it had given itself still more secure, humanity provided itself with other arrangements in addition to the religious systems that from time immemorial and in every place arose and ensured that it was passed on. Though discovered only in the nineteenth century, these arrangements were very ancient. They were outlined as kinship systems.

KINSHIP SYSTEMS

Without most of us ever knowing it or realizing it, or clearly understanding its consequences, it appears that human societies since time immemorial have been organized in accordance with relational structures recognized as kinship systems. Although all of us are involved in such systems, which without our noticing it partly modulate our ways of thinking and acting, they were not discovered and described until the second half of the nineteenth century.

Asked what a kinship system was and what purpose it served, I should be tempted to reply that it was a management regime, or rather a response, discrete and different from those of neighbours, to the central question posed by application of the Law. In other words, it is a collection of provisions intended to inform any individual (ego, in the language of anthropology) in clear, precise terms of the matrimonial alliances that are either permitted or proscribed. Such provisions are accompanied by indications about how ego names his close and distant relations, establishing with them hierarchical links that are obviously affectively charged.

For reasons that are not entirely clear, there are six kinship systems called 'elementary' - hence the most widely spread and certainly the oldest - and a certain number of others called 'complex' or 'semi-complex'. In the light of the huge numbers of codes of communication that *Homo* has been driven to invent during his long adventure of conquering the planet - not least the multitude of languages, of which so many have disappeared (and continue to disappear) - it is surprising how few kinship systems there are. Yet our only option is to accept that it is so, for although the environmental factors might on their own impose many solutions, the organization of parental links, inasmuch as they relate a limited number of individuals, creates many fewer combinations. It is true that the combination of dual relations of the three terms constituted by father, mother, and child give only six possibilities!

The systems we are to look at are not specific to the populations after which they are named. No one knows precisely why or how they came about, or why they exist in the places they do, but they apply to populations that are totally foreign to one another, some of them being geographically very far flung indeed. After all, what connection is there between the Inuits, the Saxons, the Sardinians, and the Savoyards, all of whom obey the same kinship system? The name that describes their system is simply derived from the first population study to formally identify it.

The so-called 'Eskimo' system, to which we in the west belong, privileges the nuclear family; it does not use separate terms to identify whether the grandparents or uncles and aunts are maternal, paternal, or by marriage, and it assigns the same name and rank to cousins. It may be a source of surprise that the system has a peculiarity that most people will never have had occasion to remark upon, namely that we use the same term 'uncle' to describe our father's brother and our mother's brother, as well as the husband of our mother's or father's sister. The prohibition of marriage between cousins characterizes this system, though as far as France is concerned that particular provision was amended in the 1920s. Be that as it may, this system is but one of six.

In the so-called 'Hawaiian' system, all the aunts and uncles are called mother and father, and all the cousins are called brother and sister: it is as if the whole of one generation regards it as its common task to raise the whole of the next generation. Although the genitors are perfectly identifiable, ego in this system has at his disposal several mothers and several fathers who have the same prerogatives and functions regarding him as regarding all the children of his generation. This system, however, contains more internal barriers than the Eskimo system, since no state legal arrangements exist to enable ego to marry the offspring of his genitors' brothers and sisters, i.e., those he sees as his brothers and sisters.

The 'Iroquoian' system names the biological father and all his brothers father, and calls the biological mother and all her sisters mother. On the other hand, the father's sisters are called aunts, and the mother's brothers uncle. The children of all these fathers and mothers are designated brothers and sisters, while the term cousin is reserved to the children of the genitor's sisters (the aunts), and to those of the genetrix's brothers (the uncles). In this system, it is as if ego has to identify himself according to two family gatherings united by him, a male branch and a female; since all the issue of these two branches are considered his brothers and sisters, he must find a conjugal partner among the children of other family gatherings.

Things are more complex in the 'Crow' system. As in the Iroquoian system, all the father's brothers are called father, all the mother's sisters are called mother, and their respective children, i.e., those of the father's brothers and those of the mother's sisters, are called brothers and sisters, and hence ego cannot marry them. Special terms are reserved for the father's sisters and the mother's brothers. These peculiarities mean that the children of the mother's brothers are called sons and daughters, while the father's sisters' sons are called father, and their daughters are called father's sisters. Here again, regardless of personal wishes, marriage can only be with a child from a distant group.

In the 'Omaha' system, the father's brothers are, as in the two last systems, called father, and the mother's sisters called mothers; all their respective children are called brothers and sisters. The mothers' brothers are called mother's brothers, and their sons inherit the same title, while their daughters are called mothers - which can mean that an adult man, even quite an old man, may address his maternal aunt's granddaughter as 'mother'. Only the father's sisters' children - who would simply be cousins in the Eskimo system - receive the curious title of nephews and nieces. Here, similarly, everything is done to equip the system with internal bars to marriage.

Finally, the 'Sudanese' system gives different names to the uncles and aunts according to whether they are maternal or paternal, and names the cousins according to their position (mother's brother's or sister's son, or father's brother's or sister's daughter, for example). In this system, the reverse occurs of what happens in the other systems, since marriages between collaterals are not simply accepted, but actually encouraged.

If to the existence of such systems we add house rules for new couples adopted by the various cultures, customs, or traditions, we are confronted by arrangements that make the relocation of individuals from their group of origin extremely problematic - it is as though their group alone saved them from infringing the Law. All this is not without consequence in our modern world, where the mixing of populations favours love pairings between individuals from mutually foreign systems and cultures; these on occasions go nowhere owing to the unconscious pressure of such elements. The fact is that an individual's vision of the world is formatted (to borrow from computer-speak) by the system and culture in which he or she has been raised.

While the differences in the terms and conditions governing marriage are striking enough, the consequences of differences in those according to which children are reared are not always so obvious.[13] True, it is difficult for us, who live according to the logic established by the Eskimo system, to conceive how the ideal marriage within cultures obeying the Sudanese system, which includes North Africa, could be that of a niece with her paternal uncle, or his son. Indeed, western colonizers wasted no time in exploiting such a discovery to justify their mission to those they regarded as savages in need of civilization. But later on, this same mentality was seen to go into reverse when westerners, with similarly exaggerated enthusiasm, took to advocating that lessons were to be drawn from these hitherto despised populations on the ground that they were authentically closer to nature. I remember, for instance, how around 1960, demand feeding was imported from sub-Saharan Africa. Films showed babies being held close to their mothers until quite late on and availing themselves freely of the breast that was at their easy disposal. From this it was argued that these happy babies, having satisfied their need to suck, did not suck their thumbs. The conclusion was immediately drawn that we, too, needed to return to the healthy laws of wonderful Mother Nature and allow ourselves to be guided by our own bambinos, who were certainly as bright and had the same potentialities as those we were shown. I could date from that period the regrettable drift of our societies towards enthronement of the *enfant-roi*, the 'sovereign child'. We may wonder how such good intentions could have such a wretched effect. The simple answer surely is that because differences across cultures and kinship systems were ignored, totally erroneous conclusions were drawn on the basis of facts specific to a given culture and system. Mistakenly, demand sucking at the breast was associated with nonsucking of the thumb, whereas what was being unremarkably evidenced was that the baby, having a close and continual contact with the mother, never

---

[13] I had a couple to see me one day to ask me to arbitrate on the rearing of their three children. The mother was Swedish, the father Japanese; their opinions were radically divergent on nineteen points, which they meticulously listed opposite French opinions that were evidently different again. It was a very instructive consultation.

felt the need to hallucinate her presence by sucking its thumb. Our ideological drift towards the 'sovereign child' results from just such serious failures to look at imported cultures and systems in the round. The deference of African women in this respect to their children was due to a whole host of factors - not least a shortage of resources - that are absolutely different from those applying to western mothers. In any event, the African situation is not of indefinite duration. Whether or not forced out by a new arrival, the African child will soon be required to distance himself somewhat from his natural mother, who will be relayed by all the women in the group, and assume his status as a child, i.e., in the logic of his generation. Such conditions avoid the overinvestment which our little westerners suffer, being the cherished and exclusive objects of mothers often prepared to live only for and through them.

Approximations, misunderstandings, and confusions of this sort are probably due to interactions between the various styles of parental definition attested by the dispositions of the various systems outlined above. It cannot be irrelevant that in one of them all the men of one generation constitute so many fathers, and all the women so many mothers, while in another only the genitor and his brothers are regarded as fathers, and only the genetrix and her sisters count as mothers; meanwhile, in a third, the titles of father and mother are strictly reserved to the genitor and genetrix alone. My own reading has no more offered a ready explanation for these variations than it has indicated factors likely to have brought them about. But geography, with all that it means in terms of climate and subsistence economy, will certainly have played a part, encouraging adaptive, quasi-reflex forms of conduct which will have been retained or amended, when not abandoned. Prevailing arrangements will certainly therefore not be an outcome of whim or chance, but rather of a deliberate decision to adopt the economically most advantageous solution to situations of inextricable conflict. This subsequently will have been passed on through a linguistic code which will never cease to be active, even though common usage down the generations may allow original meanings to be forgotten.

Kinship systems, and the cultures that are associated with them, thus enclose individuals in the mesh of a logic that is not always easy to decipher.

I will not expand on the difficulties encountered by mixed couples formed by the union of a native with a partner having an immigrant background.[14] But they cannot be explained simply by differences in culture and religion. What counts also is the pressure produced by the differences in logic between the two kinship systems present; in France, the two systems most frequently involved are the Sudanese and the Eskimo. The pressures produced often sweep all before them and can sometimes wear down the best wills in the world. The truth of this has been confirmed to me by the borderline cases that I have encountered, and which involved - as no outsider would ever imagine - certain Jewish couples who might have been expected to be spared by a solid commonalty of religion and ways of thought from the sort of problems they told me about. Most often, they were 'mixed' couples, i.e., though both Jewish, one would be Sephardic and the other Ashkenazi in origin. Within the Jewish community, the Ashkenazis (the word meaning 'German' in Hebrew) comprise Jews of essentially ancient European origin, while the Sephardics (meaning 'Spanish' in Hebrew) are the Jews of Mediterranean, Middle Eastern, and North African origin, even though many of them can trace their European origins back to before the Inquisition. The Jews, who have lived and continue to live in different cultural zones, have always adopted most of the arrangements that go with them, so that the Ashkenazis in Europe obey the sort of cultural rules that are prevalent in the Eskimo system, whereas the Sephardics, having lived or living still in an Arabo-Islamic zone, adhere to those of the cultures prevalent in the Sudanese system. In these last, patrilocality is the rule.[15] What this means is that the couple that the son forms is integrated into his family of origin, i.e., it integrates his bride, and the couple that the daughter forms devolves on her husband's family of origin. In the cases I came across, there were always problems when an Ashkenazi bride of a Sephardic husband refused to be integrated into her in-laws' family, claiming the prevalence of her links to her original family, or when the Sephardic bride of an Ashkenazi felt rejected because she was not integrated into her in-laws' family in the way that her brother's wife would have been by her own family. Of course problems of this

---

[14] Such marriages are never the effect of chance but rather of necessity dictated by a history that the subjects cannot always access but which governs them nonetheless.

[15] Even so, this is not always the case; it is possible to find widely divergent uses and customs even within the same kinship system.

sort do tend to fade down the generations, and the immediate prevalent culture wins out in the end and imposes its own logic. But such resolution takes time, and cannot help throwing up problems along the way whose unsuspected outworkings may sometimes wreak havoc.

It may help understanding of problems of this sort, if appeal is made to the notion of identity that is clutched at more and more these days by our contemporaries. Yet in saying that, it is not always possible to account for the phenomenal energy powering the claims made. But if we bear in mind that the kinship system, culture, even uses and customs, are so many complementary points of reference, all of which help to lessen the pressure of the fear of death, then full allowance can be made for the ferocity of the confrontations that take place. Perhaps that alone, and nothing else, is what underlies the hackneyed notion of demands for identity, of which phenomenon the recent debate in France over the display of religious symbols and the Islamic headscarf affords one of the best developed illustrations.

CULTURAL CODES

When account is taken of all the many curious inventions that our species has come up with down the hundreds of thousands of years of its evolution, it seems hardly necessary to draw attention to the degree of ingenuity it has shown since our distant *Homo* ancestor walked the earth. Through the exponential multiplication of *Homo*'s neuron connections, evolution has fashioned a brain that is capable of passing on its developed state from one generation to another. Human education does not date from yesterday; both passively and actively it has always existed, geared to passing on beliefs and knowledge to a lineage that watches out for them, demands them, and is by definition permeable to them. This long drawn-out process could not avoid using trial and error, which always succeeds in the end; it has brought us to what we even today imagine is the unsurpassable truth about our world, although the recent developments of atomic physics, genetics, and molecular biology among other things invite us to regard the least of our certainties as relative. Extrapolating back almost no distance in time, we are forced to recognize that human progress has always groped along, and that doubts expressed about this or that view today do not imply that our ways of thinking as a whole are invalid. The fact that Aristotle, Euclid, Homer, Pythagoras, and Marcus Aurelius did not know that the earth went round the sun or that the American continent existed does not diminish the importance of their works for us today. However one views the time distance separating us from them, we are bound to acknowledge that we continue to be indebted and closely linked to them.

It is certain that human cultures, in response to their particular environmental imperatives, very long ago created their own modes of thought, exchange, and being, as well as rules of behaviour of which no tangible trace remains since writing is barely five thousand years old. I would posit, however, that these modes and rules will assuredly have imprinted themselves upon the language spoken by the particular group in an extraordinarily precise, efficient, and irremovable way, for all languages confer on their speakers, without their realizing it, a vision and understanding of the world that are specific to them. When it comes to translating a language, the concrete register generally poses few difficulties - spoon, boat, house, or garden have equivalents in all languages - while the same cannot be said of the abstract register through which vision of the world is mediated.

The verb 'to be', that all-important linguistic component, which is frequently irregular in languages derived from Indo-European, affords an excellent illustration of the variants that arise from the history and geographical location of the populations that use it. Thus it is possible to track back that the French *je suis* (equivalent to the English 'I am') is derived from the Latin *sum*, which in turn is derived from the Greek *eisum*, while this last connects to the Latin infinitive *esse* in its sense of 'to be found', 'to be oneself', i.e., 'to be what one is' - something found in the English *I am*, a contraction of the ancient expression *I as me*, a joining together of the two expressions of simple identity *I* and *me*. But the English *to be*, as in all the uses of *be*, just like like the German *bin*, are related to the Greek stem *phuo*, which gave the Latin perfect *fui*, and all originate from the radical *phusis*, which means 'to grow'. Thus we 'are' because we 'have grown'; we *shall* be when we 'shall have grown' so to speak. As for the German *sein*, which replaced the old *wesen*, this connoted tarrying, i.e., ceasing to wander or lead a nomadic life, as it were. The notion of being to which this referred was conveyed in Latin by *habitus* - the same notion exists in French and English - corresponding to the Greek *ethos* (hence the English word *ethic*), and which connoted a 'way of being through remaining longterm'. This same notion of stability is moreover found in certain French dialects, where *Où restez-vous?* (literally, 'Where are you staying?') is used in place of the standard French *Où habitez-vous?* (literally, 'Where do you dwell?'). Compared to all this, it is all the more striking that the nomadic Semitic populations did not have a verb 'to be' in the present tense, the notion being conveyed by simple apposition: *ana mrid* means 'I [am] ill' in Arabic; *ani gadol* means 'I [am] big' in Hebrew; *ana fi lmadarssa* means 'I [am] at school' in Arabic; *ani babaït* means 'I [am] at home' in Hebrew. It is as though the apposition was intended to signal the ubiquitousness of the nomad's presence, signifying his atopic way of life and at the same time legitimizing it. Modern Hebrew has curiously preserved this construction. It is perhaps due to the sedentary past of the populations in place and their use of a present tense of 'to be' that dialectal Arabic, derived from Classical Arabic after the conquest, acquired a present tense of 'to be', and even used it as an auxiliary verb, by saying *rabi* for 'I am', this *rabi* actually meaning literally, 'He saw me'. This model thus provides a present tense of 'to be' that is literally conjugated as 'He saw me', 'He saw you', 'He saw him', and so on, whereby the speaker appeals to a third party to witness to his being - or to his sedentary state? - and sees himself as separate from him. Hence perhaps can be understood, if not deduced, the behavioural differences that can be observed between the distant coolness, not to say disdain, of the Europeans, confident in their certainties and the security encouraged by their rich environment, and the Mediterraneans, hailing all and sundry with gesture and voice, hoping by a look to be granted the right to be where they are and be able simply to assure themselves that they are.

Unfortunately, I do not have enough specialized knowledge to be able to extrapolate these examples to other world populations, but I am sure that my hypothesis could be verified. I am regularly amazed by what my etymological dictionary reveals to me, and have long taken pleasure in collecting the various names given to the various family relationships represented in the over forty languages spoken by my clients. Despite regular differences in the signifiers, the sense they convey is broadly similar;

thus the grandparent, in all its grammatical forms, is 'great', 'ancient', 'distant', or even 'from before', and so on. What is striking, however, is the *homo*nymy that the Arabic word for the male grandparent shares with the word for 'powerful', which is understandable in fact if one bears in mind that the word for 'father' in that language equally connotes 'possessor' or 'owner'. At the same time, there are some amusing variants from district to district, since the term 'powerful' that is *homonymic* with 'grandfather' is relevant only to the paternal grandfather, his maternal counterpart being addressed by his grandchildren as 'father + his forename'. This phenomenon could correspond to those places in our northern latitudes where, as in some circles in France, the distinction is made between maternal and paternal grandparents by addressing one side as *papy* and *mamy* and the other side as *pépé* and *mémé*. But to address the maternal grandfather as another father is not insignificant: it is indicative of an arrangement of whose place in the unconscious we are not unaware.

Clearly there is scope for a good deal of commentary, on the basis of apparently trivial examples like these, about the attitudes of speakers of these different languages and their inherent expectations from the least exchange. Yet it would seem that only the filiations of languages have been studied by linguistic science, while the circumstances and necessity of their creation have been no more successfully grasped than the genesis of word formation itself. All the same, is there anything to prevent our envisaging languages as so many codes capable of facilitating communication among speakers through the sheer arbitrariness or conventionality of signifiers? Little ones, when they begin linguistic communication, do not ask so many questions when they coin neologisms in order to refer to objects or actions. In France, they may twist *chaussure* (shoe) into *totu*, *bouteille* (bottle) into *batil*, or *voiture* (automobile) into *vroumtu*, using such coinages without any worries or hesitation, and do not give up such formations in exchange for ordinary forms unless and until they feel that they have not been sufficiently understood - failing that, they linger in a system that is their own, the advantage of which is that it enables them to have special communication with their mothers. As for the way in which the different pidgins have grown up all over the world, it seems to attest if nothing else how easy it is for humans to devise the codes of communication that serve them, even if that includes needing to borrow - and corrupt - linguistic material provided by neighbours or invaders.

The peculiarities that I have tried to list here are not products of chance. They all have a history that legitimizes them and to which, it seems to me, insufficient attention has been paid, given that such histories are implicated in the forging of so many specific visions of the world.

Now a vision of the world is no meagre thing. It is neither whim nor fantasy, still less a minor detail. It is what people cling to passionately, seeing it as *the* supreme truth, to the point where they almost lose all possibility of imagining how there can be - if only for others than themselves - some other truth or perspective. They may even go so far as to be ready to fight to the death for their vision and try to force others to adhere to it, as though the existence of another vision represented an intolerable threat to their own. Nor is this so incomprehensible, if one remembers that such visions of the world do nothing less in their construction than articulate all that enables their adherents to mitigate the pressure that comes from the fear of death that continually besets them.

What, then, has been achieved through the accumulation of precautions and procedures that have continued to evolve and which (to cite merely their most important elements) range from a burial to myths and religions, and embrace a Law, legal dispositions, kinship systems, moral codes, and linguistics? It is a question that is all the more valid, since whole libraries are devoted to individual aspects of what I here can only paint schematically using the broadest of brushstrokes. At its heart can be discerned the coming and goings of some shadowy figures: a worrying mother, an irritable father, and a child who waits. But to repeat the question: What have all these accumulated precautions and procedures achieved for human beings? It cannot be denied that they have helped them to provide for their subsistence and reproduction. They have also surely assisted their socialization. If it is unclear how all this has operated, then surely the answer lies in the way all these elements have helped human beings throughout history to manage the pressure caused by the fear of death and to cope as best they could with the time-span in which, whether they liked it or not, they were fixed. For what we learn first and foremost from the various stages over which I have lingered in this discussion, is that for each and every person there is a strict correlation between the stress provoked by anxiety about dying and the quality of life that can be attained. When that pressure reaches a maximum, human beings are literally no longer capable of living; when it reaches its lowest level, they are able to view the time they have to live as an inestimable gift and can at once occupy it with a joy that seeks only to be expressed.

Such is doubtless the most obvious benefit that we owe to this long, complex adventure, in which our own era is but a stage that might be regarded as run-of-the-mill, if it did not concern us directly and force us to take stock, however crudely, of where we are in it.

Now we need to ask whether the sustained, unidirectional cultural activity of which we have been talking happened by chance or whether it had an agent - whether or not he was conscious of what he was about.

THE GIFT OF THE FATHER

If we had to sum up everything that has been contributed down to the present, we should have to confess that until and including our own era, evolution has never ceased to confront, albeit without too much success, the problematic complexity of relations between the males and females of our species.

From their earliest beginnings, human males - men - had always given top priority to the (perhaps consolatory) satisfaction of their sexual needs by mating with their females, the women who, in common with all animal females, alone had the capacity to bring children of the two sexes into the species and therefore ensure its reproduction.

One day the men formed themselves into a band of malefactors. The crime they committed, though it reinforced their cohesion, afflicted them with a lasting fear of death and created in them a more or less hazy consciousness of the timescale within which their spans of life were contained. The violence of that discovery no doubt left them for centuries if not millennia in what could be likened to a form of disarray. This would have been all the greater inasmuch as they surely could not have shared anything about the experience with their partners, who in any case could not, one imagines, have said anything to console them. Their females had doubtless long faced this problem themselves, and they had ended up resolving it in their own way, by deliberately banishing all awareness of time in an effort to reject the death of their children. We may wonder what sort of audience they would have made for their males' discovery. That death strikes? Big deal! They had always known that: had they not experienced it in the flesh of their flesh? Moreover, what did they have to gain by such a realization, when the subtle system of denial that they had arrived at offered them some protection? Despite its inadequacy, they had managed to gain some benefit from it, for it enabled them to go on devoting the same energy to their living children. There was once and for all no question of death's being presented to them as something ineluctable. Such an appraisal, such a dialogue, both imaginary, never took place, never could, and moreover never has.

The women - the mothers - thus kept to themselves, continuing to fulfil the tasks that were essential to their progeny. The men - the genitors - kept to themselves, too, weighed down by the unbearable stress caused by the anxiety of which we have spoken. But in order to rid themselves of it, or at least lighten its load, they were led to master their animal drives, deal with the impulsive side of their make-up, enter into exchange with their fellows, and devise ways of managing these new relationships. Their agreement over the exchange of potential partners was sealed by the establishment of the Law of the Species. Dimly perceiving, however, that this Law, which they had wilfully imposed on their female companions, had need of fully enforceable terms, they missed no opportunity, especially when driven by necessity, to augment its provisions with linguistic codes, the construction of kinship systems, the elaboration of legal measures, and the invention of cultural or cult constructs. All of this gave rise to mythologies that bore the obscured memory of the stages traversed, as well as the highly problematic realization of the fixedness of our species within time - that dimension which was uncontrollable, yet contained the outworking of the species within it. The men neither desired nor even knew what they were doing, being simply driven by what could be styled their fundamental self-centredness. Even so, they were the agents of our species's extraction from the animal kingdom, and thus of its humanization.

They had always been there, the men, facing the women whom they treated as they wished and whom - without intending it or for a long time realizing it - they turned into mothers, the devoted, attentive, protective, comforting and strenuous guardians of their children; sometimes, perhaps, they already recognized their own mothers among the women. Yes, they had always been there, the men, who were much less well qualified than the women, whether mothers or not, for the care their offspring required. Not that they were that concerned, for they always reserved priority for themselves, refusing to sacrifice the satisfaction of the least of their needs, particularly the sexual. But, over thousands of years, as they adapted unceasingly to environmental conditions and to those imposed by the practice of exchange, they laboured to perfect the organization of their most intimate and most immediate group, the one with which they spent most of their time and which they took with them in their wanderings, comprising their female companion(s) and their offspring. Taken together, these no doubt increasingly clearly assumed the profile of what would later be dubbed 'family'. Thus the males of the species, the men, anxious to gain admission to their partners, one day definitively accepted, or rather ruled upon, the substantive bonds that they had forged with their partners and the children whom they had begotten by them. They created the conditions likely to ensure the recognition of their status, not the least of which conditions was the support the couple would gain from external recognition. It may be said in this connection that the evolution of our species now bestowed upon it a gift, the gift of the authority that is specific to it, the gift of the father.

The fact that this resulted from an adaptive process that was perfectible and endlessly revisable did not prevent its leaving a deep and universal imprint on the human psyche. That imprint has come right down to us, for, having assumed the position of guarantor of a Law by which he knew that he also was bound, this father was radically different from an animal genitor, even if the animal male genitor could be acknowledged in some species as having a role and function oriented to the protection of his offspring and the prolonging of life. Being constantly confronted by his children's mother's consubstantial animality, which continually contended with him in the name of the tyrannical love she bore for her children and of the incommunicable knowledge she possibly always had concerning death, the father had to deal with any number of problems, which he endeavoured to solve through innovations and discoveries that were always oriented toward building the awareness of time and accepting the mortal condition.

Even so it must not be thought that this evolutionary process - which took an ignorant and selfish genitor, like the one buried in the very first grave, and turned him into a father conscious of his place and prerogatives, like the Roman *paterfamilias*, having led him through the stage of the essentially sociological father, like the one who pioneered the exchange of women and thereby the establishment of the Law of the Species - is only of historiographical interest, being a chapter of past accidents that probably changed history and caused it to go off suddenly in a new direction. Rather, the lesson learned at every stage remains alive within us and is robustly active - as is revealed by the following clinical vignette which I was fortunate to come by.

The Other Side Of The World

I wasn't particularly pleased, that afternoon, to have to go to my consulting-room on my weekly day off. But I couldn't dodge the urgent request of my lawyer friend either when, without giving me any further detail, she told me how desperate she was to have my opinion about the complex situation of a family whose case she was responsible for.

They came into my office: a lady of at least 40, a tall girl of about 12, a gentleman no older than 30, and two other, smaller children, a boy of about 5 and a girl between 3 and 4 years old. The lady and the tall girl spontaneously took the seats that were facing my desk, while the gentleman and the two smaller children sat closely together on the sofa.

The lady was the first to speak, and told me the following story. Years before, she had had what she believed was a significant relationship for some months, when her partner suddenly disappeared. She tried to contact him at home, and then at his office, where she was told that nobody had seen him. The friends they had in common and his family had had no news from him either, and they were as surprised and worried as she was. She therefore went to the police to report him as missing. After a long interview, they recorded her deposition and promised to keep her informed of developments. Weeks went by, during which her anxiety gave way to a form of sadness and weary resignation.

Such was her state of mind when she answered the telephone to her erstwhile partner, calling her from the other side of the world. He had found a job about which the words tumbled out as he described how wonderful it was. He was in lyrical mode, telling her how mild the climate was, how blue the sky, what colour the sea was, how magic the light, and how like paradise the atmosphere he had found there was. Hearing all this, she didn't know whether to be relieved or irritated, and wondered what this sudden phone-call was in aid of. He, meanwhile, was asking her to join him and, if she was agreeable, to marry him. She couldn't believe her ears, and had him repeat his proposal several times. The call lasted a long time. He ended up convincing her. In less than a week, she had made arrangements with her parents, put her affairs in order, given notice to her employers, and settled all the details of her life in Paris. Then she made off to the sunshine of the south seas. Hardly a month went by before she found it necessary to escape, in the middle of the night, on the first plane she could catch, to an island some two and a half thousand kilometres away. Her life had turned into a hell: an unexpected and serious change of mood had come over her new husband, who had suddenly started drinking heavily and battering her every evening. In the town where she landed, she several days later found a job as a secretary. She was sufficiently happy with her new post and the friends she had made to abandon, at least temporarily, any plans to return to France. Months went by. She got over her lamentable marriage. The life she now led was easy and agreeable. Still more time went by, without her fully realizing the fact. Relations and friends came to visit; none were able to persuade her to go back with them. Then one evening, in the bar of the only hotel on the island, she met *a man who made himself agreeable to her and whom she found charming. Although she had slept with no one since her marriage, she spent the night with him. The next day, he had gone, and she realized she didn't even know his first name. He nevertheless left her something to remember him by, because over the coming week she discovered that she was pregnant. Far from being upset about it, she felt the pregnancy could supply her life with new direction. She had a little girl - the tall girl who now accompanied her to my consulting-room - whose upbringing brought her immense pleasure. Three or four years later, her material situation had continued to improve, and she acquired a house with a garden so large that she needed to take on a gardener to look after it. After several months, she became attached to the gardener; he moved in with her, and they had two children - he was none other than the younger gentleman who had accompanied her to the consultation, and their two children were the younger children who now sat pressed against him on the sofa.*

All went very well indeed, and things might have gone on that way but for a letter that came from France, telling her that she was the beneficiary of a very large legacy. She returned to Paris with her partner and their children. They were so delighted with what they discovered - the bequest was indeed large, and included a magnificent house in a smart suburb - that they decided to stay and get married.

She took herself off to the mairie, the town-hall, to see to the formalities. Here, however, they pointed out to her that she was already married, and that in order to make what she seemed to want to do at all realistic, she would need beforehand to divorce her first husband. To set about this she consulted a lawyer - the friend who sent her to me - who managed to trace the first husband, something that was not a foregone certainty at the outset. Things however became complicated when the husband - doubtless to create trouble for her out of revenge for their past history - demanded, as a quid pro quo for his consent to the divorce, contact with the tall girl, whom she had nevertheless locally declared at the birth as hers alone - paternity of the two younger children was acknowledged by the gardener.

Although she was able to martial the appropriate dates and told her story with plenty of corroborating testimonies and supporting documents, the judge would not rule in her favour. Her daughter, born in marriage and unacknowledged by any other man, was identified by the court as the child of her husband. Accordingly, she would have to be entrusted to him, as was customary, for one weekend in two, and for half the school holidays. The girl in question, being old enough to be heard according to the International Convention on the Rights of the Child, shouted at the judge that she did not want to visit that man, who was unknown to her, and that she already had a father - the gardener, whom she pointed to as such - and wanted no other. The judge decided therefore to withdraw her from her mother and place her in an institution where psychologists were charged with the task of obtaining her consent by giving her an ultimatum: the law was the law, and as long as she remained fixed in her attitude, she would not be able to see her mother more than two hours a week - which fell during my afternoon off - whereas she could return and live full-time with her mother if she would only agree to accept the judge's decisions.

The benefit of this story from our point of view is that its episodic structure in time and space brings out very clear distinctions between the genitor (of whom nobody had any knowledge, the mother not even knowing his forename), the social father (the mother's husband, whose status the law and the judge charged with safeguarding its application were concerned to protect jealously), and the man the girl herself pointed to as her father, to whom, although he was neither her genitor nor her social father, she attached so much importance that she was prepared to defend his status at the cost of her own freedom.

Whilst our incursion into anthropology has helped to throw some light on the category of genitor (the first paternal category in the history of our species), as also on that of social father (the category at the root of the Law of the Species), we are still some way from understanding what it is that made our gardener so precious, and apparently so clearly defined, for a big girl with whom he in principle had not the smallest direct attachment.

Put another way, fatherhood is much more complex than it might have seemed at first sight. Yet fatherhood is, for all the confusion from which we have not succeeded in rescuing it, the phenomenon that essentially explains not only the differences in the ways that societies and peoples organize themselves but also the convulsive changes experienced by our western societies in recent decades. If we want to achieve greater clarity, we need first to study the strange relationship which, from far back in our long history, has always, for better or worse, both united the child's two parents and pitted them against each other.

Chapter 4
Solid Mothers Versus Nebulous Fathers[16]

Solidity was always their salient characteristic - I speak of mothers - even before they were called upon to submit to the transformations demanded by the new species as it established its hold over them. They only barely tolerated having to adapt the animal dispositions that had always been their buttress to the new conditions that were created for them. Subjected to the violence of the sexual drive of males sent crazy by continual female availability, the females resigned themselves to being the stake in male quarrels, and kept their distance from male devices, the male perspective being one that remained alien to them and of which they doubtless wanted no knowledge. Is it possible that they derived advantages and compensations from this situation, inasmuch as they continued with it, without appearing to react, for millions of years? They must have had remarkable energy reserves to persist in so recalcitrant an attitude. Unless they alone knew what pleasure, as well as pain, it could bring them. Perhaps they were aware of the happiness, strength, and power that was theirs, and it was unthinkable that they should be deprived of all that, should speak of it - how could they? - or reveal its nature. Dependable, resolute, economical, efficient and, more than discreet, confidential, they constituted that 'dark continent' to which Freud would one day compare the quintessential female,

---

[16] Translator's note. The French title to this chapter is 'La Mère sûre et le Père flou', which could be translated into English in many different ways. However, all renderings of the author's opposition *sûre–flou* other than 'solid–nebulous' fall down because too specific. It will appear from the author's discussion that the core contrast is between maternal *tangibility* (definiteness) on the one hand and paternal *intangibility* (not to say mystique) on the other.

Fathers and Mothers

when he accepted his own inability to answer the question - one that remains unanswered to this day - of female desire. What, in short, does the female being, the being she has been since the dawn of time and in principle still is, want when she becomes a mother? She is still as solid as ever she was, and she bids fair to being so for ever. She has the permanence of the air, the sky, and the earth: she is as it were simply the foundation stone of life itself.

On the other hand, it was nebulosity that typified those others - the fathers - all down the long history of the males who did not even know that they were fathers. Nebulous. Indefinite. Undecided. Lumpish and clumsy. Wandering, too. Venturing to the very limits of all they encountered. Laying themselves open, unreserved and unrestrained in all they set about. Eccentric. Extravagant. Untidy. We can imagine a typical example: pursuing without order or hierarchy all the paths that presented themselves to him, even though it should bring him to grief and, occasionally, be the death of the group he had dragged along with him; or else, at other times, managing, with luck on his side, to help his group benefit from some new adaptation or invention. All of this resulted from the pressure of those sexual drives that he had never successfully mastered - and never would entirely. Then, one day, after millions of years of such directionless behaviour, perhaps during the course of some still more crazy project not unconnected with those drives of his, he committed an act that would change his behaviour root and branch: under a heap of rocks he crushed a being who was both hated and feared. This act led him to discover the dimension of time, owing to the fearful anticipation that there would be a reaction to the crime he had just accomplished. Within him it created a fear of death that would never thereafter leave him. Conceiving, and one day confirming, the existence of a hierarchy of relationships, he was induced to perceive his life as fixed in a limited time-span. He therefore set about organizing it, with ever the same crude and precarious means, before endeavouring to give it a sense. Gradually feeling his way through the same nebulosity, never knowing quite where it was taking him, he one day decreed a Law for the species, realizing only somewhat late in the day that its imposition on his female partner would not be so simple in practice. Continuing to feel his way, he tried therefore to improve it with any number of complementary arrangements coloured by the specific environmental conditions obtaining in different places; these colourizations would in turn compromise the Law's integrity or hamper its efficiency, leading to further measures that would lead to yet more refinements, and so on. It might almost be said that, clouded as he himself had always been, he seemed destined forever to inhabit the dimension of nebulosity, never mind where he went or what circumstances he found himself in.

Once cultures had started to develop and were able to spread through writing, various tendencies appeared here and there. One such was that embodied by the Roman *paterfamilias*, who topped the pyramidal family edifice that that society had constructed for him; this gave him the power of life and death over his entire household. Another example was that of the Arabo-Islamic father or *abu*, whose name was synonymous with *owner*; he indeed did own his children, for the legal provisions of the Arabo-Islamic region always gave him custody in divorce proceedings, regardless of fault. When we look at what influence these initiatives had, it seems that while they might be imitated or adapted, they were also open to challenge, if not total opposition. Such a lack of uniformity suggests a universal acceptance and understanding that the sort of solidity associated with mothers could not and should not in any way be counterbalanced or matched by the attribution of an equivalent solidity to the father. It was essential for the wellbeing of the species and of the individuals it comprised that fathers should forever be nebulous - a fact that, yet again, is verifiable from the many studies that have retraced the history of fathers and fatherhood.

The fact that this paternal nebulosity was imposed, preached, advocated, and adopted almost universally as the only possible counterpart to the definiteness or solidity of motherhood is explained by something which I shall return to later. For the moment, let me say that I would never have embarked upon this book, if the father had remained simply nebulous and were not on the verge of disappearing altogether, whether owing to his removal by changes in the contemporary world or to his having removed himself from a position that had become decidedly intolerable. I shall return to this evolution and its contributory factors in due course. Before then, we need more understanding of these twin notions of solidity and nebulosity. To do this we need to look to the behavioural logic - since actions and words alike are gender-related - of the two beings whose destinies are propelled by this evolution.

THE FEMALE AND THE MATERNAL

The title to this section expressly connects two ideas, and is intended to underline the fact that mothers are female beings and that it cannot be otherwise. Lest it be thought that I have fallen prey to a banal and unjustifiable tautology, I am prepared not simply to defend it but to hammer it home. I remember being violently taken to task during a public lecture at the Sorbonne a few years back by a vengeful member of the audience who violently reacted to this linkage by clearly articulating her hope - which was loudly applauded! - that she would soon see me quite properly ... disappear.

Yet it really is essential to labour this point before going on to look at what it is to be a mother, because there is actually huge confusion in this area, not least because technical progress has fed the aberrant notion that mothers are interchangeable, and that motherhood, which has always defined them and continues to characterize them, can be assumed by a non-female. There is not simply the claim of male homosexual partners to have a right to adopt; today's serious debate over human cloning, which is constantly in the media and may be just around the corner, was preceded in the 1970s and 1980s by research into, of all things, male pregnancy. Such research, though ostensibly predicated, as is the case of cloning itself, on veterinary considerations relating to livestock production, has nevertheless fed fantasies about its being extended to our own species.

By voicing what seems obvious to some and insulting to others, I mean to make it possible to re-examine what is specifically female, i.e., to review those characteristics that cannot be referred to the male and have no connection with the male. Neither sex is actually deducible from the other, and it is only feasible to study the two together insofar as we have a detailed inventory of their respective differences. That is why I wish here to sideline the sort of approach that clearly differentiates between the female being and the mother on the one hand, and that of the male being, whether a father or

Fathers and Mothers

not, on the other. Rather, my purpose is to provide a symmetrical and comparative approach that tackles, one after another, the peculiarities of these two characters, both of whom are equally indispensable to the physical health and the correct psychic structuring of all children.

Now at this point I find I cannot resist mentioning an association that has been insisting itself on my consciousness as I write. It may seem a rather trivial observation to make about the differences we are weighing up, but it is something I have been aware of for a long time without ever knowing precisely where it comes from. I have long been struck by the fact that on beaches, café terraces, in the street, or at public gatherings, men never pass up a chance to look at women and that they derive obvious pleasure from doing so - and this does not leave the objects of their attention indifferent either. I have observed, however, that in similar circumstances women, too, look more often at women than at men, i.e., the converse of the effect that mere symmetry would imply. If what is at work here simply related to the capture of the image of the other in order to nurture erotic fantasy, then the fact that women's magazines mostly contain photos of women would equally be difficult to explain.[17] It would be tempting to explain the phenomenon as having a unique function, namely, to enable women who feel unattractive, as often happens, to think about ways in which they could enhance their powers of attraction and thereby attract more attention, either by drawing lessons from those they look at or by drawing inspiration from the models illustrating the full-page spreads. But I do not believe that this explanation, while doubtless partly true, is all there is to it. I think that women (no less than men), when they look at other women, are rewarded by a radiancy of vital energy that female beings, especially when beautiful, manage to provide for the benefit of all and which all seize readily because it costs nothing. It seems to me that beauty ought almost to be seen as a public utility - witness the happiness that infuses us when we stand before a work of art, a fine building, when visiting a beautiful city or gazing at a lovely landscape, and, conversely, the sinking feeling we get when we see a scene of devastation, a grim urban district, or buildings in which aesthetics have

---

[17] This is also true of the men's magazines that seek to imitate them, though in that case it is more to be expected and more understandable.

Fathers and Mothers

been sacrificed to functionality.[18] Aesthetics would seem undeniably to have an erotic effect useful to all because it is accessible to all. As Plato maintained, we humans have definitively associated beauty with life and ugliness with death, inasmuch as life is populated by exchanges and punctuated by love, Eros.

The interest of all this goes well beyond the anecdotal. Without our realizing it, aesthetics infiltrate the most ordinary aspects of everyday life. They explain, for example, the deep emotions stirred up, yet never clarified, by the heated debate in France over the wearing of the Islamic headscarf. Some regard the practice as a manoeuvre designed to perpetuate the oppression of women through a regressive attitude towards the sort of relationships that the majority society encourages them to aspire to. There is some truth in that. But it should not blind us to the time-honoured status of such arrangements, which were probably established on an empirical basis because they proved themselves in practice. We can just imagine how the Mediterranean societies of two thousand years ago that generally prevented women from displaying their beauty, or even showing their face, did so in order to frustrate the men, rather than the women, of the life force that they might draw from it. They were consequently deprived of the forces that could temper their aggression and abandoned to the violence of their death drive; this fostered within them a warlike disposition capable of turning them into determined fighters, ready to embrace any undertaking that might assuage their intolerable inner agitation. Such arrangements, which in their day must have forwarded the campaigns of all empires, from Darius the Great to Alexander, followed by the proselytizing conquests of Islam, are nowadays entirely out of phase with the less overtly bellicose logic of today's international relations. We see then how apt the declarations are of those women struggling in many of the Arabo-Islamic countries who maintain that their open-faced emancipation is a prerequisite for the progress that is desired within their societies.

Having digressed to the point where I find myself propounding the life-

---

[18] By way of a practical demonstration, compare, for instance, the effect of a visit to the city of Dubrovnik with that produced by visiting one of the many Stalinist-style towns thrown up overnight inland of the Dalmatian coast. Alternatively, compare the courtyard of the Louvre in Paris with certain districts in some of the suburbs!

giving and peace-enhancing power of aesthetics, I can only rejoice at the fact that humans come into the world by the mediation of those women who become mothers. They have always been beautiful, are still, and will ever be so. As the popular song has it, *Maman, c'est toi la plus belle du monde* - 'Mum, you are the most beautiful woman in the world.'[19] They may not realize it, but by virtue of this very fact they are broadcasters of life force in abundance.

But is beauty the only thing that unites, virtually fusing in one, the female and the maternal? Or is it possible to link the two dimensions still more profoundly through the solid certainty that seems, under both heads, to express itself in so many strikingly different ways? I would say, in fact, that beauty, life force, certainty, balance, and harmony never cease to be conjoined in the female being, since they are established early, very early indeed, in life, in what is the physically localized source of her body's future development. From the 160th day of her life in the womb, the hollow being created by genetic determinism comes under the influence of a tiny neurological apparatus, the gonadostat, which is made of a mere few dozen cells located in certain nuclei in the hypothalamus. This process, which is as old as humankind itself, provides the emerging ovary with some sixty thousand follicles, of which only about fifteen hundred will persist into puberty, and of which only between three and four hundred will become sufficiently mature to produce at best a handful of children.

This anatomy, which Freud likened to destiny itself, is thus already in place even before the female child enters the world, together with all the intermediate organs to fulfil its mission and the function with which it is entrusted. It is a function whose features all flow from the solidity that upholds them; they are security, reserve, economy, reliability, efficiency, moderation, and consistency.

Security, the first of these features, is easy to see and understand, insofar as everything relative to the development of what the female body will one day contain after fertilization occurs inside it. There it is housed and

---

[19] [Words and music by François Bonifay and Marino Marini (1957), sung by Tino Rossi among others, and originally entitled, *Più bella del mondo* - trans.] Cf. the conversation I had with the cherub of chapter 3, above: the eyes of love behold no ugliness! That said, love does require to be anchored in reality.

serviced by the automatic processing of a machine that has been admirably set by the long, slow, adaptive process of this type of life invented several tens of millions of years ago.

The characteristic of reserve, which directly serves the female body's security is ironically nothing if not blatant in the way it advertises itself. Just one simple sign is required to indicate that a number of things take place therein, without the necessity to specify their nature or spell them out in detail: the most immediate, literally prominent, thing about the female body is the breasts. The message they convey, aside from their unquestionable power of erotic attraction, is that the female body is primarily designed to procreate and even to look after the issue of its pregnancies. It is as though, despite wishes and actions, the splitting off of simple genitality from its procreative potential came up against a natural impossibility, and always required a mental operation or at least an intellectual effort, involving the partners in a prior commitment to the precise course they chose. I shall come back to this issue later, when I discuss the transformation in the status of the child. My reason for lingering on the subject here has absolutely nothing to do with denying that women have purely sexual desire - far be it from me to suggest anything so invidious! It is simply to point out that prior to the comparatively recent perfecting of contraception, the procreative potential signalled by the breasts could never be set aside. Actually, I am not sure that it can even today, given that, in spite of all the contraceptive means available in present-day France, there are still around 250,000 voluntary abortions carried out every year (against an annual live birth rate of 800,000). One might be forgiven for surmising that something within the female unconsciousness stops the decision-making power of the will from blocking the even more powerful faculty of desire. Although these terminated pregnancies are unwanted, they are indisputably desired; otherwise they would not have occurred. Similarly it is an abuse of language when, in France, unwanted children (*enfants non voulus*) are described as 'undesired' (*enfants non désirés*). Their true status is rather of having been desired to such an extent that they have managed to overcome the lack of will that threatened their existence. In order to gauge the extent of the phenomenon, it should be borne in mind that a fully consummated act of sexual intercourse occurring in optimal conditions, i.e., between a fertile woman on the day of ovulation and a male partner with an excellent sperm count, has only a one in four chance of initiating a pregnancy.

But to continue with the dimension of female reserve - which we have not yet fully expounded - that characteristic extends to the female genital organ itself. While the breasts are a prominent feature, the vulva is quite different. It hides away, avoids the eye, as though aware that it cannot get away from the fact of its constant availability to penetration and wished to protect itself. Masked, tucked away, closely inserted between the thighs, it maintains its mystery and shape, so barely guessable that sculptors need only join two curves to suggest it. This reserve, allied to security, in the end probably endows it with a sort of modest reassurance and serenity, since it lacks any site in the unconscious mind where its shape is presented. For, in the unconscious mind, genital representation is effectively scaled down for both sexes to the penis alone. This offends some protesting feminist sensibilities. They make use of it in order to discredit and denounce psychoanalysis as male-chauvinist, as if it were to be expected, indeed to be insisted upon, that a slide projector should simultaneously appear on the screen. It is hard to understand why people should require the representation of the genitals of one sex, with which they cannot maintain that they have not had direct contact right from the start of life, when the representation of the genitals of the other sex is there only to supplement the information and recall the existence of difference.

As I have just said, this reserve adds to the vulva's mystery - a mystery renowned for generating fear to the extent that during the Middle Ages in some central European countries, witches were accused of casting spells when they displayed it. It is a mystery that has not failed to obsess artists of all periods and levels, including those who, tens of thousands of years ago, were no more capable of stopping themselves from representing it on the walls of their caves than today's scrawlers on the lavatory walls of stations, cafés, and colleges are from obsessively representing it in the stylized form of a discreet, yet always recognizable slit. Think of Gustave Courbet's famous painting 'The Origin of the World' (1866; Musée d'Orsay, Paris), the history of its execution and that of its various owners, and it becomes easy to see how the current dramatic expansion in the pornography industry is about feeding an illusory search for deliverance from the fascination mingled with fear that this primal reserve arouses. This is all the more clear because however much it may be hustled or assaulted by concentrated gawping, this famous reserve never yields or fails. Absolutely nothing can be established, seen, or verified that proves excitement, desire, or even indifference at the moment of coition. This clearly does not in the least exclude appreciable physical phenomena affecting the female sexual apparatus: its lubrication, the engorgement of the clitoral and perivaginal vascular networks that turn the coalescent layers of the vagina into a tube in anticipation that the perceived lack created by the space thereby generated may be filled. Yet all that remains strictly private to the woman, and can never conspicuously demonstrate her mood towards her partner. Similarly, there is nothing conspicuous or objective to signal to the partner the finality of desire or the reality of orgasm, accompanied or not by the sighs and groans that sometimes enable the woman to fake them without remotely experiencing them - a form of generosity which sometimes manages to attach a man by the confidence in him that the woman manages to confer on him. In the face of a partner exposed by an anatomy and physiology that speak eloquently for him, this reserve is capable either of feeding into formidable power, of which some women make full use, or of creating an air of doubt and uneasy assurance that undermines the lives of others, leading to poor self-esteem, if not depression: none of all this is accidental, but always comes out of personal histories. We cannot leave the subject of female reserve, however, without mentioning the fact that it helps to furnish the silence with possibilities or suppositions that are unsaid; the trace of this is detectable in conversations with children, when they say that their mother can read their minds or knows all about them and their thoughts.

To the extent that female reserve comes from another of the female traits listed earlier, namely economy, it reinforces that dimension, which expresses itself at every level. We see it, first, in material and number, for, as mentioned earlier, continual selection reduces the sixty thousand follicles laid down in the mother's womb to fifteen hundred, of which only three to four hundred reach maturity. This is scarcely profligate on the part of evolution, given the major purpose for which they are intended. Considerations of security make even greater use of economy, when it comes to managing the eggs; from the remaining stock of follicles, generally only one is produced each month. A new egg is produced in the following cycle on a uterine mucous lining that - in the interests of efficiency perhaps? - will have been entirely renewed. It is an extraordinary biological clock that can punctuate time with such regularity. Does the awareness of chronology that it confers affect the nature of the female experience of time? Is it conceivable that it might encourage a belief that time could be mastered, or even denied? Whatever the answers to those questions, the clock does not continue to tick indefinitely, since it is programmed to function only during a limited part of life, from puberty to the menopause. The menopause is the age when the body, modestly and realistically acknowledging the limitations to its performance - invoking the criterion of efficiency once again? - no longer seeks to go after the goals to which it had been accustomed. Significantly, some African societies allow widowed menopausal women to take a wife [sic], choose an impregnator for her, and bring up children for whom she will be deemed the father and to whom she will be able to bequeath her property.[20] It is as though, having once left the temporal rhythm that heretofore was dictated by the menstrual cycle, she were being enabled to join the men in their specific relationship with time.

Yet the precise moment when - to recall three of the traits in our list - the reliability, moderation, and admirable behavioural coherence of the female being is most evident has to be the time when fertilization has taken place. For the day does indeed arrive when this perfectly conceived and gifted organism is finally fertilized. It is the realization of a promise that is consubstantial with the creation of that organism from its own conception and through its own development. But that is not all. It also represents the wholesale validation of a host of behavioural characteristics that will have informed the female being from its earliest years. I am not simply speaking of the inexhaustible play that little girls have with dolls that come ready-equipped with all kinds of paraphernalia. I am thinking rather of the little girls one sees in parks, playgrounds, and nursery schools - or indeed in paediatricians' waiting-rooms - who are ready with help or comfort for any child, boy or girl, who is hurt or crying. Whereas little boys of the same age will take advantage of the situation to give the sufferer an extra thump or

---

[20] This practice draws attention to the minimal role that genitors, if no more than that, play in the life stories of the children they procreate.

pinch a dropped toy off him (or her), they on the other hand will return his toy to him or offer him another, any available, using words and voice to make it more attractive. 'You're a real little mother!' is what bystanders are liable to whisper in her ear, masking the emotion that such genius stirs up. Are they simply imitating their own mothers? That is what the resolute negationists of gender difference would have us believe, even though they themselves have occasioned so much misery by blaming an excessively conformist society for manufacturing this type of behaviour, and refusing to acknowledge that it is related to fundamental sexual difference effective from the embryonic stage on. What is happening in the little girl's behaviour is the early dawning of what will be the general direction of the adult female's behaviour, i.e., to find a being liable to be needy, undertake to satisfy that being's needs, and draw from satisfying those needs, in addition to pleasure and benefit both of which are generators of energy and of a strictly incommunicable nature, an authentic feeling of power. It is the adventure or passage through pregnancy that will cause that early disposition to glow white-hot, for the being conceived is by definition a being in constant need. There is no need to go and look for such a being or hope to find one, for it is closer than close, it is actually inside, nestling within a body that it knows is wholly available to it. All female behavioural traits are henceforth legitimated and are focused by a supreme and healthy coherence. The environment encourages the project and applauds it unreservedly because its execution will give birth to a new life. Power is therefore not simply perceived and felt; it is conceded and recognized without the least hesitation.

While the undisputed encapsulation of the foetus by her body is pre-eminent in giving the mother the solid certainty on which her dimension is founded, it conveys another sort of certainty, one already mentioned, which is anatomically supported and has considerable symbolic consequences. It is that despite being always penetrable regardless of how she feels, and not requiring the least anatomical modification for this purpose, the woman knows that she harbours close within her this considerable potential for power. It is for this and for all the other reasons given, that I have now for a long time described the focus of all female anatomical, physiological, and behavioural characteristics without exception by using the term 'pregnancy logic'.

Beyond the strict construction of the formula I have just given, it is possible to invoke the same logic in order to explain the nature of the work entrusted to women - imposed upon them, some would say - since time immemorial and in all latitudes: those tasks which have ended up being repugned as humiliating and thankless, in which women, regardless of their sector of activity, nevertheless excel inasmuch as those activities offer immediate results. There is a strong echo here of the commitment to the immediate satisfaction of need that is expressed in pregnancy and in the mother's subsequent relationship to her child. Both activities share a common ingredient that does not so much have existence within them as occupy the status of an intolerable intruder. The response offered is not to ignore it or reject it but rather to be vigilant lest it should intervene: to deprive it of space, to avoid all risk of being affected by it. This ingredient is quite simply either wished out of existence - wished out of having ever existed - or made to vanish through wish-fulfilment if its unwarranted interference has peradventure not been forestalled. Its identity must be obvious, even if I have not named it. It is time itself, in all its components and with all its characteristics. Real time, chronological time, the time that passes with imbecilic fixation, always in the same direction: time that is dangerously liable to be perceived, integrated, lived, interiorized, both by the female protagonist of the action and by her beneficiary. Time the enemy, the big enemy, the one to whom no concessions can ever be made, whose ruses must be watched out for, the one that must be kept under continuous surveillance - My goodness, a wrinkle! A new grey hair! Horrendous! And the ad that repeatedly announces the latest cream with wonder ingredients! - the enemy against which there can never be enough insurgency or energy and resources spent. The enemy whose defeat always brings pleasure, when need is immediately satisfied and no quarter offered, as when with a broom the obedient dust is swept from the room and the tiled floor is finally clean - an achievement that is down to you alone and what you have just accomplished. For you are the single agent of the result you at once obtain and which witnesses to the power you have.

Time, the enemy. Time - and death at the end. Death that is to be fought, to be faced down without flinching. Death that must be denied, with the determination not to let it win.

Mothers against death.

Courageous. Determined. Unrealistic. Crazy. Possessed of that wondrous foolishness - ingenious, creative, and poetic - that no one will complain of, and for which everybody, from the bottom of their being, is humbly grateful.

For mothers are solid against death, though death be more solid still!

To preserve life, whatever the cost - the Greek *Zoe* - in whatever state and whatever the result, throbbing, roaring life, life in its raw state, be it reducible to mere survival.

The reader will recall how I lingered on the conscious awareness of time that broke in upon the species at a particular moment in our evolution. We have perhaps now reached the point in our story where the insistence I laid upon that moment is likely to prove most useful. We are back with the earliest human burial, with its cascade of perceptions and emotions. I emphasized how it was an entirely male matter, and did not concern the women. Let me repeat my hypothesis here, namely, that *Homo* was unable to impart to his female companion any of what he had discovered, just as she was never able to tell him what she had known for millions of years: that death, which had so often hit her in the flesh of her flesh, was her closest enemy, and that she had armed herself, however futile she ultimately might know it to be, with denial. It was as if she said to herself: I refuse to admit to the logic of the passing of time: it will defeat me; it will force my submission; but I will never be its accessory in the death of my children. Let it not count on me! Even rational admission of the fact would be for me to betray myself and destroy the coherence of my being. And my partner had better not try to impose on me what I reject. For I will go on rejecting it with all my might. And if he should put pressure on me to submit to the societal arrangements that he and his associates put together, he will find me no less determined to resist. I shall make sure I pass on my convictions and my message to my children, particularly my daughters, and I shall enjoin them to pass them on to their own. One day, perhaps, will see triumph? One day, perhaps, will be victorious?

I wonder whether I am beginning to say that the female being may be humanly different from the male being, with a psychic organization that is

Fathers and Mothers

rather different at a fairly fundamental level? How could one advance a hypothesis which, on the face of it, seems aberrant and runs the risk of suggesting that men and women belong to different species? Unless what is meant, after all, is nothing more than the unsuspected and oft-denied consequences of a difference between the sexes whose true extent has never been properly taken into account and which might entail the reassessment of men and women as two sharply differentiated subspecies of one common species? Why not? Would it mean that there are different ways of listening to men and women, for example in psychoanalysis? That is one hell of a question, and it belongs to the category of questions one is not supposed to ask. Yet are we really doing any more than returning once again to Freud, to his unending questioning of the female mystique and his no less obsessive image of women as a 'dark continent'? Of course, his day knew nothing of mitochondrial DNA, the genetic material which is passed down from mother to daughter, linking every female offspring back in an unbroken chain to her most distant ancestors more effectively even than is suggested by the system of encapsulation that links a given series of Russian dolls.[21] How could this particular form of genetic material, the mitochondrial DNA, transport an inheritance that could account for, among other things, the different relationship that men, as opposed to women, have with time and which I trace to the experience of the earliest burial? I cannot say, any more than I can insist that it is so. I simply suggest it as a factor that is just beginning to be looked at, whose effects and consequences are as yet unknown. But nothing prevents me imagining that one day a gene may be discovered, containing within it coding for this or that disposition regarding time or space. My position may appear somewhat presumptuous, even dishonest. I make no apology for that. As a doctor with a long career behind me, I have seen far too many advances and revisions in my own field to allow absence of proof to block the venturing of hypotheses. Over forty years of paediatric practice I have counselled the parents of my little patients to take care of their own ties with each other, including, in particular, their sexual

---

[21] The mitochondria are vacuoles (tiny pockets) within the cells, involved in various metabolic processes and, like the cell's nucleus itself, they are constructed of genetic material made up of deoxyribonucleic acid (DNA), the discovery of which is quite recent. Mitochondrial DNA is peculiar in that it is transmitted to children without alteration or mixing with the genetic material contributed by the father, and hence as such passes from mother to daughter.

relationship; it can function as an admirable circuit-breaker in the inevitable conflicts that arise in a couple's life. I now read that recent research has found that oxytocin, the hormone that intervenes to stimulate the uterine contractions of parturition or the ejection of milk from the breasts in infant-feeding, is considered to be the molecule that promotes attachment and that it reaches peaks of secretion in both partners during coition. My long held recommendation, which was purely intuitive and pragmatic, thus finds itself now supported by biology. Ought I to have held back from my advice because no biological proof was to hand? Of course not: the results I saw for myself inclined me never to neglect that particular prescription. It is experiences of that sort that lead me to risk certain hypotheses when I am persuaded that they could help towards a better understanding of the obstacles we keep stumbling over.

If, ultimately, this question of time and the first burial is not DNA-linked, this need not trouble us unduly. Transmission could conceivably be attributed to an educative process based on a similarity of biological functioning between one female body and another. That would be an even simpler and more economic process than the one invoked a moment ago, which appealed to sexual differences. It would probably need to be linked to the operation of pheromones, the mysterious airborne molecules whose power is such that, for example, all the women working in a particular workshop will end up in a relatively short space of time with coinciding menstrual periods. After all, is not all biology subject to 'timers' of one kind or another? Besides the circadian rhythm that exceeds the boundaries between day and night, cortisol and growth hormone, like melatonine, are secreted during the night; the pylorus opens every fifteen seconds to allow the stomach to empty; the pancreas discharges insulin into the general circulation every twelve minutes; cells are programmed to live a precise length of time and then die - a phenomenon called apoptosis[22] - for example three months in the case of red blood cells and two days only in the case of the oral mucosa.

Even so, I am not happy about too systematically invoking processes of this order to provide a total explanation for the female disposition that so

---

[22] When for various reasons this programming is not respected, the cell fails to die and becomes cancerous.

strongly resists all challenges in regard to time. On the other hand, if we interpret that resistance as an ontological factor deriving from the evolution of the species - possibly resulting in establishing two subspecies - then this may not just explain it, but actually encourage us to wonder whether it had a purpose and a usefulness that have thus far escaped notice. Let us be frank: having been exchanged by the men among themselves with a view to settling their own relationships with one another after the first burial, the women had no objective option other than submission; yet they never accepted it or subscribed to it. They therefore contented themselves with remaining aloof from the famous Law of the Species, were ready to contravene it whenever they could do so safely, were resolute within the close, even merging relationship they had with their children to preserve the benefits that they had always had from their animal dispositions, and took, among other precautions, that of maintaining a discreet distance from all that implied a conscious awareness of time.

I can already hear the vehement reactions that these words will engender, and can imagine myself being charged with denying women the capacity or opportunity of running businesses or having the sort of careers that men always used to reserve to themselves. I refute in advance any such accusation; indeed I submit that nothing can, or ever should, limit women who have the potential for such activities in any way whatever. What I am saying, to be perfectly clear, is that such women may well have a sense and conception of time, manage it, dominate it, and make use of it without the least apparent problem, and yet, like other women, they preserve - and ever will preserve - independent of any actions they may undertake, a specific life-experience and relationship in regard to time totally different from those of men.

I cite as proof their relationship with fear of death. I maintain that they are infinitely less oppressed by it than men. Mind you, I am not saying that they are wholly without it. Only that they are less oppressed by it, i.e., that the pressure that it causes them is certainly, as they experience it, relatively low, less subject to variation and, above all, infinitely less subject to wide fluctuations. If anyone doubts this, let them go and talk to male nursing officers. Which of them will not confess his surprise when, as a novice, he will have discovered how soft men, the so-called stronger sex, are. 'Like big kids,' is the sort of comment one sometimes hears made of them, before the speaker goes on to laud the courage of sick women with every bit as much reason as their partners to fear their end. This sort of relative serenity stems from relatively stable pressure due to fear of death regardless of circumstance, and is yet again a question about time. For, being female, and because the subspecies to which they belong has lived tens of millions of years, they know what men do not and cannot know of the specific way in which they experience the division of time. They know, in the most intimate and least communicable way possible, that their lives do not end with their physical death, but that they go on in the children they have borne in their bodies - those children whom they have brought into the world through their bodies, and to whom, with life itself, they have given bodies that will themselves bear the enduring mark of their mothers. They know that their intrinsic wisdom has led them to invest not simply in themselves, but to widen the spectrum of their investments in others. Their genius is to adhere spontaneously to the advice of the best financial advisors: 'Don't put all your eggs in one basket.' They know that their lives have always been split between what they know themselves to be - incomplete - and what they know they can be - complete, or almost - through successfully satisfying without limit or delay the needs of a third party, whether it come in the guise of the impatience that is permanently excited and mad to possess her body or in the even more extraordinary and moving guise of heart-rending helplessness, ready to give itself up unreservedly to her.

In order to find fault with my approach, objectors will undoubtedly want to point to models that supposedly contradict it. That, for example, of the women who have always exercised their talents throughout history, before going into print, as they have recently started to do, about their sexual performances. Yet can it be said of them that, apart from the pleasure they themselves obtained, they did not profit from the pleasure they gave to their numerous partners, about whom they have the capacity to hold forth with such expertise? As for those who never have sex with a man or who never procreate, so what! Even if they never exploit the potential of their sexual identity, they are nonetheless bearers of it: they know that they could have made use of this potential, if they had not sublimated that direction, or if circumstances had not intervened to prevent their taking that course. If what I have said still seems inadequate or unconvincing, then consideration should be given to the extreme infrequency with which women have laboured on death's side in human history, how seldom they have been warriors or war-leaders. How often, in contrast, have they risen up to denounce murderous folly! Personally, I am sorry that they do not do this more often still. When American suffragettes rose up against the murderous folly of their menfolk, they succeeding in effecting a remarkable change in the political landscape. Moreover, if account is taken of the explanations I gave earlier, when discussing the death drive, it should be apparent to what extent my current argument is closely connected to the shallow fluctuations that women experience in stress due to fear of death.

Could I be thought to be saying that in view of their anatomy, physiology, and behavioural characteristics, all women are uniformly identical? I certainly hope not! On the contrary, it seems extremely important to me to emphasize that no one woman is like another, that each fortunately is unique, to the point sometimes where, unhappily, her singularity is viewed with suspicion. In drawing attention to the common ontological substrate, it was never my intention to diminish the effect of individual history or the product of a particular experience or relationship network. But so as to avoid misunderstanding it seems important to point out that I am saying that however wide the spectrum embracing individual women and mothers may be, be they timid, crushing, engaging, surly, devoted, inconsistent, impatient or domineering, none can, even today, claim to be able to be aloof or unconcerned by the elements that I have said they carry as a group.

Could I nevertheless be thought to be saying that, in relation to the fear of death, all women share the same common level of anxiety, i.e., they are somewhat protected and live relatively more serenely in this respect than men? My answer is: On many occasions, certainly - yet not always. For, of whatever stuff they are made and whatever they do, the moment comes when the fear of death no longer lets them off lightly; it finally invades and overwhelms them, creating real 'disturbance'. The moment I have in mind is when they cease to be merely women and become mothers - especially mothers of boys. For that is the end of their relative serenity. It is the end of small variations in the stress occasioned by fear of death. Their reactivity intensifies. They become unbearable, ungovernable, totally unreasonable, and are increasingly liable these days to turn into the category of mothers of boys that I call 'worrier mothers'. It is such a strongly pathogenic category that its identification and recognition have become an essential component of what my paediatric career has taught me; I have come to see that the most serious sickness that can strike an emerging male human being is to be encumbered with such a mother. For the 'worrier mother' is stuck in a maelstrom of ambivalence, at the centre of which gnaws away the remnant of the muted struggle that her subspecies has never stopped having with the other subspecies. Since her son belongs to the other subspecies, the question arises of how in spite of all she will preserve him and manage to check the drives and other aggressive movements (if only within herself) that she has obscurely inherited as a disposition from her mother and, without realizing it, cultivated throughout her life against her father, her brother, or her male partner? Will not such a child be disproportionately exposed to the dangers that naturally menace his existence? What she goes on to do is to develop a series of strategies - including, among others, such as keep him indefinitely 'in' her - and she guards him jealously by doing his living for him and, though he himself asks nothing, she exaggerates the least threat whose existence she simply imagines. The effect of this on him, meanwhile, is to heighten his own sensitivity to the least variation in stress attributable to fear of death.

People may be surprised by the difference that I have found, and now highlight, relative to the children's sex; they may wonder whether this is a reflection of statistical bias affecting my client-base, which, as I have said, comprises speakers of over forty different languages. Strange as it may seem, this statistical bias does not distort my analysis but rather offers additional enlightenment. It is true, for example, that the difference in the way that migrant communities from North Africa treat boys as opposed to girls is striking, flagrant, and verges upon caricature. But it does not produce the effects that might quite reasonably have been expected, since it falls within a whole context of arrangements coded and conveyed by the language itself relating to the culture of the populations concerned. Hence the verb 'to give birth' is commonly rendered in dialectal Arabic in a way that literally means 'to boy'. Instead of asking, 'When is your daughter due to give birth?', people ask, 'When is your daughter due to boy?' This daughter will have 'boyed' - the verb is intransitive - when she has brought a boy into the world; if she has a girl, she will be said to have 'borne' - the verb is transitive and expects a direct object - 'a daughter'. The upshot of this is that the law of the Arabo-Islamic zone causes parents to come out with such expressions as: 'I have three children and two girls' - a formula and mindset which seems aberrant, even monstrous, to us in view of the inequality it encapsulates. And rightly so, were we not to remember that within the logic of that culture, independently of inequalities of inheritance yet coherent with the rest of its cultural logic, women ultimately occupy the highest rank in the social hierarchy when they become 'ladies', i.e., when they have a daughter-in-law to serve them and who will patiently await her own similar hour of glory.

This brief incursion into ethnology reveals to us how some cultural systems have dealt with the different ways in which men and women experience time, and how such systems manage the differential levels of stress due to the fear of death closely associated with that experience. 'Pregnancy logic', which concentrates upon the immediate satisfaction of need, automatically results in a virtually exclusive investment in the present, with much less concern for the medium and longer term. This contrasts with the totally contrary investment that the male being operates. The organization of societies having been till now directed by men, males have imposed their rules and, as demonstrated particularly in the Arabo-Islamic scenario just mentioned, inflicted upon women what could be considered a trial of patience that has marked the language. The reason it surprises us is simply explained by the radical differences in system of reference: our language, cultures, and evolving dominant kinship system do not prescribe such arrangements for us. That said, nothing prevents us from recognizing the radical difference between a mother's relationship to a son and her relationship to a daughter. It is surely not irrelevant to point out in this connection that the statistics of child morbidity reveal that out of every 100 sick children, boys account for some 70 to 75 per cent. I would happily concede that two X chromosomes perhaps confer better defence than a single one albeit accompanied by a Y chromosome. But I find it hard to believe that this is the only factor worthy of consideration. It seems no less relevant to bear in mind that a mother may feel less awkward with the more familiar body of her daughter than with the more foreign (to her) body of her son, and that this awkwardness could lead to different handling liable to be a source of trouble for the mother as well as the child. It is easy to imagine that the genital similarity between her daughter and herself is enough to enable a mother to accept her daughter, just as she accepts herself, secure from variations in the intensity of the fear of death; her son, meanwhile, she will see in reference to the other males in her life - father, brother, partner - whose most commonplace behaviour flagrantly betrays that kind of preoccupation. It could almost be inferred from this hypothesis that this might be one way, scarcely less effective than any other way, in which a mother confers on her offspring its gender identity as well as a legitimate part of its history. The only problem is the balance of such transmission. For what the morbidity statistics may imply is that mothers draw their daughters into their own history alone, thereby enclosing them in an identity dilemma which the daughters will have great difficulty extricating themselves from; meanwhile, they cannot transmit to their sons a share in history other than their own without developing in regard to the sons an anxiety that is not neutral in its effects. An indirect consequence of this process would be to confer on the boy the male characteristics of his later relationship with the fear of death.

The paradox inherent in this attitude is, however, as hard to demonstrate as it is to understand. Essentially it operates thus. If fear of death and experience of time are so closely linked that the one generates the other and vice versa, then the maternal attitude that I have just described could turn out to be almost salutary. If a mother were able, in relating to her son, to experience time differently and conceive of the existence of wider variations in stress due to anxiety about death, or if, conversely, she herself were to perceive such variations and were induced to recognize another way of experiencing time, then it might be hoped that such a process would enable her to approach, even if not access, a more intense experience of time. Perhaps things would turn out like that if the process were left to itself and could evolve according to its own logic. But what takes place generally leads to a converse result, inasmuch as the mother violently intervenes in such circumstances in order, deliberately, to reduce the least variation in anxiety stress; this immediately smothers the beginnings of an experience or greater awareness of time that might have come on its own and been of benefit to the child. Normally, what is involved is a totally senseless reflex action, encouraged these days by an ambient message that goes completely unchecked by mothers whose primary concern is to preserve their child as a simple complement of themselves; in their heads, the child essentially often has no independent existence of its own. This is why so many psychoanalysts, from the top of the profession down, have striven to get the message across to mothers that babies, like children, are not pure objects, but subjects whose singularity as much as their stature is to be infinitely respected. Yet that very message has given rise to the most perfect of misunderstandings, with mothers interpreting it as confirming their own view that children are immensely precious, and understanding that that they should become more devoted mothers still, and keep up a bond with their offspring that they could no more relinquish than allow the child to do so.

The current context, which has already witnessed all kinds of developments over recent decades, now sees mothers' rejection of the dimension of time for themselves and their children winning new recruits. Why do I say this? Simply because that rejection fits in with what has become the ideology of the contemporary western world, which has been seduced and won over by all the qualities I lately defined as pertaining to the female. We might begin with the great and noble dimension of certainty, which belongs to mothers and to Queen Science herself! Then there is the dimension of security or safety, whose concerns now so invade our everyday life - for to drive without a seatbelt, smoke, or drink all now indicate fecklessness and offend our newly framed 'precautionary principle' - that we may suspect that we are being enjoined to organize our survival for want of knowing how to organize our life. After that, there is the dimension of efficiency, which is advocated as an indispensable measure of worth: everything must be assessed according to predefined criteria, a phenomenon that recalls the maternal obsession with the weight and height of children. Lastly, when it comes to the economic sphere of life, efficiency has become such an obsession with our politicians that it no longer needs to be pointed out to what extent it has become the essential concern. Everything is supposed to happen just so - as in the immediate preoccupations of the maternal sphere - with very short-term societal objectives determined by the timing of the next election, which entirely rules out consideration of longer-term projects.

Suspicion will no doubt be cast upon the connections in the argument I have just outlined, and it will be pointed out that society's choices are still predominantly governed and directed by men: hence women in general, and mothers in particular, cannot be accused of promoting those choices. The objection is relevant and admissible. But my intention is not to detract from the behaviour of men, who in general are deeply enmeshed in both their desire to seduce and their relationships with their mothers, but to highlight the collusion that exists between the choices men go for and the general orientations set by maternal behaviours. It is as if the men were looking over their shoulders in case they might disappoint their mothers. You might say that they had jumped aboard their mothers' method of dealing with the stress due to fear of death, judging it to be cleverer, more effective, assuredly more profitable, and better adapted to an increasingly cruel world.

In so doing, today's men commit a miscalculation which would not be so grave, were they to be its only rather than earliest victims, fated to drag their progeniture into it after them. For what does a mother do when abandoned without any let or hindrance to her own devices and sole propensity in the face of the fear of death? She shuts herself up in an isolation of deceptive immediate advantage. The expectant mother does no less, as she exercises the extraordinary power that the experience of pregnancy confers upon her: the power to expel time and experience the coherence of her behavioural logic that will be forever stamped with the mark of what I call 'intrauterine non-time'. Since that 'non-time' process has always furnished tangible proof of its efficacy, why question it? On the contrary, why not extend it indefinitely? The final upshot of this debate is the establishment by the mother, once her child is born, of a virtual womb, patiently woven, constantly maintained, and strong yet limitlessly elastic, inside which the same laws obtain as in the real womb. Though born to reality and to air-breathing life, the child must never know the trials of waiting, the torments of time, but must be always satisfied immediately and not know the least restriction in the satisfaction of its demands, whatever their nature or extent. In short, the child must never, ever lack anything.

What a superb bargain this is! For it is nothing less. No one walks away from an offer of this sort. Yes, madam, how right you are: your child really must not lack anything. We agree with you there right down the line! And we would encourage you to keep matters under review so that your child does not go short of anything through inadvertence or want of foresight. And for your further assistance, we shall ourselves take care to provide a comprehensive survey of all the child's possible needs, leaving none in doubt. Indeed, we would go so far as to anticipate needs that you yourself will not have foreseen, as well as others which would not have been anticipated without our determination to enumerate them. As you can see, we are of one mind with you: we shall be happy to cobble together needs that your child possibly would not have had spontaneously, just so that you may be able to give yourself all the more happiness in fulfilling them!

When the market latches onto a want, there is no holding its urge to fulfil it. And here we have something to satisfy everyone. A truly remarkable equilibrium has been reached - except that language, once again, must stick its oar in, to reveal, even if it cannot restrain, the drifting current into which everything is being thrown with blithe abandon. For, of the one 'who lacks nothing', the Latin language speaks as of an *incestus*, an 'incested' one.[23] We might say, on the basis of this, that what the type of behaviour that we have been discussing reveals itself to be is yet another offence against the famous Law of the Species. Similarly unmasked is the ontological difference which I postulated earlier, when I said that the female being that the Law targeted always distanced herself from it, never subscribed to it, has always been and remains resolutely restive towards it. But how is that articulated?

Let me recall what I said earlier and in much greater detail, and it will perhaps become plain why I lingered so long over that discussion. The Law against incest indirectly gave human beings, by virtue of the generational difference that was to be respected, the clearest possible awareness of the way that humans are fixed in a framework of advancing time, a realization that should enable them to accept themselves as mortal and hence focus

---

[23] The English word 'incest' derives from the Latin *incestus*, which is itself forged from *incastus*, a composite of *in* and *castus*, i.e. *non-castus*. *Castus* signified 'pure', 'chaste', and *incastus*, unremarkably so, 'impure' or 'not chaste'. *Castus* was, however, quickly replaced by *cassus*, which signified 'empty', being already a past participle formed from the supine of the verb *careo*, 'I lack'. *Incestus* thus had a double resonance, that of 'non-pure' or 'non-chaste' on the one hand, and that, which subsequently prevailed, of 'not lacking', on the other. Thus in the outlook of the Latin language, sexual 'lack' became a paradigm of 'lack' itself.

upon the correct organization of their lives. Nevertheless, that her child, however much she concedes his or her human condition, is mortal is something that every mother, like her most distant ancestors, continues to reject.. It is something that she rejects with all her strength, with all her being, with all her head, with all her guts. There is not one mother, not even part of one, whoever or wherever she be, who could spontaneously experience things differently or reckon her experience illegitimate or unreasonable, save that, as I have said, there is a difference of maternal disposition according to the child's sex: confident in her daughter's ready adherence to her outlook, the mother will probably set about converting her son to it by anticipating and experiencing on his behalf, exaggerating even, the variations in intensity of the fear of death that he might be called upon to live through. This is something that lends her conversation or attitude an affecting coloration that is almost convincing - life, whatever its quality and whatever it may cost! Nothing touches us more, whoever we are and whatever our age and condition, than this maternal caring. None can claim to be indifferent to it, since it is what resources each one of us again and again, because after the fashion of beauty, which I said earlier mothers also radiate, they can power everyone to their highest level of performance. Nothing does us so much good as the denial of our mortality by our mother. Even if she makes us smile and we know exactly what makes her tick, she warms us with the most moving of love's proofs. That somebody should wish us eternal is no mean thing, and insofar as wishes of this kind are uncommon, we can only show gratitude for being able to benefit from them. My career has enabled me to meet many such maternal figures. The memory of one of them comes back to me now. She astounded me by the scale of her achievements.

A Breast ... With Conviction!

> *She surprised me from the word go. She refused to come into the waiting room when I invited her to do so, rather than hang about in the entrance, impressing on me that she didn't want to expose her*

baby, even for a few minutes, to the germs my sick little patients might give him. When hygienism goes that far, you wonder what is coming next. I was not disappointed. For I had to submit myself to a Draconian law that began with discreet but suspicious examination to check that my shirt was spotless and extended to how carefully I washed my hands, the prior disinfection of the end of my stethoscope, and the freshness of the cloth placed on the baby scales. As this was an intelligent and cultured women, I became quite taken with the situation: a phobic-obsessional of that sort offered by her co-therapist baby could not fail to be of interest, if only technically, because it was outside my normal routine. I waited for the moment to arrive when the authentic investment which she had begun to make in my person would allow me to intervene. Several well-judged answers to her questions, the resolution of issues that were minor and straightforward yet were ruining her life, and the fact that I accepted her as she was - she never did enter the waiting room - in the end produced a relatively relaxed atmosphere, and I even managed to tease her about the bees in her bonnet without making her angry, though I ought to have worried more about their staying power. There was, of course, no question of using any vaccine without prior discussion, or of prescribing any medicine without evaluating its drawbacks and justifying its relevance and effectiveness. By putting out tiny feelers, I ventured to discover something of her life, her history, and the relationship with the child's father, whom I had never met. All was carefully catalogued, filed, and meticulously shelved, except that the files were empty! I was put in mind of one of those libraries where you wonder whether the books they contain, which you are bidden not to touch, really are books or blocks of wood!

Months went by, and I suggested to her one day that her baby, now almost ten or eleven months old, might taste something apart from milk from her breast. The very thought! She quoted statistics at me, and ways of doing things related to the history of peoples, regions, and civilization; the many authorized opinions she cited even included my own writings! Was she a well of information? No, she was a fortress - and an unassailable one at that, I thought to myself. I saw that my methodology had pitifully failed, and that I had probably allowed myself to be manipulated without realizing it - doubtless to punish me for my impropriety in thinking that I could rise to the formidable therapeutic challenge she represented. I was ready to throw down the gauntlet, when she started talking to me about the possibility of returning to studying. While she was talking about the logistic problems she faced, I inwardly rejoiced about the space this would at last create between her and her child. But I was careful to keep quiet. Weeks and months went by without the subject coming up again, until one day she mentioned that she was planning to visit the university administration to see whether she could keep the baby with her during the examinations; these each lasted six hours and were phased over four consecutive days. I admit sincerely and unashamedly that I could not help stamping my foot and almost cheered. However, I bit my lip, thinking to myself that Madam Fortress would at last be forced to surrender to an authority far more neutral and distant than I had been.

She left no avenue unexplored, and assailed so many administrative officers that she finally achieved the right during the exams to be called on her mobile phone by her mother, who would stay in the courtyard with the baby and let her know when he demanded her breast, so that she could leave the exam and feed him.

She left Paris one day for the provinces. I admit I wasn't sorry. But my relief was short-lived, as for months and months she continued to say in phone-calls and letters how much she missed our talks! Doubtless she had run up against a practitioner who was less ambitious and more structuring - for her and even more so for her son - than I had been, and hence she was appealing to me for support of her crazy ways of doing things. The day eventually came when she stopped calling. I felt relief, though I did feel remorse for my own conceit, clumsiness, and pique.

I could leave this woman's story there, on the grounds that what I have said is edifying enough as it stands. Nevertheless I would like to remain with her a moment longer in view of the stature she has acquired in this chapter. Fortified by her obduracy, she effectively occupied the essential portion of a space in which her baby had no place other than as a pure object - an object delivered up to a power that she had every opportunity to deny because it was masked by her solicitude and the care she devoted to satisfying his needs, known or supposed, wholly and immediately. Is it not significant that virtually nothing has been said about the baby, apart from the fact that he had an existence that did not seem even to belong to him? The story raises a number of questions about the notion of need. For, while it is important to identify that a child has needs and that these require satisfaction, there is no getting away from the need this mother displayed for her child to be just that and nothing else.

What therefore constitutes a need? Is it not naturally expressed in order primarily to achieve its satisfaction, especially when it comes from an immature? How could its immediate satisfaction perhaps be prejudicial, and how would deferred satisfaction differ? If it is possible for one method of satisfaction to be better than another, which is it? Who says so? How would be it be better? Why? All of these questions relate to an area of maternal behaviour that, for all my deconstruction of it, everyone is probably happy to receive with tender emotions! Yet each of these questions concern that behaviour and deserve a clear, well-argued response.

What is a need? It is a sensation or perception manifested in the body or in the psyche, in a form recognizable from the fact that to gratify it is to cause it to disappear. I need water, I feel it, I know it, I identify it through saying that I am thirsty, and I even have the proof that my perception was well-grounded, since the absorption of water causes the one-time need to disappear. I can replace the example of water by whatever I might wish, and the same obtains. Whatever the nature of the thing I perceive I need, it is still a matter of need. And there is no more sense in disputing the appearance of a need than in denying its legitimacy and necessity of satisfaction. I am thirsty, I lack water, there is water available, I get some, I drink it, I assuage my thirst, my need disappears. There is nothing complicated in that. The biological mechanisms of our daily life overall never stop appealing for the satisfaction of our multifarious needs. When, earlier, I evoked what happens during gestation, I emphasized to what extent the mother's body continually monitors the foetal body so as to satisfy, even anticipate, its every need. The expression and satisfaction of need is thus written into the maintenance of biological life, life in the raw, and there can be no question of our denying the importance of that.

There is no point in denying, either, that my patient's baby will assuredly never have ceased experiencing needs - all of which, moreover, will have been satisfied immediately. Indeed, of him it could be said that he was never anything but a being with immediately satisfied needs, and even more aptly, that he never lacked anything, because his mother, whatever she might say, would never have it otherwise. He was the object of her attention, the object she could second-guess, the object that fitted perfectly the sole mission she recognized as hers and the power she knew she had for achieving it, i.e., to keep him alive and make him a living object allotted to her and to her exercise of power. Whether he had autonomy or not was not something she either thought about or worried about. Indeed, she was incapable of imagining that he was not autonomous, or not autonomous enough: autonomy was something that within her understanding had an equivalent status to teeth or hair; it always grew eventually.

Considerations of this kind place us squarely in the frontier zone between biology and rearing. Continuation of the fulfilment of needs intuited even before they manifest themselves, is a perpetuation of the mechanisms of intrauterine biology and is explained by what I described earlier as a virtual womb, limitlessly elastic, woven around the child. The child's arrival in air-breathing life involves a break with those mechanisms: if the baby automatically breathes with his own lungs, he is compelled to use them when he is hungry. He has left intrauterine non-time and has in principle entered time.

If the baby's hunger, or any other need of a similar order, is not satisfied, he will cry louder - which is not always very pleasant, I have to concede - but he will perceive more sharply what he is feeling. He will therefore be 'lacking' - that notion I slipped in a little earlier without explaining myself. Now it so happens that the perception of lack is fundamental to the constitution of self-perception. For it is by identifying lack in all its many and various manifestations, that the baby will be able to register the characteristics of his own body, those of his mood, and even those of the environment in which he is fixed. Little by little he will acquire consciousness of what he is, in terms of himself, and not as an object to be stuffed and pampered in order to give the one responsible for these kindnesses the consciousness of a duty discharged well.

Now if need is a sensation, lack is this same sensation rendered more perceptible by its having not been satisfied. The experiencing of lack is a prelude to that of desire, something which is radically different from need. Desire is not conveyed by a sensation evoking need. Desire is a state of tension. It is a motor, the nub of which consists in the consciousness of a need that the individual perceives as pertinent yet knows cannot be satisfied immediately. An individual feels desire rise within, when a need, perfectly identified as such, just allows the possibility of deferred satisfaction to spring up marked by waiting. Inasmuch as the manner in which I tolerate this waiting is mine alone, my desire will characterize me more than anything else as what I am, singular by definition and different from any other, since I alone experience what I experience and have experienced what I have experienced.

Yet that is not the end of the story, for the notion of waiting invokes once again that of time, the famous dimension that never stops cropping up in all sort of guises in our discussions. I laid great stress upon the conditions in which humans became consciously aware of its existence and laws, when, earlier in this book, I spoke of the murder perpetrated by our *Homo* ancestor. I also clearly showed how closely the gaining of this consciousness was allied to the birth of the fear of death. All that is needed therefore, at this point, is to close the discussion of the points I raised earlier by showing the different ways in which these notions of need, desire, time, the fear of death, and the death drive are linked together.

Need, the satisfaction of which is not always automatic in the way that it is in biological mechanisms, is the perception, generally physical in nature, of a lack that satisfaction forthwith effaces, thereby engendering a pleasure that can create a genuine state of addiction: a mother who unremittingly satisfies her child is sure to appropriate him entirely to herself and maintain him indefinitely as much within her dependency as within the dependency of pleasure. One might say of this seductive attitude that it is quite simply destructive, since it endeavours to perpetuate non-time. Sadly, it is no longer today the province merely of indulgent, albeit often well-intentioned mothers. Plenty of grandparents believe they can 'spoil' their grandchildren, because 'being a grandparent is the pleasure without the responsibility' - such a subtle way they have of denying responsibility for the damage they cause! How many fathers, too, especially separated fathers, use such means literally to buy their children's love, because they think they have to!

Desire comes from a need, physical or other, which has been perceived, but whose satisfaction has been deferred to the point where the trace of the lack of satisfaction has persisted. Its satisfaction equally generates pleasure, frequently more intense than the former, but whose addictive potential is much less by reason of the suffering produced by the time of waiting and of habituation to that waiting. The trace of the lack that signalled the emergence of the desire is therefore, in this regard, the best guard possible against addiction to pleasure.

Time therefore is the ingredient that intervenes to differentiate the categories of need and desire. To the extent that time has no hold over him, the individual who experiences it more or less perceives its passing as the bearer of a threat of death. But the consciousness he has of it, since he is not dead, establishes him as a living being and makes him all the more conscious of being so.

The fear of death emerges automatically in everyone from the perception that time is passing; through touches that vary in length and intensity, it confers on all the awareness of their mortality. That awareness, frightening as it is, is of course always violently repudiated, and this is never truer than when it has not been prepared for by any habituating phenomenon. If because of the excessive prolongation of the immediate satisfying of needs, the individual is for a long time shielded from the perception of the passing of time, then the least portion of that time that passes unoccupied by the satisfaction of a need, and therefore of a pleasure, generates pressure of anxiety that is intolerable enough to engender fear of the danger of immediate death. This is what underlies the propensity of today's children, who have been and continue to be sated, to tyrannize their environment with demands to be put in possession of everything - anything, something - straight away.

In chapter 2, I explained that the death drive is an unconscious mechanism that throughout our lives draws us toward regaining the mineral existence from which we have come. I used the metaphor of a slippery slope that we spent our whole lives climbing, and I mentioned that the life drive was built upon it. Now, when time passes and need is not satisfied, the lack that becomes thereby more urgent more or less quickly and more or less powerfully invokes death, in terms of both the fear of it that is perceived and the drive towards it that is manifested. This experience, once it has been overcome by deferred satisfaction of the need, which will have left its mark in the form of an imprint of the lack, is perceived as a victory, not simply over death but over the fear of death and the death drive as well, and confers on the subject - all the more so if he has not experienced it before, the certainty of his status as a living being.

I conclude from this that, while working to a method apparently irreproachable in her own eyes, my patient had not curtailed the addiction of her child to pleasure and continued to defer the moment when she might have enabled him to see himself fully as a living being, i.e., as one who has correctly and sufficiently early perceived the existence of time, since the mere perception of its passing will reduce the stress due to fear of death. Without presuming upon his future development, it is a fair bet that her child will later become one of the little tyrants whose numbers only increase.

Am I to conclude that this mother was a sort of animal mother? Decidedly not; quite the opposite! For animal mothers are programmed to harden their offspring and enable them to live in a world that is naturally hostile, where every creature runs the risk of being eaten; hence they do not flinch, if need be, from knocking them about to get them to leave, even though, as is true in the majority of species, they may not refuse to be mated by them subsequently. No, this particular mother was a human mother, one abandoned to the inexhaustible enjoyment that she derived from the solidity of her function and status in a society that had adopted, in a wholly unlimited and uncounterbalanced way, the totality of the values of which she was a carrier. She was a human mother equally in that her behaviour was consistent with the hidden struggle that the two sexes have carried on since the earliest times of humankind - the struggle, using different and unequal arms, that women have ever waged against men. It was men who placed constraints on them through the Law of the Species, the law that enacted their exchange and whose terms they no more accepted than they did the dispositions that would have forced them to admit the ineluctability of death. It is men who continue to impose constraints on them and whom, though they often deplore the fact, they need to involve in order to access the maternal status that has throughout all time made them so powerful. Always those wretched men...

From this it should now be clearer than ever that the struggle that, despite the various aspects it has taken down the ages, has gone on all this time is actually reducible to a conflict between two self-centred dispositions both as excessive and unreasonable as each other. The mother defends her right to repudiate time, the only way for her to be and continue to procreate. The father seeks to impose his person, his sexual desire, and his consciousness of passing time. Today, in our western societies, this confrontation appears to have reached a new phase for which neither party is ready, yet they will need to adapt to it by possibly inventing new forms of relationships. This has not yet happened, even if today's new forms of parenthood are ascribed to such inventive efforts. Women, having achieved a far greater degree of autonomy, are demonstrating a capacity to dispense with the partnership of men. Men, on the other hand, overawed by this development, may well try to follow close on their heels, copy them in everything, and thereby risk losing their own identity and taking the whole species with them. Will time be defeated because its passing is denied? And will death be vanquished by this stratagem? Against the winds of folly that seem to have risen, the best defence is still probably to return to the simplest definitions in order to learn and appreciate what may be going on in the difficult combat that is taking place at every moment and in almost every family unit.

THE MALE AND THE PATERNAL

We have already more than glimpsed them in these pages, the men, the human males, whose long, complex, and almost pitiful adventure has already been described. In this book, they have been on the receiving end of quite a few fairly unflattering epithets. The reader may wonder whether these are literary effects on my part. Or a manoeuvre designed surreptitiously to ingratiate me with female readers who have for some decades now been fully engaged in tortured questionings about their place and being? Or do they simply arise from elements of my own history and personal relationships with women and men, with mothers and fathers? People must draw their own conclusions. These days, no sooner do people discover a talent for interpretation than they become deaf and cancel out anything that might excite negative comment - technically speaking, this is a form of resistance. Personally, I do not intend to let what others might think put me off stating my formulations in the way I do. Although my observations may have a derisive air or seem sometimes to proceed from bitterness, the tone adopted is meant simply to give an edge to the questioning of criteria that have dominated the choices our western societies have made. For while many among us see current criteria as an outworking of determined progress, I view them as extremely harmful and regressive. But it is hard to know how to get this point across clearly when the commotion created forces everyone to retreat into their own personal unhappiness and take cover in deafening silence, waiting for the miracle that will not come. Won over to maternalizing values and encased in the certainty of their perceptions, our western societies have become ferociously resistant to all that unsettles their routine. While lip service is paid to the forms dictated by the democratic ideal, according to which all opinions are debatable, this comes with the demand that rational explanation must be provided for the least analysis or proposition designed to modify current options, even though the reality is that there is no willingness to question them in any way whatever. Due process thus will have been seen to be followed, and the demands of logic above all else apparently correctly served. Impossible as it is to dissent from the demand for logic, it needs to be understood that even in purely logical terms there are things that may be heard and other things that may not - and at all events certainly will not - be heard. Here again we are up against resistance. It is a dispiritingly notorious fact that to confront resistance is to reinforce it and indeed join forces with it to construct the barricade it seeks. I will, however, try not to fall into that trap.

Since here only rationality will do and every proposition needs to be backed by convincing argument, it will be best if I proceed, as in the last section, by spending some time on the time-honoured evidence provided by anatomy and physiology. This category of evidence is never given sufficient consideration. I said earlier that fathers were nebulous and had long been so, and I said that this was actually a good thing and that it would be good if it continued to be so. So let me try to demonstrate this. In outlining men's historic adventure earlier in this book, I repeatedly showed how the dimension of their maleness was always at the forefront of their activity. The discussion of the last section closely linked the nature of womanhood to that of motherhood. Now we must show how it is similarly true that the father is a father because he is first and foremost a man. It is probably this conjunction of the male and the paternal that is not just at the root of the nebulosity characterizing his status but also at the root of what makes that nebulosity reasonable, necessary, and above all healthgiving.

In the parallel that flows from this option, the sexual anatomical difference between men and women reveals a fundamental asymmetry in their relative positions that is sufficiently great to imply that their capacity to reach understanding between them is something of a miracle. 'Like a marriage between a carp and a rabbit' is a popular French way of saying that two things don't go together. But in view of all the differences between men and women, the marriage between a man and a woman is scarcely less problematic or practicable.

Of necessity, this leads me directly to a strange paradox in the confrontation of the two notions, solidity and nebulousness, that is relevant to the issues raised in this chapter. While the secret, discreet, mysterious (nebulous?) character of the female genitalia do not stop women from becoming solid mothers, the concrete, evident, observable, and sometimes blatantly obvious - quite the opposite of nebulous! - character of the male genitalia do not give him in respect of parenthood any advantage whatever, and leave him, when he becomes a father, with no certainty or solidity at all, unable to assume his position save by wandering into the zone of the undecidable, in other words into that famous 'nebulosity', both in regard to his own self-perception and as reflected in the way he is perceived by his offspring and their mother.

Fathers and Mothers

I cannot say whether this odd interplay between the two qualities makes sense in rational terms, or whether it is just a piece of argumentative opportunism on my part. I simply voice it here as an interweaving element that may mean something to someone, yet without imposing any particular reading on it or insisting that it has a particular applied usefulness. That said, it is nonetheless possible to interpret it in terms of the time-honoured realities of anatomy, whereby the female body provides itself with a child that it bears and brings into the world, whereas male genitals are never more than instrumental to that operation, and are ad hoc, interchangeable, even virtually anonymous.[24]

All of this should confirm the idea previously mentioned that although the evolution of the species created the father to discharge a function, and although fathers themselves have taken it on and sought unceasingly to perfect it, it has never been - far from it - what it has been for the mother, a function issuing directly from her animality. In other words, it is in no way natural to him, i.e., it tends rather to the cultural, though I do not wish to debate these terms, which are simply intended to draw a contrast between nature and culture. It is, as far as he is concerned, a derivative function, one in fact grafted upon what he has always been essentially - or naturally? - namely, a being highly susceptible to a sexual drive that never goes away and gives him no respite. After all, it is only because one day he determined to manage this drive as best he could that, having recognized his role in reproduction, he took to organizing exchanges, including that of women, and decreed the Law of the Species. But he was doubtless little concerned to measure the effect that that Law might or would have upon his environment and descendance. Let us not flatter ourselves: right down to this decisive discovery for the future of his species, he never made plans, only ever thought of himself, made his own arrangements, and was firmly of the mindset that he was to satisfy his drives as best he could and at the least risk.

He went on being a man, no less and no more: a self-centred male basically impervious to anything outside his essential preoccupation and always ready to make use of his physical strength to achieve his ends - a

---

[24] This instrumentality, as experience of some decades shows, may on occasions be reduced to a syringe, a flake of frozen sperm, or, in private, a spoon...

Fathers and Mothers

brute beast, in sum. He may have evolved just a little over time and lost the odd rough edge, gaining a veneer of culture, thought, and propriety, yet he remained at bottom a brutish lout. Though he certainly used his intelligence and was interested in other fields of activity, he was motivated by neither generosity nor self-sacrifice, which were always fundamentally foreign to him. No, all outward behaviour on this brutish fellow's part was a function of calculation - the phenomenon flatteringly termed 'sublimation' - simply to enhance his powers of attraction and thus multiply his opportunities to satisfy his needs.

The shape of his confrontation with his partner, the object of his desire, should be immediately discernible. There was no question of her avoiding him: she could think what she liked, he would do everything to force her to his will; he would endlessly perfect strategies for her oppression. The visceral attachment that characterized her animal function as a mother he countered with his own no less animal attachment, that of the sexual drive, which tormented him much more than her. As he was physically the stronger partner, she clearly had no choice in the matter.

It was ever thus. All brawn and no brain - a sentiment that still finds utterance today, even if applied somewhat hastily and not without a touch of pitying tenderness. To my mind, however, the formula is too limited. For the head of a man, whether the man of long ago or today's man, however urbane and civilized he may now have become, is not as empty as this hasty judgement would have us believe. On the contrary, it is full to overflowing, filled up with an organ, the most important in his eyes, be he a farmer, a workman, a management executive, an academic, an intellectual, a priest, or whatever - his genitals. To realize this truth is to be well on the way to understanding the tragic life he leads.[25]

There, and there alone, he stands, with his extremely plain morphology and a physiology that almost begs the assessment that it was thrown together in a hurry by nature, as if she wanted a vague tool, a rough addition, rather than a well-designed instrument conceived within a well-defined perspective. Such is man, encumbered by a sexual apparatus that constantly reminds him of its existence because driven by an imperious need to which

---

[25] Yes, tragedy! The word comes from the Greek *tragoidia*, and refers to the lament of a male goat ... without a she-goat!

he would one day ascribe the more complex status of desire. Because the excitability threshold of this organ in which his need reveals itself is so low, the perception of need often verges on obsession. This obsessiveness is not always easy to live with, especially at times when it becomes overlaid with fears caused by the exaggerated influence of factors significant since the rise of cultures: the inner censor, personal inhibitions, or the taint of prevalent normative discourse. But there he is, as I have said, encumbered by that protuberant sexual apparatus, whose existence, presence, and performances have never ceased to absorb him. For him and his fellows it has always been a subject for representation, whether on the walls of caves long ago or, as now, in all those places where they can give free rein to their graphomania; it is always erect, of course, as if to ward off the failure of that essential power - a preoccupation that in all places and in every period is evidenced by cults or ithyphallic representations. The pride the father took in it seemingly incited him to confiscate the mother's children from her in the name of the begetting potential he abusively arrogated to himself and which he continued to turn unduly to his advantage. What abuses did he not exploit during his long history? Think of the violence he constantly resorted to in order to lend credence to the least of his prerogatives once he had used it to impose on all of his species a Law contested by one half of its members. This is a story of arrogance, deliberate cruelty, and manifest indifference to the effects of abuse.

Was this an effect of nature - a nature that was both animal and possibly cruel for that very reason? Yet it is hard to find a zoological comparison. Not the lion. Not the great or most fearsome apes, his close cousins. None of them ever set up what man, though he took a long time to achieve it, eventually constructed. Perhaps all these attitudes were simply so many compensations designed to combat the deep ontological doubt that worried him in everything he did, a doubt that, wherever it intervened, was never anything more than the offspring of the fundamental doubt that ever tormented him around the sexual apparatus upon which the entire architecture of his identity was based. We can say, then, of him, that he himself was constructed on and around a core of doubt.

Whether we have in mind a close relation to the *Homo* ancestor or one of today's playboys or hard-porn actors, the anxiety-ridden male preoccupation of which we have been speaking is a constant.[26] Psychoanalysis, which has spent a long time exploring its content, teaches us that it was probably always the product of the same mechanism. Having discovered his sexual reality in the very early part of his life, the infant male is unable to stop falling into a major misunderstanding. At this time, when he becomes aware of the strange and invasive feelings he has for his mother, he wants to merge with her and become her, as happens in the violence of any passionate affair. In a burst of irrepressible imprudence, he vents the desire to lose the embarrassing appendage that makes him different from her. Clearly, he quickly gets over this. But this fantasy, reinforced scarcely any time after by the conviction that his sister has lost hers, leaves an enduring trace which is so deep that he never manages entirely to exorcize the threat of that loss. This strange obsession, which is virtually graven into the male destiny, may well - we know so little about it - be ultimately traceable to the period in the womb itself. The embryological process begins with the formation in the foetus of rudimentary undifferentiated gonads, which are acted upon by the Y chromosome. If the Y chromosome does its job properly, the gonads becomes testes, and they immediately start secreting the male hormone testosterone. This secretion in turn enables development of the penis. If for some reason the process fails to take place as it should, the penis never gets under way, and the genital apparatus evolves in female mode. You might say that, from the launch of the Y chromosome and the secretion of testosterone on, the male being is condemned to make an effortful existence - seen later in his erections and activism - if he does not want to lose his status. Hence the importance of the messages he receives from his sexuality. Every erection - how attentive he is to them! - gives him a grain of security, which disappears along with it and forces him to wait, with the same anxiety, for the next one, and the next, and the next, and the one after that, for it is true that *post coitum animal triste* - after coition the animal is sad. Thus he goes on indefinitely, in a pitiful state of dependence on the woman or women who know how to incite, sustain, and maintain such erections, and with whom he maintains an ambivalent

---

[26] I recall reading an interview in which a female porn star expressed her surprise at how regularly her male partners, after demonstrating their prowess, spoke to her of their concern about the quality of their equipment!

relationship. His body is forever a stranger to wisdom and moderation; it is on the basis of such activity, kept up till death strikes, that he will keep himself feeling on top. Those who think I am exaggerating here should bear in mind how often those men who are most creative into ripe old age reveal their continuing strong taste for sex, even addiction to it. The opposite phenomenon also exists, and is extremely badly tolerated. Around ten years ago medical science identified a distinct clinical syndrome labelled ADAM (Androgen Decline in the Ageing Male), which bore a detailed resemblance to deep depression (lassitude, extreme physical fatigue, impotence, black thoughts, loss of taste for life, suicidal obsession, and so on), save that it did not respond to antidepressant treatments. This clinical picture is due to the definitive failure of the endocrine testicle to produce testosterone. Once recognized and correctly treated with testosterone, which is for the rest of life like all endocrine deficiency treatments, the patients appear to come back to life after just a few days, including a return of sexual interest, and even activity. This increasingly common condition is found alongside a rise in male sterility and sharply lowered sperm counts across the spectrum of the male population. A correlation has been drawn with the regression of male genital organs in a number of animal species, and some authors attribute these effects to the environmental presence of volatile oestrogen-like substances emitted by various sectors of the chemical industry; these substances act like female hormones. What I am trying to bring out by interjecting this information is that while the menopause, once it has worked through, only temporarily affects female mood and can end up bringing a certain serenity, its male equivalent is always of pathologic origin - it is not ideology to say that in principle the andropause does not exist - and produces a serious clinical symptomology that can lead to death. This helps to explain the phenomenal success of Viagra and its equivalents, and the explosion in market solutions promising a bigger penis and longer-lasting erections. Is not all that instructive?

Man, then, has always had this encumbrance, and has either dealt with his problem with a minimum of soul-searching or laid himself open with total awareness to dependency on a partner for whom he has no mystery, to whom he cannot present himself otherwise than by the need he has of her, and from whom he, betrayed by his ejaculation, cannot hide the satisfaction he derives from their intercourse. He is both vulnerable because predictable, and pitiful because so transparent and artless.

Some might wonder at this point, with possibly a note of irritation, what purpose is served by deconstructing this anxiety that men have around their sexual activity. Equally, why speak of men's sexual drive alone, as though their female partners had none, as though they experienced nothing like it and were, moreover, spared the anxiety it occasioned their males?

Lest there be any misunderstanding here, I have never said that women are not subject to a sexual drive - that would be appalling if it were true. They quite clearly are, but it is in a different mode, to which I have already alluded; it is scarcely less complex than the male mode, but generally less problematic. While the infant female, like her brother, has to struggle with the desire to merge with her mother, she never develops the fantasy about losing her organ. She is rescued from the error to which she is no less subject than her brother, by cultivating nostalgia for the personal possession of a penis that might give her the certainty of a difference she might like to re-establish. Whether subsequently she sets about asking her father for one or hopes to get one from him, this is no straightforward matter and cannot fail to create serious and long-lasting problems between her and her mother. But while I would not underestimate the gravity of this, it is nonetheless of a different order. The fact of having her partner's penis in her may unknowingly take her back to this distant period, but can only be experienced by her in a highly satisfying mode, signifying to her that she is certainly herself and different from her mother, an experience that will be stamped and validated by orgasm. Perhaps that is why her orgiastic potential has been programmed to be so high. There is, however, nothing anxiety-producing in all this; quite the contrary. Then again, we noted earlier that women follow a behavioural logic according to which their agency in satisfying the needs of others gives them a feeling of power and coherence of being: to be the one by whom her partner satisfies his need can only satisfy her and slightly enhance her own sense of power. I mentioned earlier that a woman's frigidity, where it occurs, is less destabilizing to the couple than the impotence of her partner. Lastly, let us not forget how the characteristics of the female body are conducive to the efficient management of this aspect of her activity: her arousal threshold being higher than that of her partner, she is not put under the same pressure from a need which, in any event, she alone has the luxury of being able to supplement with the pleasure she specifically derives from her relationship to her child. There is nothing in this picture of multiple benefits to trigger anxiety.

We have not yet finished in this area, however. For, given that we have mentioned how intolerable is the anxiety inherent in a man's exercise of his sexuality compared to its relative absence in his partner's exercise of hers, we really ought to question that other anxiety, the fear of death, which men and women experience differently, as we have already established.

The question arises whether men and women experience two different forms of anxiety or one form of anxiety with different timing and modes of expression. The essential answer would seem to be that the same anxiety is involved, irrespective of when and in what circumstances it occurs. It surely has to be the same, although the stress it occasions women is so slight that it does not impinge strongly upon them when they exercise their sexuality. The woman indeed, as she relentlessly encases her male partner, energetically renews herself on and in him in the exercise of that same sexuality, as if to remind him that when, as a baby, he played with the fantasy of his castration, he was truly fantasizing about his disappearance as a differentiated being. To couch matters in such terms as these seems to me to be the harshest way of understanding how very differently the men and women who will in turn become fathers and mothers connect sex and death. Women, as I have often said before, having not participated in the first burial, are involved symbolically in sexuality as the means given to them of propagating life (*Zoe*) and of prolonging their own lives through the children they carry and bring into the world. I have often observed the wonder on the faces of young women who breastfeed, when I point out to them how much weight their babies have gained and that these kilos have come from them and them alone. There is absolutely nothing comparable to this on the male side; merely an endeavour that could be likened to a continuous personal operation to survive, which explains equally the focus upon sex and the compulsion to satisfy the need for it which is associated with a low threshold of arousal. Alongside this operation, and only after a fruitful result, will the man's relationship to the child be constructed, yet in an intellectual and affective mode, never in an instinctual, body-marking mode, since he, unlike his female partner, does not bring the child into the world out of his own body. Be that as it may, fathers are not thereby disqualified from participation in their children's future, since they, by remaining what they basically are and without seeking to fulfil any preconceived model, are empowered to do useful work on their children's behalf through the capacity, which they alone have, of correctly placing their children in time and of giving them to time - in other words, the capacity to give their children their essential human condition.

This is what men and their forebears have done for millions of years, following the basic, uncomplicated self-centredness governing their essential activity, which might vulgarly be styled that of an 'animal with a tail obsessed with its own disappearance'. For millions of years these males have been at the epicentre of all relational systems in which they are involved, and have gone along with the reality that without their will and consent nothing can happen. Here again they have been consistent with the stark realities of their anatomy and physiology: the erection, indispensable to coition, may or may not happen, making the male the unavoidable initiator of the operation. Contrary to his ever-penetrable partner, he can physically withdraw, say 'no' to penetration - and here we are faced with another paradox, the reality being that he has always been mentally ready for sexual play and generally unlikely to say 'no' to it, whereas his partner, who in principle cannot withdraw from it, has almost always refused, being very sparing with the possibilities of a 'yes'. For millions of years it has therefore been the male's way to organize his environment so that nothing stands in the way of satisfying his drive. It never bothered him, therefore, that his physiology was so extravagant, that he might ejaculate, usually to no purpose whatever, some five million spermatozoa per millilitre in a volume of several millilitres renewable several times a day from puberty until the end of life - the capacity, in short, to broadcast his seed far and wide. This was never too high a price to pay in order to stifle his recurrent fear - to buy the traveller a well-earned rest. No, it was not too high a price, when the treasury was constantly refilled as long as life lasted; when it helped to wage war on his doubt and on the uncertain status that was linked to his function; when it gave so much pleasure, charm, serenity, peace and self-image and, to cap it all, the possible attachment of a valued woman whom he undertook to look after materially and of children who were endearing and so often useful. This line of conduct also had a consistent and faultless underlying behavioural logic, which I term 'coition logic'. It is the natural counterpart of the female behavioural logic that I earlier named 'pregnancy logic'.

To state things as unambiguously as this entails various consequences, not least for the way in which everyone appears to feel the need to draw, either mentally or diagrammatically, the classic 'triangle' linking parents to their child. It is today generally drawn with each of the characters placed at one angle with their relationships shown by a arrow joining them and going in both directions: thus the mother has exchanges with the father on one side and the child on the other; the father has exchanges with the mother and with the child; lastly, the child has exchanges with his father and his mother. This representation is quite simply false, because totally untrue to reality. It is an ideological construction with grave consequences. For to establish any sort of relational symmetry between the different relationships can only lead the relevant persons astray in the way that they experience their respective, very different, conditions and dual relationships. Why the pretence that one can attribute the same standing and logic to the relationship between a mother and child, forged through such a momentous experience as pregnancy is for them both, as to a relationship derived simply from the sexual relationship between a man and woman, even if the desire for a child was an integral part of it? A more accurate way to represent the triangularity - assuming we retain the model of a triangle with each of the characters at one corner - is no longer to link them all in the same manner; instead, the mother is linked to the child along one side, and to the father along the other, while the father and child have no link between them, since the communication they establish with each other goes through the mother, as we shall see later. This responds exactly to the bodily reality, and it is from this bodily reality that the protagonists take their cue. The woman, having become a mother through a man to whom she concedes a place that is always impugnable in this adventure, gives birth to a child with whom she establishes an intimate relationship already invested in to the tune of nine long months; this relationship is something whose dimension she will endeavour to sustain indefinitely. She is the pivot of the relationship that may or may not become established subsequently between the father and the child; in terms of the triangle it could be shown, for example, by a dotted arrow. Such a representation would be all the more appropriate inasmuch as it is a perfect illustration of the 'nebulous' quality I earlier ascribed to the father. The child is able to attain perception of the father only through the filter constituted by the mother. The mother, equally, is able to perceive the father - and then in the most favourable cases - only in one half of her visual field, the other half being captured by the fascinating spectacle of her child. The father himself, to begin with, sees himself merely as a man with a relationship to his partner; only subsequently, by relating to his child, does he see himself as father, and this also is always and necessarily mediated by the same indispensable partner who made him a father in the first place.

In case anyone wonders why I am lingering over details like this, it is for the simple reason that during the history of the species, including its cultural history, the male, who was always concerned to manage his sexual drive to his advantage, quickly realized how much this drive of his could be compromised by the arrival of a child. Hence his care to build societal and relational systems likely to give him effective, not to say strict, control over the relationship of his female companion to their common child. Instances of such development, which are worth mentioning again, are the concept of paternity, the relative confiscation of the children, kinship systems, the Roman *paterfamilias*, the Arab *abu*, the enormous quantity of legislation that constitutes family law in all countries, and the history of fatherhood itself. All these phenomena are examples of the busy construction of societal support, including containment around the couple itself. The goal has always been to enforce the mother's submission to the Law of the Species, to get her to resist her incestuous drive as well as the huge stress of fear she has of her child's possible death especially if it is a boy, and finally to prevent her rushing with him into the virtual womb that she has a perfectly natural tendency to construct for their joint use.

The reader will see from this that the debate joined here is actually as old as humanity - except that today's younger generations know nothing of it and have launched headlong into the adventure of parenthood on the basis of a dubious ideology which, taking its cue from the changed status of women in the workplace, believes it possible to change in every respect a relational system that is, like it or not, liable to the laws and rules that are written in everyone's unconscious. This produces two wayward currents each opposed to the other and both of them as dangerous and pathogenic as the other because they depart from the model of the nebulous father. They are, first, 'the vindictive father', who, keen to assert his rights, thinks he can usefully take up a position of solidity, and, secondly, 'the seductive father', who competes openly with the mother, models himself on her, and therefore disappears completely as a father without even realizing it.

The first of these is not an invention of our times, but has always existed. He is the abusive father, the father who controls everything and behaves in an unboundaried manner in the life of his partner, whom he reduces to powerlessness, that is if he does not knock her about or throw her out, and more especially in the life of his child, whom he turns into a hostage. He tramples everything and everybody in his path, behaving like the famous father of the primitive horde who ended up under the rocks in the first burial; he seems to display such immense sexual energy that he overwhelms his child with it. The damage perpetrated by this type of father's behaviour is exemplified in the writings of Daniel Paul Schreber's father, or in Scott Hicks's excellent film *Shine* (1996), where the father strives to turn his son into a virtuoso pianist.[27] It is the excesses of such fathers as these that have conspired to discredit a function that has been decried in this manifestation over the last few decades, all the more inasmuch as it has been arrogated by a number of 'little fathers of the people' in recent history whose deeds are well enough known not to need elaboration.

In case it should be doubted whether there is much point in spending time on this model, it needs to be said, first of all, that there are still plenty of such fathers about, and we do not want to congratulate them on prerogatives that verge on psychological murder. Secondly, these fathers cause great harm because their claim to solidity is particularly corrosive to the societal environment, and damages the very cause they claim to be

---

[27] Daniel Paul Schreber was appointed to a high office in the judiciary of the German region where he lived, only to resign and become a voluntary patient in a psychiatric hospital. During this time he wrote and published a book which was used by Freud to illustrate paranoid psychosis. Years later, the writings of his father surfaced, a paediatrician who had spent his career inventing all kinds of containing contraptions intended to 'train' children how to sit straight at table, not to masturbate, touch their genitals, and so on. Edifying reading!

defending. This claim has given rise to, for example, some highly regrettable judicial decisions in France. The powers that be, having in recent times recognized the damage attributable to the disorganization of the traditional family and to the weakening of its paternal focus, have decided - without understanding the basics of the situation - to 'restore' the role of the father. In addition to disparate measures like the new *carnet de paternité* and paternity leave, modelled on the *carnet de maternité*[28] and maternity leave, which expressly attribute to the father an equivalent status of solidity - the French authorities have instructed the courts to pay greater heed to fathers' grievances. This is the orientation that produced the decision in the case I described towards the end of the last chapter. Even more lamentable decisions take place, for example, that of the case of a child of 4, who, having been given up by his abandoned genetrix to a couple with a view to their adopting him, was removed from those with whom he had built the essentials of his future life, and placed with his genitor. To cap it all, there is the consequence of the French national Law of March 2002, which enabled separated fathers, on their own initiative or that of their partner, to obtain alternate custody of babies barely a few months old, in the face of all we know about the huge need they have of their mothers.

The other unfortunate model, that of 'the seductive father', is several decades old. Dubbed equally 'the new father', he made his appearance in the post-1968 social context, which determined to have done with the sort of iron paternal figure that no one wanted any more of. It was a time of campaigning for 'true values', not just liberty, equality, and fraternity, but exchange, joy, and the true democracy that was intended to sweep away capitalism and its inequalities, the source of all evils. Each of these ideals had their prophets, who spoke persuasively at the time, and among whom were some - such is the irony of history - who later went on to chair the very firms they had earlier attacked. It was felt that traditional fathers had often abused their power, and it was not a particularly good thing to build on their heritage. What was needed was for those who wished it to invent a new way of being a father. Those who had the courage of their convictions rushed

---

[28] The *carnet de paternité*, introduced by law in 2002, is a sort of health and administrative log given by the French authorities to expectant fathers; the *carnet de maternité* is the classic health documentation given to all pregnant women in France - trans.

generously to defend the legitimacy of maternal demands for a sharing of domestic tasks. They were, moreover, not backward at coming forward in this - though it is noteworthy that in these days many of the heirs to their innovations are more faithful to the word than to the deed.[29] It is with this style of father in mind - unless such a one indeed should be its author - that the famous triangular representation that I objected to was invented. Attentive and maternalizing, he not only applauds his female partner's creation of a virtual womb for their child, he goes on to ensure that it is watertight, and even adds an extra layer of his own. The child, kept away from all experience of time and satisfied to satiety, becomes the sort of tyrant we are all familiar with. Indeed the phenomenon has become so common that, seeing it, one can infer the sort of father that has promoted it. This type of family configuration has low resistance: when the couple break up, having followed its contextual logic and believed that they must build upon the foundation provided by the highly toxic model of romantic love, the father is seen to demand his rights; this sometimes even includes a demand for exclusive custody of his child, backed up by statements of witness to his excellence, attendance, and devotion.

How have we come to this? The answer is that we think we can ignore the emotional level and get by through relying on our intelligence and reason alone, without realizing that we are nothing if not individual members of a species whose rules of functioning have neither changed, nor admitted of any accommodation. Every transgression of those rules by the generations that have gone before us comes down to us in the form of a history to which we become heirs at birth; this history affects us far more than we are ready to believe.

A random selection of clinical anecdotes may help to illustrate the extreme patterns into which fathers can sometimes fall.

William spent time and effort setting out to relieve his female partner by taking over a large proportion of the care of their son Franky. As soon as Franky learned to talk, William began to treat him as a

---

[29] Perhaps they cling so instinctively to their experience of time that they can no longer even make the effort to relieve their partners!

confidant, availing himself of every opportunity to show his son that he, William, loved him much more than his mother did. When the inevitable crisis in the couple's relationship came along, William made Franky the witness of his misery, even dragging Franky out of bed at night to join him on the sofa in the living room where he spent his nights. It was tragic to behold this child, not even four years old, holding his father's hand, consoling him and confiding to me that his 'daddy' was very unhappy.

One wonders what sort of blind alley this man must have found himself in so as not to see the enormity of the dilemma he was locking his son into.

When Jacques learned of his wife's extramarital relationship, he did everything, in appearance at least, to cut the figure of a perfect gentleman. When he left, he gave his wife custody of the children together with generous maintenance. His arrangements obtained the endorsement of the judge, who was surprised to hear him make only one stipulation, namely the right to telephone his children every evening, wherever he might be. His wife, too, was taken aback, and was left wondering whether the display of such generosity of spirit was not intended to make her feel even more guilty than she felt already. That is, until one day she lifted one of the extension receivers and overheard the conversation. Her ex-husband was explaining to each of the three children, as they took turns to come to the telephone, that they should be wary of their mother; she was a whore who had betrayed him, and she was likely to betray them too sooner or later. One easy imagines the difficulties facing the social agencies to protect these children, drawn as they were into the torments emanating from the narcissistic wounds of a distinguished man who was unable to remember his children's status.

While not seeming to belong to the category of fathers who laid claim to a status of solidity, Jacques was nonetheless not far off it, as he masked the damage he was having on his children.

It didn't take Romain long to put his oar in where the breastfeeding of his daughter was concerned. Having gone on about the frustration he felt, he insisted that his partner express milk at least once a day and put it in a feeding bottle for him to give his daughter. To begin with, his partner didn't mind doing this, but things took another turn when she tried to get him to drop the ritual he had adopted for this. He had chosen to give the last feed of the day. The fact that he did this in his pyjamas did not bother her. What she found much more difficult to take, however, was that over his pyjamas he would slip his late mother's nightdress.

Every man, when a baby or young child, will have found himself in the arms of a mother. Indeed his early identification will have been with her, before he goes on to complete his identification with his father or at least some other male figure. It is commonplace for the arrival of a baby to reawaken this primary identification in a father, yet not for it to be taken this far!

The reason I have such a sharp memory of Daniel is not simply because his history was so unusual, but because he had no sooner entered my consulting-room than he said, 'I'm Daniel' - no surname or 'Mr' - offered me his hand, and addressed me, a complete stranger, like a friend of long date. I'd been thinking that this had bothered me more than it should have done, when I saw him several days later. I couldn't remember either his partner or the baby, and it took me several minutes, with my secretary's help, to understand what was going on: the woman with him and the baby she had in her arms were not the ones I had seen before. This performance was renewed a further three times in the five weeks that followed. In other words, I saw Daniel with four women and four babies with different names but similar ages. I eventually acclimatized myself to the situation, but it took me several months to understand the status of this harem! Daniel was the genitor of only one of the babies and the partner of only one of the mothers, who, just like the others, believed she was the only woman he had brought to see me. Daniel had simply

> decided, as I discovered later, to help women who found themselves on their own towards the end of a pregnancy, and to substitute for the absent genitor. As others collect paintings or hunting trophies, Daniel collected mothers: he made them dependent upon him simply by virtue of his devotion and attentiveness; as I learned, he had no desire or sexual end in mind. Over the following months he brought three more along to see me. He was, so to speak, addicted to the exercise of fatherhood. One day I asked what lay behind it. He said, 'When I was eight, I saw how my mother treated my father, and I vowed that when I grew up I would act in such a way as to be better respected. Among all these mothers, there is bound to be one who will understand that I am important and will agree to give me the credit for it.'
>
> Another man, Simon, gave me a similar explanation after he had been to me over several years with six babies belonging to six different women, with each of whom he had broken off as soon as the baby he fathered was born. When I expressed surprise that in spite of his propensity he had not given his name to any of these children, he replied: 'What name would that be? When I was ten, my mother told me that my father wasn't my father. Now she's dead, the bitch - and she always refused to tell me whose son I was!'

These two men had both seized upon ways of reclaiming their history with a view to repairing it. Is that not something that drives all procreation?

> When I saw little Gérard with his mother Michèle and his father Frédéric, it was just at the beginning of the 'new fathers' movement. What interested me about their story was that their family unit reversed the more usual set-up. Frédéric, hoping to make it as a painter, looked after the baby and the house, while Michèle, a management secretary, left for work in the morning and came home to a cooked meal in the evening. I looked in vain for signs that the untraditional division of tasks had produced any effects. One day, they arrived with a pink Moses' basket and introduced me to Chimène. When I enquired after the original choice of forename,

> Frédéric said to me, 'Well, I'm called Rodrigue.' In view of my surprise and the fact that I had myself used the name Frédéric, which I had often heard his wife call him by, he began a long explanation about how his father had always wanted to call him Rodrigue, but that his mother had objected. He told me he knew Corneille's Le Cid by heart, and never missed a performance, wherever it took place, if he could help it. The last one he had seen was just the previous month, played by the final-year students at a lycée in Châteauroux in central western France. Then he added: 'The finest performance I ever saw was undoubtedly the one at the Théâtre National Populaire. I was ten years old, and I'll never forget Gérard Philippe.' Suddenly I knew why his eldest was called Gérard, and I was just observing to myself that, although he was a 'househusband', Frédéric had never lost sight of the fact that he was a man, a father, and his own father's son, when suddenly Michèle, undressing Chimène, scolded him, saying, 'I always tell you not to fasten the nappies too tight.' As if echoing my own private thoughts, he retorted, 'Hang on a minute. I'm just a bloke.' And he continued, addressing his son, 'Hey, Gérard, we're just blokes, aren't we?'

The ideal way of being a father, then, is to stand in the filiation of one's own father, which entails being able to transcend all the conflicts that may have taken place with him - which is, of course, not always that simple. It is possible, then, for a father to substitute for a mother without competing for her position, and thereby allow the child to have the possibility of reliable markers.

Two other fathers come to mind -

> Cyprien came to see me. He was furious, sad, and disorientated. He wanted to know whether he should tell off his eleven-year-old son for stealing a high-denomination banknote from his wallet or carry on as if he hadn't noticed it. He was naturally inclined to come down hard, but was worried about what other people would say if he did, especially the reaction of his partner, who had already minimized the

incident and decreed that they mustn't react.

Jérôme was a voluble philosophizer about the generation gap and the influences of trends. Nonetheless he was concerned about what was going to happen to his fourteen-year-old daughter, who was a collector of boyfriends and would bring them home for the night. Up to now he had thought he could get away with a familiar approach, with quips like 'If you can't be good be careful' as the adolescent's bedroom-door closed in his face! But this was at great cost to himself, and it worried him even more.

Very difficult all that - and yet so very common!

I could go on multiplying examples like these without exhausting my stock of them or indeed without getting to the bottom of what they have to teach us and the questions they raise. What manner of fathers are these? What can be said of them - other than that against a background of societal change that has removed both the old framework of supports around the couple and the implicit recognition of the father's importance, they seem bewildered, disorientated, angry, lost, as if wandering in search of a solution that they know beforehand will elude them? In other times, their behaviour would have been seen as abject. The essentially maladjusted way in which they feel themselves forced to act testifies to both their awkwardness and their loss of landmarks. They cannot even be nebulous any more; their fear is of becoming - that is, if they do not deem themselves to be already - non-entities. Each one feels he is on his own and under threat, without the least societal support; he therefore devises his own solution in the face of a female partner who becomes all the more detestable and frightening as she moves across a stage over whose backdrop is cast the shadow of another mother, his own, and he hears still ringing in his ears the echoes of the struggle in which he witnessed his own father defeated.

Every parent is the child of his or her parents, and each rediscovers in the adventure that they live through with their own children not simply the life they experienced as a child but also the distortions in it that affected the course of their life and made them a unique individual, outside of the norm so to speak. Now if they believe themselves to be outside of the norm, it must be that they believe that there actually are norms towards which they, with only their own resources, are groping. It is as though norms existed about which no one would have any knowledge at all unless they came across them and recognized them as such.

We are left, therefore, wondering whether such norms actually exist, norms fundamental to a form of harmony that might be intuitively accessible to everyone, a form of harmony capable of embracing both the stubborn resistance of a mother to the Law on the one hand and the pressure that the Law is duty-bound to exert on the other. If such norms exist, and if, possibly, everyone sets about searching for them, we have to believe that everyone must come near at least once to perceiving the possibility that such norms exist. If so, when? At the age when people believe that all is possible? Do people brush up against them, then lose sight of them for ever?

Freud was certainly right when he said that to be a parent was one of three impossible callings. He was right, too, when, in response to Marie Bonaparte's enquiry about the best way to bring up children, he observed, 'However you tackle it, it will be done badly.' As I have already suggested, the desire to disprove this assessment remains, even today, a key motive for procreation. Everyone believes that what he or she suffered was due to mistakes made by his or her parents, and that the way to get even is to have children of one's own and not repeat those mistakes. We know what this leads to.

Where are we, then, in relation to this obstinate tendency? If some form of harmony existed or was simply conceivable, what would be its connection with the history of our species and with the consequences of the ways in which parents, albeit now in a more civilized fashion, continue to oppose each other along gender lines? If we allow the possibility that a form of harmony may exist, then the recent organizational changes to our western societies could be seen as precursors of its imminent advent, with the new parental configurations as its prophets. Alternatively, it may be that quite the opposite is the case, that these new figures of parenthood are signs of a chaos into which we risk seeing our descendents sink, along with our own souls. What can we do, or at least try to do, to escape such distressing uncertainty

Chapter 5
Children At Stake

So, firm in her convictions and confident in her power, she managed to obtain leave to go and breastfeed her baby in the middle of the examinations. Nothing - nobody - had been able to dent her determination. It was as though her condition had rendered her such that in all circumstances she could take account only of her own appreciation of things. I acknowledged my own defeat when I told this story in the last chapter. I also mentioned how frustrated I felt and how impossible it was to predict when, eventually, this young woman might agree to open the infinitely expandable virtual womb that she had constructed around her child, so that - but under what conditions? - he might finally enter the world.

Yet it has to be wondered whether she herself had ever succeeded in entering the world, especially in the light of the solicitous collusion of her own mother and the silent approbation of her child's father. How could she have done so, with a mother who invited her to follow in her own footsteps, and who viewed such an arrangement as fully justified, being in effect the rightful and healthy extension of her own history? Had she herself, one wonders, had any other sort of childhood than the one she put in place for her son? Had her own father been anything other than silent? It is through such details that histories are passed on. It is in ways like this that what is carved deep within the memory of individuals takes on an apparent impassability, to the extent even of bending the direction of life-stages that they enter on their own account. 'Why change a strategy that has worked - you are yourself the living proof!' is a message her mother may well have given her. And what could she have found to say against that? It was extremely easy, therefore, for her to confuse reproduction with repetition, and to turn the opportunity to reproduce into one of simply repeating the past.

How many are aware that such repetition, with the underlying laziness on which it relies, spells the death of invention, if not death itself? Reproduction, on the other hand, because it integrates a strange new party into the adventure opens the way to change, innovation, and life. For every new generation, it is the outworking, at the level of the individual couple, of the interbreeding generalized by the Law of the Species. Many understand that the passage from one generation to another is an opportunity to make good the losses of the past, yet they allow themselves to be boxed into a past that has still not released its hold over them, and they run for cover, frightened by the risks they imagine their offspring to be running.

How many realize that they are going up a dead end, yet will not allow themselves to be born into a life that they are too terrified to assume? How many take advantage of the longevity and availability of their parents - both novel aspects of life today - and are content to sprawl indefinitely in the prolonged comfort of a childhood that has totally lulled them? After all, is it not a worthwhile aim, to invest in simple existence? And why be suspicious of such a state on the ground that it would feed the fearsome pleasure of grandparents - the pleasure pre-eminently of the maternal grandmother, with the silent complicity of the paternal grandmother who, though often at a remove from her developing grandchildren, seems particularly gifted in understanding how formidable female determination can be in the service of pleasure? Grandmothers on both sides have been successful for several generations past in winning over their male partners to their views, that is when they have not simply reduced them to silence. The father of the child in question will himself have been converted by his own life-story to a belief in the pertinence of a strategy that implicitly received his own approbation. Must he not himself have had a mother as formidably determined as the mother of his child, and a father as silent as he now was? How else is one to explain his passivity? Perhaps he lived a life that functioned from day to day without ups and downs? What cause did he have to worry? The long term? Would there not always be time later to address any consequences that might arise? Is it not simpler and better to take things as they come and live from day to day? What reason could there be for him to listen to all kinds of prophets of doom that would cast doubt on the happiness offered, when all the precautions surrounding this mother and her child self-evidently flowed from goodness and love? And to cap it all, why be wary, when such an approach was in total contradiction with the current ideology of our societies, which are so satisfied with themselves and their attainments? Such thinking suggests to me that we have reached a crucial point. All the signs are that it is a point of no return.

I need do no more than list some of the striking features of this situation: the lack of an adult dimension in the general behaviour of our contemporaries, invited as they are to let themselves be lulled indefinitely; adolescences that go on and on; the rise in the average age at which women have their first baby; disaffection with marriage; instability of the couple; the large rise in divorce. I do not need to labour these points, because everyone is aware that they exist; everyone is exposed to them to a greater or lesser degree, whether or not they think they might sooner or later be directly affected by them. Besides, these are things that media analysts go on about endlessly, as they do similarly from time to time in regard to the exponential rise in single-parent - 'monoparental' or 'lone-parent' - families.[30] We accept all these features as simply objective realities of the times we live in without ever asking ourselves how they managed to come about or whether sooner or later they might affect us or threaten the quest for balance that humankind has always preoccupied itself with. But it seems hardly feasible to go on idly putting these upheavals down to what is deemed to be a new, yet unextraordinary change in our species, and not even register, still less investigate, the multiple factors that have led to it.

The current triumph of the maternal dimension includes not least its relationship to time. This is demonstrable both in the way that children are currently brought up and in the dynamic of societies dedicated to consumption, which focus on the immediate and ephemeral - the 'mother effect', as the French pun (*éphémère–effet-mère*) ironically suggests - to the detriment of the lasting and longterm. This triumph of the maternal

---

[30] Eighty-eight per cent of lone-parent households in France are headed by women; numbers have exploded in the last quarter-century. From 79,000 in 1979, there were 1,390,000 in 1993, 1,750,000 in 1999, and passed the 2 million mark in 2002. This is equivalent to an increase of 2,531 per cent in 23 years.

dimension might incline us to think that a serious challenge to the Law of the Species is under way, if not an effort to throw it over entirely. Our western societies do not yet advocate the practice of incest, but they give the appearance of having gone soft in their condemnation of it, when they can contemplate plenty of its equivalents, as if they had reconciled themselves either to its irrepressible emergence or to its inevitability in at least a statistical sense. It is regrettable, to take just one example, how the message of psychoanalysis is so filtered and twisted that mothers can frequently and openly demonstrate their delight at the incestuous declarations of their sons, while certain fathers announce to all and sundry that they want to be the only men in their daughters' lives!

Perhaps we have to admit that, if matters have not already gone too far, we may be on the brink of a decisive phase in the long, hard confrontation, dating from time immemorial, between men and women, whom I in the last chapter likened to two fundamentally mutually alien subspecies of our common species. And perhaps we should admit also that that phase, which could surreptitiously signal the emancipation of women from subjection to a Law that they never thus far ratified, might bear witness to their victory. Perhaps, thirdly, we ought to admit that we are dealing not with a sudden and inexplicable societal change, but rather with the consequences of an evolution for which preceding generations are as responsible as we are, one whose possible implications were never at any stage grasped. We do no good by self-deception or evasive self-justification. A better policy is to take stock of what was believed to be risk-free but which has nevertheless, without any desire or foresight on anyone's part, profoundly altered the relative balance that prevailed till now. Even so, that is no straightforward task! For the situation in which we all find ourselves continues to be so emotionally frayed, that the attempt to make even a rudimentary assessment exposes one to the charge of being unbearably nostalgic about the past, as though any questioning of the current drift is liable to be taken as a dubious invitation to turn the clock back. Yet the acknowledgement of progress in some areas should not preclude drawing attention to possible drawbacks or unforeseen side-effects in others. The system of public healthcare in France, for instance, has made major progress. But to recognize that it is expensive and that its finances need looking at is not the same as wanting to do away with it.

Without going too far back, we might note, for example, that problems confronting our western industrial economies - run by men, as some will interject - linked to their promotion of desire for material gain gave rise to a massive entry of women into the workplace. Yet no thought was given to the disequilibrium that this would create, at the very least at a symbolic level, in the relationship between the men and women concerned. There had always been a symbolic balance in their relationships: till then, work had provided men with an anchorage point for a creative potential that enabled them to counterbalance that which women had always held by virtue of their procreative capacity; simultaneously it enabled men to keep women within their dependency and thereby have some influence, however slight, over the development of their common progeny. Once women entered the workplace, their potential was immediately doubled by the addition of new creative potential to their existing procreative potential, while the creative potential of men neither changed nor grew. It is worth wondering in fact whether the deficit thus opened up on the male side is not responsible for the inequalities that women have continued to suffer at work in terms of rights, career prospects, and pay compared with their male colleagues. Yet in spite of being victims of discrimination, women have nonetheless fairly quickly acquired economic independence. This progressive economic self-sufficiency has meant that, whether or not they have children, they are able to contemplate the possible break-up of their couple, a phenomenon attested by the fact that throughout all social classes the majority of petitioners for divorce are female.

The sense of material well-being created by the new arrangements in the workplace could hardly fail to engender across all social strata - such is the homogenizing effect of industrial ideology - a truly obsessional desire for the same feel-good state at every level and in every area of life. It is similar, to take another example, with the sexual appetite that was supposed only to exercise the male members of the species. It had always been a male dream to be able to enjoy unlimited sex and not to need constantly to conquer the fear of pregnancy that put a brake on female enthusiasm and long deterred women from yielding to male entreaties. Although research into contraception was motivated in the first instance by demographic concerns, it was nonetheless looked to and promoted for the relief - and pleasure without nagging worries - that it would provide. No wonder, then, that women, whose genitality as we have seen was less disorganized than men's, should claim the same freedom as their male partners. How could they fail to take advantage of this advance? Most of them cheerfully did, yet with one important difference. For, while today's men continue to behave like the butterflies they always were, many women are still not prepared to indulge themselves so lightly, despite the possibilities afforded by contraception and more liberal standards of behaviour. Such a difference in approach is explicable only by unconscious factors that remain at work. Because both men and women bear the mark of their gestation in their mothers' wombs, a man's encounter with the body of a woman is always for him a kind of homecoming, so that the last woman, whatever her rank, counts as a second; on the other hand, a woman's encounter with the body of a man is always for her a kind of discovery, so that the last man, whatever his rank, counts as a first who effaces all who have gone before; the risk she incurs is therefore too great a one to be taken lightly.

Meanwhile, what has happened in the case of the children? Here the hold of their mothers over them has become so blatant and all but total in families of all configurations as to be a matter less for demonstration than for evaluation. Far from affording children the comfort, happiness, and security that some imagine or assert, it locks them and their mothers into sometimes disturbing problems. I do not think it can be repeated too often that the advance of our species can be summed up in terms of the confrontation of two heterogeneous forms of self-centredness that neutralize each other to the benefit of their offspring. The situation now, however, appears to be rather one in which the voices that rise to condemn men for their patent self-centredness and their concern with their own satisfaction alone choose to be dewy-eyed about the stranglehold of mothers, as though it were a model expression of disinterestedness. In reality, it stems from a form of self-centredness that is even more to be condemned than its male equivalent, since, left to itself, it does not simply destroy individuals, it jeopardizes all the progress the species has made over hundreds of thousands of years.

The consequences of this situation cannot be regarded as momentary, individual, minimal, or negligible. They seem to be sufficiently beyond us as to threaten to turn our planet upside down. It will not be the first time in our history that small causes will have had major effects.

FROM THE NEWBORN OESOPHAGUS TO AL-QUAIDA

However much of a non sequitur it may seem to link these two things under one head, I do so after a period of reflection that has lasted many years. Halfway through my career as a paediatrician, I found myself confronted by the emergence of a clinical picture that quickly went on to become an insistent and then regular feature of my practice. There is nothing remarkable about the fact that babies, particularly small babies, often regurgitate and occasionally vomit; the phenomenon is referred to in medical texts dating right back into early Antiquity. It is less usual for them to vomit continually and suffer so badly that they become poorly nourished and wake several times a night. Having come across the phenomenon several times in the early days, I was surprised to encounter it more and more often: from one baby in five, it went to one in four, then one in three, and now, as I reach the end of my career, it accounts for almost nine babies in ten, a truly staggering statistic. I have therefore lived through what some of my colleagues, with a sideways glance at some successful contemporary political sloganeering, have dubbed 'the reflux generation'. For some unknown reason, the junction between the stomach and the oesophagus stopped fulfilling its antireflux function, thereby allowing gastric acid into the oesophagus, where it caused intolerable burning and, in some cases, ulcers of varying degrees of severity.

Having realized what was happening, especially the strange increase in the phenomenon, I was sufficiently mystified to want to do something about it. I not only went through the literature exhaustively, I also discussed the matter with colleagues, who were as astonished and nonplussed as I was. I also questioned a number of teachers of medicine, old and not so old, to try to understand what we were dealing with. They too had registered the phenomenon, but had no explanation to offer for it. The increasing frequency of the symptomology meant that eventually I had enough data of my own, and decided to do my own investigation, to gauge the influence of differences in infant milk - artificial versus maternal, older types of barely half-skimmed bottle-milk versus the various newer formulas - as well as in sex, conditions of birth and birth rank, family configuration, and the like. The data was not simply time-consuming to collect, it was also difficult to analyze, since I had defined certain parameters, and some of these intersected with others. At the same time, rapid advances in the commercialization of effective dietetic and pharmacopoeic treatments made the drawing of conclusions even more problematic. Finally, there was the new prominence given to the hitherto unobtrusive subspecialism of infantile gastroenterology; this began to lay down guidelines that could not be set aside, yet which did not serve my ends, since their focus was upon improving diagnostic methods and therapeutic results. I remember trying to convince the young, recently qualified medics on the platform at a French national colloquium that my alarm and questionings around the rise in this new pathology was based on long clinical experience. Their response was that it must have always existed, but that years ago we certainly did not have the expertise to diagnose it. My colleagues and I of similar years were really quite incensed by this attitude, which deliberately set aside our aptitude as clinicians. It was with some degree of bitterness that we recognized the regression that had resulted from the rise of a form of medicine that, for all its scientific pretensions, had harnessed itself to instrumental technique alone.

As time went by, I went back to my own statistics. I had to conclude, first of all, that the type of milk-feeding had nothing to do with the question. Nor had sibling rank, any more than family structure and configuration, term, weight at birth, or birthing conditions. There was a distinct bias towards boys in the distribution of cases, but this was in line with general male morbidity, i.e., 70–75 per cent boys as against 25–30 per cent girls in all areas, and was therefore not particularly significant. Eventually, I recognized a factor that I previously had not noticed or previously considered noteworthy. This was that the symptoms did not occur among babies of recent immigrants (Black Africans, North Africans, Sinhalese, Cambodians, Madagascans, Indians, Chinese, etc.), but did occur, and to virtually the same extent as in the historically indigenous population, among babies born to parents of ex-migrant, well-integrated stock. I was disinclined to conclude that it was our country, or its climate, that made babies sick! At first I just recorded the fact. Later, I began to think that this had to be significant, especially when I realized that I had never come across a single case of infantile reflux among my Lubavitcher Jewish clients: extremely devout Jews meticulously observant of all the customs, in many cases established in France over several generations. Linking this fact with my observations of other groups, I was forced to concede that the particular populations in which this clinical picture never appeared had one thing in common due to their original, albeit very diverse cultures: a solid symbolic system and a family structure that was sufficiently hierarchic for the father to have a recognized and well-defined role. As integration helped to remove this background in the generation after immigration, so the symptomology of infantile reflux appeared.

Distressed by these findings, I looked back from a distance over all my professional experience, trying to pull all the diverse strands together. It was evident to me that I needed to consider another important detail, the fact that the rise and increasing frequency of the symptom dated from the second half of the 1970s. I hesitated for some time over whether these dates were a matter of chance or worthy of greater consideration. However, it has to be acknowledged that something far from insignificant took place in France in 1975: the legalization of voluntary abortion or, to put it another way, the last word in birth control techniques.

All the same, I did not see how this could have a connection with what I was investigating, until I had to acknowledge that the achievement of total birth control could not fail to have affected the status of the child. Until then, including the time of the Ogino ('rhythm') method and even the pill, there still remained a degree of risk with all contraceptive methods. The child once conceived, whether wanted or not, programmed or not, retained the status he or she had always had: the fruit of (unconscious) desire, which could impose itself on the (conscious) will; the child was definable as a by-product, partly assisted by chance, of its parents' sexual activity. Because of that fact and regardless of whatever love or enthusiasm they might conceive for their child, the parents quite simply assumed the hierarchy of their relationship to him and received him as something of a surprise, which left the door open to all the reactions he was going to have. His parents were for him, as parents always have been from the earliest times, a relatively serene environment in which he could develop his own sense of security. What the legalization of abortion signified was that desire no longer predominated. Henceforth desire was entirely subject to the will; the will could censure desire in all circumstances, since the availability of abortion made it possible to suppress the effects of its intervention. Henceforth the child, programmed and willed, if not yet at the stage of being graded and predefined, no longer had the status of a by-product, but was a pure product of the parents' sexual activity. The relationships that were now created around the child were typical of the relationships surrounding products in our societies: acknowledged as rare and precious, the child was to be perfect, i.e., functioning well, never a cause of disappointment, a reliable provider of the pleasure expected from him or her, and intended never to prove a disappointment - in other words, locked into a preconceived destiny in whose service the parents unflinchingly placed themselves, inverting the classic hierarchy of relationships and hoisting him, the child, to the top of the family edifice. This was not the way to give him, the child, the least sense of security.

If this development is viewed in terms of the criteria highlighted many times in this book, it is clear that the change of status from by-product to product eliminates the dimension of time. For, in the former case, the generational hierarchy is maintained: the child remains the child; his parents are the parents. In the latter case, however, the generational hierarchy is all but abolished by the hoisting of the child to the same generational level as his parents - if indeed the hierarchy is not actually inverted by the child's being hoisted to the generational level above his parents, in that they deem themselves to have incurred a symbolic debt to the extent that their attitude is defended by the observation that the child did not ask to come into the world.

Programming of this sort, introduced by the total mastery of birth control, makes every mother susceptible to a new and remarkable anxiety. For, without actually being able to articulate the thought, she will wonder whether her child, locked in as he is to the predefinition that has fallen to him, will be capable of shouldering the task that awaits him. Whether she likes it or not, she will feel that it is largely up to her to enable, not to say underwrite, the child's performance, and she may feel remarkably alone in helping her child, even if her partner is by her side and excels in parental task-sharing. In view of the fact that such a predefinition is the expression of an expectation and a wish for innovation, both divorced from any notion of inheritance and from the effect of transmission of the parental histories, the full extent of the ambition of the project becomes apparent. Here again, it is possible to identify a real break with the past. Whereas previously the very fact of the pre-eminence of desire over will made the child a link in a history that would eventually continue through him, the pre-eminence of will over desire enabled the parents to believe that they could deliberately break with this history. Prior to this development, the dominant theme of all births was reproduction, which gave each of the parents an opportunity to put some order into their relationships with their own parents and guard against repetition. But now, the new situation allowed them to think not simply that they could draw a line under all they had hitherto experienced but that they could invent and innovate through an enterprise within which they were determined to be excellent parents, attentive, loving, and better in short than their own parents ever were toward them. To achieve this, they placed themselves entirely at their child's disposal, throwing themselves unhesitatingly into what really amounts to an exercise in seduction. But such strong repression of elements looking for the least opportunity to return naturally to the surface will lead to their re-emergence with all the greater violence. The dream whose realization was supposed to be so wonderful begins to turn into a nightmare. The parents' stress, in particular the stress of the mother, which is much more obvious to the baby, is capable on its own not simply of contributing to the rise of the problem but of maintaining it or making it worse.

It may be wondered what bearing considerations of this order could possibly have upon a symptom as physical as reflux. Yet the matter is a great deal more straightforward than might be supposed. First, even in rats, stress can create gastric ulcers: the neurological system of the gastric region, especially the perioesophageal nervous plexus (the solar plexus of ancient authors), is particularly vulnerable to changes in mood - indeed American writers have not hesitated to describe it as a second brain. Secondly, by virtue of their time in the womb infants are extraordinarily acutely sensitive to the changes in mood and even the unformulated thoughts of their mothers. This is why it is possible for a mother to communicate her history and all that may have happened within it without the least word of explanation, on the level of gesture alone - which incidentally represents a formidable advantage that she has throughout her life over the father, who in order to obtain the same result is obliged to use words that can reach the child only if the mother puts up no obstacle. Thus the conscious choice of the mother and her partner to invent and to make a more or less radical break with history will provoke a conflict, as I have suggested, with the old fundamental process of communication. Although it clearly will not torment her to the extent that she is herself aware of it, it will nonetheless continue to exercise her in the manner of a muffled, obstinate, and obsessive voice that she cannot shut out. Her gestures will be necessarily affected, making her seem more 'stressed'. Since the infant's neurological cabling lacks insulation, he will perceive the slightest current circulating above a certain intensity in one fibre spread to all the others.[31] This makes the child extraordinarily sensitive to very small changes in the muscular tonus of the person holding him, especially when that person is the mother. It is this mechanism that lies behind the apparently miraculous effects produced by certain psychoanalysts when they talk to children. The children, needless to say, do not understand what is said to them, but they unerringly register the involuntary variations in their mothers' muscular tonus associated with the emotions produced in her by those same words. Analysis of how this chain reaction works is why I myself have never followed the practice of some psychoanalysists in talking directly to very small children. In my opinion this practice is not only phoney - since it is simple enough to tell the parents directly the message one believes they need to hear - it is not entirely risk-free either. I have seen it encourage in parents a persistent and unhelpful posture of sideration, i.e., they are so impressed by the words addressed by the professional to their child, that they dread saying anything to him or her

---

[31] The material that insulates the nerve fibres, myelin, grows only from birth and at the rate of no more than three-tenths of a millimetre a day.

on their own initiative. Bereft of the artistry of the brilliant practitioner who knows how to work miracles, they become scared to get it wrong. I must say I prefer living breathing parents who communicate with their children, whatever the quality of the message delivered, to parents who have been converted to the stupid and harmful religion of babyolatry!

The reader will understand from all this that what I am saying essentially is that when the mother is calm the baby is calm, and that when she is stressed, the baby will be too - to the point of reacting with his guts. Or, to put it more clinically, through his perioesophageal nervous plexus affecting the physiological dynamic of his antireflux system.

As soon as I was able to formulate my personal deductions, I began more than ever to couple the use of drug treatments with the work of listening to parents, the results of which were always convincing. In this regard, let me say in passing, I was following no other than my normal practice. For, regardless of the nature of the children's problems about which I have been consulted, it has always been my practice to work with the parents and with them alone. Sometimes indeed, where the parents concerned have been easy to mobilize, it has proved possible to dispense altogether with drug treatments for reflux and yet still arrive at a cure for the problem within a normal period.

At this point someone may ask: Supposing all of what you have said is true, what possible connection can it have to Al-Qaida? In a direct sense, of course, there is none. But in view of all that I have described, it cannot be denied that for some decades now the structure of interpersonal relations has been deeply affected by individualistic ideology, and that this has produced permanent disruption in the relationships between individuals within families. In the absence of any kind of societal support, the families of old have been encouraged to oust the father more and more radically from his function and, in direct furtherance of the impertinent success of the consumerist option, they have put the mother in charge, even though that very development may cause her to feel alone and responsible, even culpable, for all that happens. Thus the whole of our social environment, along with the exchanges that lie within it, has been modified by the profound upset in the hierarchy of values, positions, and respective prerogatives of the two parents. The ever-extending outreach of our networks of communication (satellites and internet included) within an ever-shrinking globe has encouraged our western societies, simply through the attempt by their businesses to grab a bit more market share, to export the new model that they have created. And since that model is so attractive - how could it not be, when it advocates the primacy of the pleasure that everyone dreams of? - it has had mass appeal and entailed mass adhesion to the values it advocates. But there are individuals in the Arab-Muslim worlds for whom this is deeply shocking. How could they assent to options liable to cast doubt upon their status as *abu*, as the fathers and owners of their children, and countenance being despoiled of it?[32] Given their attachment to the sharply distinguished, time-honoured hierarchy between parents and sexes, they have undoubtedly received that subtly persuasive export as an attempt at conversion, something all the more unacceptable inasmuch as it could be viewed as motivated by base motives of mercantilism and capitalism. As the only form of proselytism acceptable to them was their own Islamic religious version, and as what the west was advocating seemed to violate its values, they successfully organized themselves, fed their resentment, co-ordinated their forces, and recruited enough fanatical candidates for suicide to undertake the new form of warfare they have initiated.

In the end what we are seeing here is one more confrontation, with resort to new ways and means, among the descendents of *Homo* between the upholders of the primacy of space, the sedentary, and those who obstinately adhere to the primacy of time, the nomads. It is difficult nowadays to conceive or accept that this is the nature of the situation, because we are blinded by the achievements of technical progress and imagine that we have left behind that type of debate. It is, however, a debate that becomes particularly fraught when it arises not between different cultures but within a single society whose choices it insistently challenges.

---

[32] A remarkable, almost prophetic illustration of this debate is to be found in Yilmaz Güney's splendid Turkish film *Sürü* (*The Flock*, 1978).

Fathers and Mothers

THE JAPANESE CONUNDRUM

I was invited one day to give a series of lectures in Japan on the changes in parental status in France over the course of the last fifty years. I gathered together plenty of documentation and carefully prepared what I wanted to say. I intended to demonstrate that although paediatricians had managed over fifty years to banish most of the scourges that had threatened childhood, they had failed to help children to blossom to the extent that their enhanced physical good health might have been expected to encourage. For, over the past twenty years, we have witnessed any number of new and worrying problems ranging from sleep difficulties to problems of emotional development, including delays in language acquisition and other behavioural difficulties. For my Japanese audience I prepared a case intended to show, with statistics and clinical histories in support, how all these problems were directly linked to the considerable change in relationships within the family and, in particular, the ousting of the father, who had now lost his societal support and was being surreptitiously solicited by his surroundings to become a second mother for his children. I wanted, in particular, to illustrate this theme by commenting upon the exponential rise in one-parent families, the vast majority of which, as is well known, are lone mothers with children.

At my first lecture in Tokyo, I was astounded to hear the child psychiatrist entrusted with the task of introducing me take the opportunity, before I could open my mouth, to praise the intelligence and appropriateness of developments in western societies, particularly France, as compared with Japan, where the numbers of one-parent families were deplorably low! To support his argument and add volume to his cry of alarm he produced a demographic projection to the effect that, unless something happened soon to change the situation, the present Japanese population of 138 million would fall to a mere 58 million by 2100. It was no consolation to him that such a shortfall might be made up, as indeed has already started to happen, by people from the Philippines, Korea, and other countries in the region; what he loudly demanded was a reform of what he constantly referred to as Japanese 'civil status'. Hearing this enigmatic term in my earphones and wondering whether it might be a semantic approximation of some sort, if not an outright error in translation, I called for a precise explanation of its meaning. I learned that every Japanese child at birth received a document giving his or her filiation over several generations, and that single women giving birth exposed their children to a bastard status that would damage the children throughout life.

It is at least conceivable that our western democracies may have long been influenced by an analysis similar to that given by my Japanese co-professional. It may be that the measures that they took in this area were simply geared towards plugging the demographic deficit into which they saw themselves plunging. These are all things that may have happened without our realizing it, either because the facts are beyond recall or because the motives were never made explicit. It is, after all, not so very long ago that among western European nations, unmarried mothers and illegitimate children were mercilessly stigmatized, a fact whose very disappearance supplies us with information about the date and grounds for the end of the containment that the social environment had hitherto placed around couples over a very long period, the institution of marriage being the most current example. A possible inference is that the obsession with demography was associated with an objective to preserve from disintegration a national identity supposedly embodying a particular vision of the world that was so strongly held that it was acceptable to sacrifice all to it. The sacrifice included what had hitherto conspired to create the relative balance between the two partners in the human couple, a balance that had been dearly bought during the course of the species's evolution. A fairly recent illustration of this development is the last revision made in France to matrimonial law in 1972. After numerous revisions to its various provisions, the only formal advantage left to a father to balance, symbolically at least, the advantages that the journey through pregnancy naturally conferred on the mother, was the right he still had to determine the family's place of residence. The abolition of that right, when it took place, was not moved by electoral considerations in order to solicit female votes or by recognition of the consequences of female accession to the workplace. It took place simply because the government of the day had passed a measure intended to reduce unemployment by giving Algerian workers allowances to return home; the problem was that, as things stood, they risked taking their children back with them. In order therefore to keep slightly fewer than six thousand children in France - of whom only a portion wanted to stay - the Code was reformed in such a way as to accept the pleas of mothers who did not want to follow their spouses. The powers that be thought they could disguise the grossness of their mistake they had made by trumpeting it as a definitive form of equality of democracy within the couple. Cheap and ineffectual words: the democracy they described could not, strictly speaking, be made to function, since, where there is dissension between two, no majority is realizable. We see, then, how it is possible for regrettable situations to arise, which everybody has to cope with as best they can, no amendment to them is considered, and those responsible for the mess are never seen again or bothered further.

Now if we cast a rapid eye over the globe to see where containment of the couple either persists or else has disappeared, we see that it closely correlates with two linked factors, namely, demography on the one hand and consumerist logic on the other. As I have said previously, consumerist logic is essentially maternalizing and geared to the immediate satisfaction of need: it could be said that it is more concerned with quality than quantity, and with the present moment, the here and now - i.e., that concentration on the immediate and ephemeral that I earlier styled the 'mother effect' - rather than the long term, which has always been at the core of worries about the perpetuation of the species, a concern that in Japan seems linked to preoccupations of a nationalistic order. It is becoming taken for granted in France, and common parlance virtually across the country, that it is better to have a few children for whom one can do a great deal rather than a lot of children for whom one cannot do enough. In poor countries, or those that have barely embarked upon development, the demography continues to gallop. By contrast, in rich countries, material wealth and the promotion of a consumerist logic have always effected a demographic slump. When countries get richer, their demography sooner or later ends up regressing, which leads to measures that previously would have seemed improper if not impossible. What seems to happen in this field is that greater consumption possibly brings the maternalizing dimension strongly to the fore, and ends up imposing it as the most intelligent and best adapted to the aspirations of everyone. Yet at the same time there is plenty of awareness of the ravages produced by unbridled consumption and unrestrained capitalism, both of them destructive in absolute terms and requiring, it would seem, some sort of regulatory element. On the other hand, there is no mystery about the lengthy dormancy that has affected countries whose ways of life have come down from the age-old nomadic options that favoured the recognition of time to the detriment of space, which was entirely rejected. It is perfectly obvious that the only possible resolution lies in compromise - just as the merit of the opposition to globalization will surely lie in any effect it may have in favour of regulating the latter. Curiously, what we might see, then, is a return to the classic model of the family, that which places in opposition the dynamics of two forms of self-centredness for the benefit of the child. The changes occurring in our western societies would therefore have the merit of giving birth not to new relationships but to new conditions for those relationships or a new style of them. The current unease in Japan witnesses to how sensitive questioning of this sort continues to be there.

What is remarkable in the case of Japan is that although it was fixed in a centuries-old model of civilization, it chose in the mid nineteenth century actively to import the western lifestyle. The logic of consumption, which has won over all social classes in Japan, today finds itself in conflict with the weight of a tradition which stubbornly refuses to give up its essentially paternal ancestral options, especially the tight containment that is put around the couple. Detailed analysis of the reasons behind this resistance reveals in the foreground the difficulty of reconciling western lifestyles with the national myth that views the emperor as the successor to the Sun god and as the mother and father of each of his subjects. What is striking about the recent changes of this society, whose demography is in sharp decline - though it displays the effects of an extraordinarily active superego, in the form of its respect for gender differences, its politeness, discipline, cleanliness, honesty, and sense of the Other - is that here again it is women who are at the forefront of the anti-establishment movement. When questioned about what drives them, some of them, the most audacious, observe that they cannot and will not any longer obey an essentially male tradition that would force them, particularly if married to an eldest or only son, to become his ageing parents' carer. It is a moot point how valid such an alleged pretext may be, since it is a scenario that, statistically speaking, is bound to affect only a proportion of them. It would seem that, at their current stage, these women are still unaware of the extent to which they have been influenced by the maternal values which are promoted and emphasized by the consumerist society all around them. But what we probably have here is a model crisis, illustrating a novel phase in the eternal combat that the sexes have always had with each other, whether or not they are united by forms of containment determined by convention for them - and perhaps in spite of them.

BACK TO THE PAST MODEL OF EXCHANGES

In the light of what was said in the last chapter about the solid mother and the nebulous father, we are duty bound to acknowledge that practically no couple, if their relationship is to survive, can manage without a minimum of containment. Otherwise it is difficult to see how such a relationship could go on being lived indefinitely when it is based on two forms of logic that are not simply heterogeneous but virtually impossible to coalesce. It is, moreover, all the less likely, if there is an expectation that the experience will provide joy and happiness, inasmuch as it is impossible to see how either joy or happiness could spring from an everyday environment polluted by the enduring confrontation of those two disparate logics. Hence we are compelled seriously to ask whether life as a couple confers any benefit, and if so, what it is.

We know that among our contemporaries, a good proportion of them at least have, for some decades already, answered in the negative. What they in effect have come to practise are forms of polygamy and polyandry - which often amount to the creation of a convenient, practical, and precarious sexual service - with partners spaced out over time, which keeps up the pretence that they have not succumbed to the aberrations of those cultures which are bold enough to practise at least polygamy on a simultaneous basis. But we have to ask whether this is a reasonable and well-founded response on the part of some of our contemporaries. Or is it circumstantial, an indirect effect produced by the logic of consumption? After all, in an era of contraception and condoms, with easy, demystified sexuality, what point is there in lumbering oneself with a single, omnipresent partner and forming a permanent couple with that person? I hope that no one will appeal to love and denounce the question as impertinent. For then we should have to embark on a quite different discussion on the nature of that love and explain, in particular, why it arrives one day, and yet so often runs out of energy before no less often disappearing altogether. We might do better to return to the original question, but phrase it differently: If life in a couple is not to be reduced to a convenient and essentially precarious sexual service, what benefit can it bring to those who risk living in a couple subject to a minimum of containment?

My view, which is both personal and founded on my practice, is that the experience of living in a couple translates into a form of ontological progress, from which each of the partners, knowingly or unknowingly, whether they like it or not, draws an undoubted benefit. In order to determine that this is true, it is enough to listen to the stories that everyone is keen to tell either on their own or in their spouse's presence. It will be evident that such an adventure is always told within a perspective of progress, insofar as each of the partners occupies within it, regardless of what they do or desire, a position that encourages true unconscious transference, with all the benefits that can accrue from the underground and insidious yet always positive working of such transference. It is as if each of them, through having the facility of projecting onto the partner the hitherto unresolved part of the problems that have never ceased to assail him or her, is setting about solving them. The process could be seen as a sort of blind man's buff, with the two partners developing in a common space with blindfolds over their eyes. Every time they meet each other, they do not immediately recognize that it is their partner, but the time spent in achieving recognition allows them to identify on each other a whole range of elements that they had forgotten and to which they can no longer attribute a precise status so as to recognize these elements and possibly free themselves from being obsessed by them. This is, incidentally, precisely what happens, though in one direction only, with the transference that operates on the psychoanalyst in the therapeutic space: the procedure enables the analysand to project on this being, behind him, the affects developed during his existence in regard to the numerous individuals with whom he has had a problematic relationship. If the space allotted to the possible encounter of the partners has no boundary, if it lacks a framework and it is understood between them that contacts will be ephemeral and skin-deep, they are unlikely to have a true encounter and gain from meeting each other. If, on the other hand, the space within which they move is bounded by a framework that affords a minimum of containment and no prior understanding has been put between them, then they will necessarily come into conflict - often violent conflict - on more than one occasion, but they will not fail to take away from these contacts a mass of information not just about the other person but about themselves too. Insofar as the process is interactive, each partner, whether willing or unwilling, aware or unaware, agreeing or disagreeing, consenting or not to pay the price for it, *always* derives substantial benefit from it.

But who is there who will willingly acknowledge the existence of a dynamic of this sort, when no one is ready to agree that the most basic choice that people make in their entire existence, namely their choice of lover, is never a matter of chance, but always an unsuspected and rigorous effect of a form of determinism to which they could in no way have access? At a time when the democratic options of western societies have lapsed into demagoguery and when all opinions are reckoned to be of equal worth, irrespective of their nature or field - far be it that ignorance, however crass, should ever be stopped from expressing itself! - how are people to be persuaded that the knowledge they think they have of themselves is as pretentious as that of any adolescent and is absolutely nothing compared to the unknown that drives them and leaves them not the least margin for manoeuvre? For, if there is one area in which it is impossible to see clearly and where everything happens in the way just described, it is in the adventure of love and in what it produces.

Why is this so? The plain and simple reason is that it concerns the touchstone of the experience of life, which started precisely in such a vein via the early exchanges that everyone has had with their own mother. It could be said, perhaps, that we all know that we came into the world through being born of her and that we are all, through our unremitting exploration of the bonds woven with her, engaged our whole life long in achieving our distance from her in order to be sure that we have finally been born - an achievement that often turns out to coincide with the end of existence itself.

However subtle and complex such expressions as these may seem, nothing can be learned, taught, or established on the basis of them without matching proofs. But do such proofs exist? Indeed they do. To discover them, we need to return to the logic that subjects every individual to the effects of his earliest bonds; these, even before they have become milestones, are the basis of his history.

I have, for example, always disconcerted those members of the public whom I have met, as also those among my patients whom I have urged to consider the matter, when I have proposed, as suggested in these last few lines, that everyone, be they man or woman, marries their mother - always and only their mother. This happens for a reason, and the choice thus made always sooner or later turns out to be the most useful and fruitful that could be made.

It may be wondered why I have thought it important to state these two propositions in this way and why they have always seemed to me to be necessarily linked, even if they can be treated only in succession. It is that people marry their mothers because they have absolutely no other option. This is due to the fact that it is upon her and her alone that they construct the primary matrix of what they will one day, sooner or later, call love. Upon this matrix all their subsequent loving encounters will be traced until one of them appears closely fitted enough to it to be finally invested in and to merit becoming longterm. This is an effect neither of chance nor of conscious, enlightened choice. It is the imposed, direct effect of what spending nine months in the womb concretely and definitively establishes in the brains of boys and girls alike.

WHAT THE VERY EARLIEST STAGE OF LIFE TEACHES US

The fetology and neonatal psychophysiology of the last three decades have not merely supported psychoanalytic theory, they have at last given it a concrete and irrefutable scientific basis. The fact that biology and theorizing about the role of the unconscious have for once apparently led to similar conclusions would be a cause for rejoicing, if as I have already mentioned with regret they had not been invaded by a societal discourse that is both well-resourced and driven by an agenda that is not always reputable.

It was always thought and propounded that the experience of pregnancy was universally neutral and devoid of consequences for its issue. Until the early 1970s, the newborn child was likened to a simple digestive tube, which responded to the single definition given to it by nineteenth-century obstetrics, namely, that it was 'the necessary and inevitable product of the workroom'. Now, in fewer than thirty years, the newborn has come to be seen as equipped with such varied and astonishing potential that a new fertile scientific field has opened up devoted to its study. In consequence many of our fellows have fallen into a daft new religion intended to make believe that newborns are endowed with such genius that they can be relied upon to discover by themselves the best way for them to develop. On the other hand, some new certainties have emerged from this exploration, and these have the potential to sustain some healthy, ideology-free reflection on the subject. Thus it is finally accepted that, far from being the dark, abyssal, silent, scary desert that was formerly believed, the uterus is a rich, complex, and stimulating environment in which the fetus very quickly becomes a formidable collector of sensations.

During their construction the sensory areas of the fetal brain (the tactile, auditory, visual, olfactory, and gustatory) are continually collecting and storing a large number of afferences, which could be likened to pieces of information stored in the database of a computer. The peculiarity of these afferences is that they come almost entirely from the maternal body. By the seventh or eighth week of pregnancy, the fetus is already equipped with fairly elaborate sensitivity to touch, temperature and depth - the last is what enables the fetus to have a sense of its spatial position. By the tenth week it can distinguish the four primary tastes: sweet, bitter, savoury, sour. By the twelfth week it has efficient hearing. By the twentieth week, through an organ that is present by the eighth week yet disappears at birth, the vomeronasal organ, it is able to distinguish by their odour all the substances dissolved for varying lengths of time in the amniotic fluid. The sensory areas of the brain do not limit their activity to the collection of sensations supplied by the sensory organs, but also constantly exchange information among themselves. This includes the visual area, even if the uterine penumbra means that it has not received much stimulation itself. Thus is prepared the sensory integration that will be perfected by the sight when the child is born. All this explains why a newborn can recognize from its earliest hours in the world the smell of its mother and distinguish her voice amid other female voices.[33] Experiments have shown that a newborn will exert itself to listen to the maternal voice from among loudspeakers placed round its ears; just as it can, simply after being held in her arms, recognize her photograph within barely eight hours.

This transnatal link therefore provides every individual with a form of 'nurture' that is strictly maternal in origin and which I have called elsewhere an 'elementary sensory alphabet'. It marks the child indelibly and, like the most precisely calibrated instrument, will continue to refract throughout life the individual's subsequent sensory collecting, and thereby contribute to his or her constructive vision of the world. The same transnatal bond explains the ease and identifiability with which the relationship of the child to the mother is established at birth and during the days that follow. If this link did not exist, it would be impossible to understand, for example, how a small child, left for twelve hours a day at a day-nursery or with a childminder and spending only an hour or two a day with its mother should continue to recognize her and value her as such. It is also easy to see how this initial bond could be reinforced over time, after birth, through the accumulated pleasure arising from the immediate satisfaction of elementary needs.

This form of primary nurture will provide the very young child with so strong a base of security as to cause the mother to be seen by the child as the unique and inexhaustible source of life. It is this conviction, attributable to the secure base, that will mould the child's first love, the love that will be, as I said earlier, the matrix for all subsequent loves. Far from being passive, vague, or neutral in this exchange, the mother will strive, as I have tried to show at length, to favour the bond, service it continuously, and strengthen it still further. The result is a sort of equation which, translating the young

---

[33] The maternal voice, speaking at a level of 60 decibels, is perceived by the fetus at 24 decibels, while other ambient voices, male and female, are perceived at only 8 to 12 decibels. The part of the maternal voice that especially enables recognition is the bass notes, since these carry the melody; thus a baby does not recognize his or her mother's voice when she reads a sentence backwards.

child's conviction, probably establishes itself in his or her head and could be expressed thus: 'Mummy = my life'.

Such a perfect source of mutual satisfaction would theoretically have no reason to run out or change direction, were it not for the interference of everyday events on the one hand and the baby's neuromotor development on the other. One or more ordinary and practically inevitable things are likely to happen by the second half-year of life, leading to a tragedy whose aftermath will show just how salutary it is that it has happened. Something frightful, horrible, unacceptable will have happened for the first time a few days or weeks before: 'Mummy's gone!' Suddenly she was not there any more - and it does not, of course, greatly signify why she was absent; it could have been any sort of impediment. At all events, she did not respond to the expectation that the child had of her! She became all at once indispensable and unavailable; she did not immediately respond to a need or a demand for care and attention. The satisfaction of need was deferred. Insofar as the child's neuromotor development will to a degree have made the need seem at once rarer and more urgent, the time - the chronological time - that has slipped in between the arising of the need and its satisfaction will suddenly be perceived, even if it has been only darkly identified. However harmless this might seem on a factual level, it will nonetheless subvert the rest of the story. The repetition of incidents like this will cause the baby to begin to sense internally his or her status as a subject cut off from his mother, separate from her, capable of suspecting the one-directional logic of the passage of time - a logic whose outline can in practice be easily reconstructed against the backdrop of repeating sequences of similarly marking events. Such a shaky new outline of the notion of the 'moment in time' begins to dawn in the child through these early experiences, in which it is experienced as a 'now' that is necessarily anxiety-provoking because it comes after what seemed a 'past century' of waiting and opens the way to a 'future' of expectation. This 'future' has nonetheless been shorn of its promise of serenity, since the 'future' that the child used to experience, the 'future in the past' so to speak, has notwithstanding produced the recent 'past' that he or she would never willingly have experienced. The process seems to be, then, that the perception of the passage of time relies in the very first instance upon a memory, however imprecise, before attempting an anticipation that is scarcely less blurred.

The feelings of distress that thus recurrently invade the very young child will eventually cause him to perceive the precariousness of his existence and to attribute to his mother not simply the capacity to maintain his life but also the power to suspend its course at will. The source of life that she had been till then is now revealed to him as a potential dispenser of death. A second form of equation now comes into play, of the type: 'Mummy - my life - my death'. The simple power that was previously attributed to the mother is thus transmuted into a formidable omnipotence, and this renders her sufficiently frightening as to modify the peaceful love of which she had earlier been the object.

It is perhaps not forcing the issue to say of these two stages that the first, the phase of the satisfaction of need without any passage of time intervening belongs to the purely animal level - the level pertaining to survival pure and simple - while the second marks the child's access to his or her human status, since the intuition of time and that of the fear of death are as intimately linked to this instance of it as they were in the case of the species at the time of the first burial. As far as very young children are concerned, they will grasp the slightest opportunity to verify the validity of their conclusions. It is the age when children try to restrain the omnipotence conferred on their mothers by the exercise of their own omnipotence - which can be identified as lying at the root of the capricious behaviour of this stage, which is known as the oppositional phase. The contest, which is energy-consuming and tiring for both partners, should sound the death-knell of the hitherto ambitious project confined to the child's private animal logic. The mother, who will have been seen till then as highly life-giving should now also be perceived by the child as possessing a sure power of death. I have said 'should' in the last two sentences because this entirely natural process is unfortunately often nowadays compromised by the exaggerated concern of the majority of mothers, indeed of parents, who will not go anywhere without their walkie-talkies and go rushing to their little one at the least sound they hear.

The sudden changed perception that the child has of the mother is not an easy experience to go through for either baby or mother. The mother, who continues to be concerned that their exchanges ought to be happy, will sometimes find herself complaining as much about the child's whims as about the relative indifference he or she may show towards her, sometimes culpabilizing her for having the nerve to seem to give the father greater priority. This goes to show what an extraordinary metaphysician the very young child is and the emotional expertise he sets about acquiring as soon as he begins to take in the upheaval that has occurred in the organization of his exchanges. What he is looking for is some sort of harmony that might regulate these exchanges and enable him to recover more or less the serenity that he remembers, that which obtained during the first phase of his existence. In order to achieve this, he will set about conferring on the people around him perfectly differentiated roles.

The man whom the mother seems to value so much, whom she points out to the child as father, the child will regard as responsible for the failure of the total availability that she is supposed to have for him and the distraction that has interrupted the satisfaction of his needs. The child will, moreover, regard the father as responsible for the perception that he, the child, has received of time and of the fear of death which has arisen in him. In consequence, the child will pledge a powerful and yet inexpressible hatred toward the father, which will extend even to wishing on occasions that the father might disappear from his as yet short life.[34] This represents an advantage for the child, because it allows him to go on experiencing his mother as the main source of life - while more or less experiencing his father as the dispenser of death. With life and death devolving on separate characters in the child's life, the fear and disarray caused by the duality of the maternal omnipotence no longer exist, and the future seems to open upon a more clearly conflictualized situation. There is no need to go any further in this analysis and consider everyone's Oedipal adventure in a different light, even supposing that some allowance might be made for its usual sexual colouring. We have all been there. We have all gone forward into life walking backward, our eyes fixed on our place of origin, refusing to do as our father would have us do, namely, turn our back on it or at least look forward over our shoulder, such is our revulsion at what might beckon in the form of our destiny as mortals.

[34] It is this unconscious pledge that explains why the death of a father is the most painful event - namely, because it is shot through with inexpressible guilt - that individuals of both sexes can experience.

THE BASIC TRIO: FATHER, MOTHER, CHILD

We are now at the point where it becomes essentially possible to identify the contribution made by the father, the functional father so often mentioned hitherto. We shall see how important he can be in the subsequent life of the child.

It will help our understanding if we cast our minds back to the outline I gave in the last chapter of the correct way to model the triangularity of the basic trio. To the extent that the urgent sexual desire of the father-man leads him to appropriate his partner in order to unite sexually with her, she will be drawn towards her exclusively female side, thereby impairing her natural disposition to be totally available to her child and becoming thereby less of an 'omnipotent mother'. If the mother derives some satisfaction from the experience and appears to show some attachment to him who is responsible for it, then he - the father - will appear to the child, from the precocious phase of his development which is termed archaic because it precedes the birth of speech, as the individual whose mere existence makes the mother seem much less omnipotent than he had spontaneously been led to believe. It will be the father, too, who, by driving the child's development of speech, will put him under orders to assume his destiny and construct his life.[35] These developments make the father, who is integrated for ever from a very young age, at once a death-bringer, an artisan, and an authentic promoter of life.

Such a definition should in no way be viewed as prejudicial either to the bonds that fathers weave with their children or to their consistency. That a baby, or an older child, should be able, without realizing it, to confer such characteristics upon his or her father - being able to pledge hatred against him, as we have seen, and even willing his disappearance from the scene - in no way means that the baby or child cannot have a strong, loving, and valued relationship with him, any more than the father is prevented from valuing, cherishing, and enabling the child to have purpose to his life. All

---

[35] Speech enables the child to create its own distance from the mother. When a mother and child remain 'too close' to each other, a form of language is created between them which is termed 'sympraxic', comprehensible only to the child and the mother and prejudicial to the child's access to articulated words.

that I have been describing unfolds only in the unconscious, and it does not automatically rise to consciousness. To compare the unconscious with the conscious is like comparing a photographic negative with a positive image. Though the former makes it possible to obtain the latter, it does not typify it, and in general gives only a rather indistinct idea of what is represented.

What this description shows - and I want to insist on it again, even though I touched on it in the last chapter - is the pivotal role that is played by the mother in such a process. In order for the child to be able to perceive her as much diminished in omnipotence vis-à-vis the father, the mother needs to be somewhat 'taken over' by the father. She needs to have somewhat internalized his importance. This was something that she would herself be committed to and would not think to oppose in those societies that ascribed a preponderant position to the father and upheld his status. It was also something that she managed at least to pay service to in societies that ascribed to the father an implicit position through a form of containment around the couple to which she belonged. Equally, it is something that she is still able to experience, and even experience intensely, when she feels a sufficiently strong love for the father to derive strong sexual satisfaction from him. This clearly encapsulates the situation. For it does not consist in an exchange of procedures in which she grants her partner the use of her body in return for the possibility to devote herself without limit to the over-satisfaction of her child. She needs to value the relationship with her man as much, if not more, than the one she has with her child. That is why I speak of 'strong sexual satisfaction' and why I have always stressed the importance of an early re-establishment of sexual relations after giving birth, so that the sexuality is not given the opportunity to 'slumber' and be thereby disinvested in. In all cases, the ongoing 'take-over' of the mother - or her commitment to the father, if the word 'take-over' shocks some - is highly beneficial. The father is thereby able to move within his unique dimension as his woman's man, of his mother-woman's man, to remain desirably 'nebulous', and not be swallowed up either in claims of solidity that are harmful to everyone or in a vain and stupid competition for maternal status.

Where the partners have space in which to bury their dissensions within a valued and well-maintained sexual relationship, they will have the possibility to explore and liquidate their own links to their respective mothers in spite of any accidental frictions entailed. This lengthy, interactive work will sooner or later help them both to move forward and closer together. Such a possibility, however, appears to be much more fragile where the union is more precarious and does not benefit from any environmental support. For, though it may survive the first episode of friction, it will not be long before the bond begins to slacken. The partners think that they are simply living what they experience and in the way they experience it. Unaware of what, despite their best efforts, is parasitizing their relationship from a past they imagine they have liquidated, they take the full impact of every confrontation full on. It does not take them long to lose trust in the feelings that brought them together, and loosen their links, if not dissolve them, on the grounds that they made a mistake. 'He/she wasn't like that before,' they will often say, as if to explain the turn-around, whereas, if the truth were told, not only was he/she indeed 'like that', it was precisely because he/she was 'like that' that they chose each other, i.e., for all the elements that the couple might have worked through, transcended, and turned into pluses, if only these elements had not seemed so threatening by virtue of all the frightening baggage they carted in from another story. The trap then closes, and the couple start to go downhill. Often they recoil from seeking help from the underused yet effective professional resources available, just as they may refuse to understand that crises can be weathered and result in good effects. They react with a fury that is proportionate to their investment. When the couple breaks up, the children most often stay with their mother, which means that they return to the obsessive orbit of her omnipotence. Fathers meanwhile, though upheld of late by the courts, lose a good deal, if not the essential part of their function, with consequences that everyone is only too aware of. Society might just muddle through, and might even make a virtue of doing so, were there not ample proof that generational succession is no repairer, but a radicalizer and reinforcer of the prevailing set-up. Hence the children of divorcees often divorce, and almost identical patterns of behaviour, including some of the worst, recur from generation to generation. It is true, even if largely unrecognized, that when things go well, they continue to improve from generation to generation. That particular message - as I hinted earlier in this book - is returning to us in France from the United States, which, in spite of the anti-American atmosphere over here, continues to be a serious point of reference. Never mind the marketing practised by certain lawyers who, to keep a hold on their client base, promise to handle third divorces on a no-fee basis, any number of studies have become available to the effect that it is a much better outcome for children if parents, even those who do not get on, stay together rather than separate. It is almost as if the children now constituted the containment around their parents that the social environment has given up on. However strange a set-up this may seem, it is worth pointing out that it might not be ineffective. For it is very common to hear elderly couples recount their former quarrels and say that in the end, through continuing to respect each other - the value that needs most importantly to be adhered to whatever the circumstances - they were able to find each other again, when they never expected to, and had the pleasure of seeing their own children grow up and steer them towards a united grand-parenthood.

Perhaps, just like the women in today's Japanese society who are seduced by the wave of consumerism, we are currently experiencing the consequences of our own haste to obtain everything straight away? Perhaps we have forgotten the long drawn-out and problematic adventure of the ancestors of our species, and have yielded to the impatience which Kafka considered was the original sin? At all events, given the pivotal role that mothers have in the totality of exchanges within the family, we have to conclude that the way in which a mother treats the father of her children will influence the way in which her daughter will treat the father of her children. Moreover, it will similarly guide the way in which her son will one day induce the mother of his future children to treat him.

BACK TO THE FATHER

The definition I have just given of the functional father should help towards better understanding of the negligible role that the father-genitor has compared to that of the social father. It also helps to demonstrate how and to what extent stepfathers - who sadly have generally no status in French law - are sometimes able to provide their partners' children with a complement of fatherhood that the children otherwise would lack owing to the dissension of the couple that gave them birth. The following clinical case is particularly instructive in this regard.

On Which Side The Delinquency?

I had for some years had as a patient the last child of a psychoanalyst mother who already had twin boys from a previous union. One day she spoke to me about them. They were now fifteen, in the third grade in the French educational system, and she was worried because their school results had plummeted and they had been identified as dealers in hashish. She had opened up to her analyst supervisor, who had advised her to see a colleague, but the boys didn't want to know: 'We're sick of psychoanalysis - we get enough of it at home!' She suggested she might bring them to see me on the pretext of their needing vaccination booster injections. As a matter of fact, they really did need to be seen for this, and in view of how matters had presented themselves, I agreed to see them for the vaccinations, but would not promise that I could do anything further. I had no idea how fascinating they would prove to be. They must have realized this, because they rated me just as much as I did them. The vaccination session proved decisive in that respect, and the adolescents agreed to participate in the programme of informal exchanges with their mother present that we immediately set up. These were due to take place every fourteen days. The experience was all the more gratifying to me inasmuch as there was real pleasure to be had in watching these two identical twins, who were difficult to tell apart, bat the ball back and forth between each other, taking advantage of their incomparable complicity and of the unusual reliability of their communication. They rejoiced in thwarting my strategy, which I deliberately made ever grosser and more identifiable. In the end they really liked me and showed how much they enjoyed our meetings, even though they denied both the delinquency that their mother alleged and their supposed poor academic performance. It was always their mother who opened our sessions, with a complaint whose possible foundation and relevance we would proceed to analyze. One day, about three months after the start of our work together, a warning from the school's disciplinary committee dropped on the mat. The twins' mother, anxious to show how seriously she took her responsibilities, told me that she had immediately informed the twins' father of the gravity of the situation. I then listened as one of the twins, whom I had already identified as the bolder of the two, retorted to his mother that he and his brother had been trying to tell her for a long time that they didn't care a straw about their father's opinion or reactions. And he added: 'D'you really think we're worried about what Dad might say? We like seeing him, and he likes seeing us! We have fun times with him - we have a good laugh together. He's not like you. He doesn't take us to the local pizzeria. He knows loads of brilliant restaurants and he's teaching us how to appreciate fine wines. We have a right skinful! OK, he might speak the lines you give him. But like us, he knows how far he can go. What you don't get, Huguette' - they always called their mother by her first name, which sometimes lent a curiously protective tone to what they said - 'is that we don't give two hoots for what Dad might say. What we worry about is what Gabriel might say!' (Gabriel was the mother's new partner.) At that, I witnessed their mother leap up and shout at them in a way I never imagined she could. She kept stating over and over again: 'Your father's your father. Gabriel's not your father!' Then sobs came and stopped her getting her words out, before she completely broke down. At this point the second twin, who had not yet opened his mouth, softly repeated almost word for word what his twin had said. I intervened in turn to ask her to listen to what had been said. At this she attacked me, and I had to raise my own voice to point out that she was flagrantly disregarding the solution to the problem that she had originally come to me with. This led to some long minutes of violent and tempestuous debate, the upshot of which I was unable to predict. Eventually, she calmed down. She agreed to my suggestion to report back to Gabriel what had happened in the session and let me know what response he intended to make to his stepsons' request. As it happened, all four of them came to the next session. Gabriel established conditions for his entry into the twins' lives, which they actually had no problem about accepting. After this the problems disappeared quite quickly. The boys became brilliant. Their studies went extremely well, and in time I had the pleasure of seeing them bring their own children to me. I never sought to probe what had moved their mother to turn such a deaf ear to her twins' demands. Had there been some sort of semantic confusion over the role devolving upon the genitor of her children, even though she was better placed than anyone to watch for that? Or was it rather that by excluding Gabriel, she had sought to keep sole control of a situation that the twins did not reckon her up to. Had they become 'delinquent' in order to draw attention to behaviour on the part of their mother that itself wasn't far off 'delinquent'?

What we have just seen shows that our fellow humans are less crazy than might be feared. There can in fact be fatherhood even in the total absence of a father: the paternal function can be fragmented and exercised simultaneously or at different times by a number of different agencies or persons. For the paternal function and its effectiveness consists in anything and everything that is perceived by the child as placing a boundary upon the power that he or she would spontaneously attribute to their mother. Hence I have often witnessed the excellent effect upon the children in stepfamilies where the father and the mother's new partner, transcending narcissistic sensitivities, can come to an agreement about their upbringing.

In this connection it is worth taking another look at kinship systems, because these can show how different societies across the world have striven to find rules for governance of these differing parental powers. A couple of examples will suffice. The 'Hawaiian' system, in order to preserve children from interparental confrontation, has them call 'mother' all the women of the lineages of their genetrix and genitor, and 'father' all the men of these same lineages. The 'Iroquois' system, meanwhile, invites them to call 'mother' all the women of their genetrix's lineage and 'father' all the men of their genitor's lineage. The aim, in sum, is always to help children to obtain the sort of harmony that they themselves strive to find, namely an identifiable balance between the two parental authorities, so that they are provided with a mother who dispenses enough well-being and a father who is sufficiently present to temper the natural maternal drive and enable the mother to be what she should always be, namely a mother whose stature has been so perfectly formulated by Winnicott as a 'good enough mother'.

Finding this balance is a challenge for every generation. Leaving aside the sort of mistakes that can arise through the use of silly slogans, each parent is inhabited by the logic of his own history. Neither therefore can ever spontaneously occupy the place that his or her spouse and child are looking for. It is here that the unconscious, which no one can seriously pretend to either escape or access, makes its presence felt. Inasmuch as the way in which the unconscious transmits its conclusions dates back many generations, the harmony sought is essentially problematic; it always looks like a more or less serious disharmony, which the child necessarily suffers and with which he will in turn spend his life trying to deal. Having spent a greater or lesser time rubbing up against other humans, in whose company he will have confronted the conclusions that the history he inherited at birth gave him, he will one day embark upon a union at whose heart he will expect his spouse, loved as was his mother, to afford him equally what he has had and what he has lacked. The experience will be one of unremitting progress through an inexhaustible series of necessarily painful reckonings. Eventually, after more or less time has passed, they will decide to procreate in their turn. They will therefore have a child concerning whom they will find themselves in the position of their own parents, drawn necessarily either to imitate them in every way or to do the complete opposite of what they experienced as children with them.

While not the express aim of this analysis, it nevertheless points us towards a vigorous denunciation of what is written more or less everywhere about the role and prerogatives of the father. He is regarded as the custodian of the Law - of the Species, needless to say: commentators generally know enough to realize that! - as well as the upholder of severity and authority, the censor, the punisher, and so on. He is told about all the situations in which he must intervene, as also sometimes about how he is to intervene. Where does all that come from, if not from what is intimated on psychiatrists' couches or may be gleaned in this or that professional writing - the belief that it is possible to mobilize and paste into reality without any comebacks elements that rise from the unconscious and yet which bear absolutely no relation to reality? The result of that kind of error - which is probably much less innocent than one might be inclined to think - does not take long to show itself, since what happens through seeking to subject the father to such norms is that his function is quite simply ruined, as he is taken out of the nebulosity in which he needs to remain and finds himself pushed into a species of solidity that has already done him appreciable harm and makes him, as I have already hinted, remarkably dangerous. Experience, validated by what can be read from it in the infant psyche, shows in addition that it is best to be sparing, if not parsimonious, in having direct recourse to paternal authority in the real world.

As a general rule, the only course to pursue in relation to the father is to uphold, unequivocally, his place and prerogatives - something that family law in our western societies is a long way from allowing. Anything else is useless blathering. For no other attitude takes serious account of what takes place, unknown to the various protagonists, in the relationship between the parents on the one hand and between the parents and the children on the other. If, as part of a therapeutic process, there is a real desire to identify the place that is occupied by a child's father, it is always to be found within the mother's discourse and there alone that research should be focused. It is there that the quality of the investment made in the father can be assessed, as well as what has become of it under the pressure of repetition and the reworking of individual histories. The life of a couple is, let me say once again, nothing if not the managing of a dual and interactive transference.

Chapter 6
Restoring The Child To Time

So there it is, the dilemma: whatever the model of fatherhood chosen - and however diverse they may seem to be these days, they always boil down to the two models I drew attention to in the last section of chapter 4 - the result always turns out to be more or less of a disappointment.

Model 1, a father who claims a solidity established by his role as begetter, with a perfect right founded upon sense of commitment and responsibility, likely to intervene out of a robust idea of his duties - opting for this type paradoxically entails at best an encounter with relative insensitivity or at worst an opportunity to create intolerable suffering. Model 2, a father with a low profile inspired by the still glowing embers of old frustrations, who throws himself into the promise of an amendable future, who patiently satisfies demands as well as needs, who seeks the much dreamt of road of rational dialogue through negotiation - opting for this type quickly entail the parents' being confronted with a tyrant that gives them no rest.

Why do things turn out like that? Or rather, why do they have to turn out like that? The answer is probably because, apart from what has already been said about the matter, the first model harks back, more or less in the unconscious, to the father of the primitive horde who was eventually murdered by his sons, while the second, by doubling up on the activity provided by the maternal model, does not differ sufficiently from it to give the child enough consciousness of having finally quit the uterine space.

The recent course of our societies, or at least a large number of them in the west, has inclined them to renounce or water down the models inspired by the authoritarian father. History has certainly vindicated them in that regard, since every time that model has placed itself at the head of a nation it has destroyed it. It is hardly necessary to put names to the phenomenon - Hitler, Stalin, Fidel Castro, Pol Pot, Mullah Omar, and so on. But it has to be wondered what could have brought these famous 'little fathers' to power over their peoples. When that question is put, what regularly emerges, among other factors at least in western countries, is a covert and diffuse yet decisive response to the prevalence of the second model of fatherhood. The 'little father' who seizes power is probably appropriating it to himself both to dominate all others and, paradoxically, paying his own allegiance to the mega-mother that everyone dreams of. Thus behind his own fascination for the firm smack of discipline, we may hear him develop a discourse that is always full of promised well-being and equity. The hypothesis is verifiable at least in the case of pre-Nazi Germany, where the Swiss J. J. Bachofen and his book *Mother Right* (*Das Mutterrecht*, 1861) inspired a circle of rapidly growing influence in the early twentieth century that campaigned for the return of matriarchy. Hitler, among other celebrities, joined their ranks in Munich in 1920.

The lesson learned from such experiences, namely that the ideal governance of a state never relies upon one relationship excessively characterized by authority, explains why democracies, which are sometimes born in the violence of rejection of such an authoritarian model, have established dualist models whose functioning is minutely organized. At the summit is a president - or in some cases a monarch - who names a head of government. The president, whose title of head of state confers on him or her an undeniable aura, always remains in principle somewhat in the background, setting the general direction of the policy that the head of government is supposed to follow and put into action. The prerogatives of these two offices naturally vary between countries. The queen of England, for instance, has less power than the German president, who in turn has infinitely less power than the French president. Whatever the country, it is always the same pattern of dual authorities that obtains.[36] And however

---

[36] As far as I am aware, there has never been any attempt to study the distributions of the respective roles of these two authorities or correlate them with the rules of law and custom current in different countries. While regrettable, it is also perhaps surprising that in these times of European integration there should similarly be no study that surveys, with a view to harmonization, the various family law provisions prevailing in countries which are coming together in other fields.

subtly different the model may be from country to country, it seems remarkably to echo the hierarchic governance of the most classic of family models. Sometimes the model's influence extends beyond the mere governance of the nation. Thus in France, for instance, bicephalous structuration is so imprinted on social organization that it has been a template for the administrative machine itself, with prefects (*préfets*) and subprefects (*sous-préfets*) being established alongside the mayors (*maires*).

No country, however, can expect to do without governance, since whenever such a situation arises, the State either atrophies or disappears entirely. There are plenty of historical and current examples to chose from. In the last analysis, countries that have been crushed by dictatorship and those that have rejected any form of authority are affected by similar defects. It is therefore not surprising that commercial companies, which deal in such serious matters as plant and finance, regardless of their size and geographical location, always make use of the same sort of hierarchic model, i.e., there is a company chairman or president who orients and oversees concrete action, and this last is entrusted to a general manager who is a presidential appointment. It is always the president who, in all circumstances, defines the objectives, arbitrates, and takes the final decisions.

Whatever might be said of them, all such formulas, whether operating in a sociopolitical or business context, work fairly satisfactorily and rarely derogate from established rules. When a French president is thought to be intervening too frequently, the press soon remind him that by so doing he is 'undermining his credibility'. Even if he has an unhealthily demagogic or narcissistic side, he will never, as a matter of principle, be seen getting involved in the sort of conflicts that arise among members of the government or in the detail of the problems of the various ministries. As for the company chairman, he will not allow himself to be dictated to by an employee, any more than he will wish to get drawn in to settling the conflicts and sticky questions that turn up in the functioning of the various sectors of his firm; at the same time, if he is dishonest, and embezzles the company, his fate is quickly sealed.

Now, all of this is reminiscent of the relationships which I have described as possible and operational between the nebulous father and the solid mother. Be that as it may, the efficiency of such a model demonstrates how important and effective it is for there to be recourse to a symbolic third party, provided that that third party remains in place and by merely existing safeguards the better management of a complicated system containing wants, opinions, stakes, and difficulties as divergent as they are numerous and complex.

In that case, we have to ask why eight million years since the differentiation of the species, one hundred thousand years since the first burial and along with it the emergence of the fear of death and of the awareness of time, thirty thousand years since the birth of culture, and ten thousand years since the stabilization of the so-called classic model of the family - why after all that time have we not found a single, satisfactory solution to the questions raised by the arrival of a child? They affect equally the parents, who are called upon to invent their role and place, and the child, whose development is directly linked to the result of that invention.

At the same time, it is worth asking how it is that the democratic political world and the world of business can both draw enduring advantage from a structure based upon that of the traditional family model, while families themselves cannot, or at any rate no longer are able to. And why, we may ask, should it now seem naive, utopian, indecent, even unseemly and retrograde, to encourage families, in the absence of anything better, to draw inspiration from the very model that efficiently runs systems that are no less formidably complex?

The simple reason has to be that it is difficult! For, inasmuch as there is a constitutional precedent for the majority of states to draw upon - just as there is an organizational mode for businesses - nothing of that order has existed for the family model since the protagonists found themselves released from the containment that had long been erected around them. Abandoned to the level of their respective propensities and nothing besides, they have constantly come into collision with each other as a result of following the dictates of their individual, heterogeneous forms of behavioural logic. It is as though the president had gone with the flow of his own individual tastes, personality, or temperament, abandoned his symbolic position, and arrogated to himself the right to install the harshest dictatorship - or, alternatively, perhaps he wanted to be kind to his struggling prime minister, and therefore decided to help him out by adopting a 'hands on' approach to all the minutiae of political life. It would be just the same if a prime minister deliberately rejected the hierarchy of powers and the need for a symbolic third party in the state apparatus, and decided to do just as he liked. The reason why such scenarios are always repudiated is that they flout the constitutional reference which, in a democracy, imposes upon leaders a scrupulous respect for the rules, and orders them, in cases of dissension, to have recourse to the electorate. Perhaps, ironically, this is what some parents imagine themselves to be doing on occasions when, in certain family models, they no longer exercise the least constitutional containment, and continually appeal for the assent of their children. The consequence of this is that they end up living in a permanent election campaign and are condemned to needing to win the children's votes through the deployment of manoeuvres of seduction, thereby unwittingly giving the children a power that they not only do not ask for, but which moreover undermines their sense of security.

It should not be thought that the description of the dead-end scenario just outlined is the sign of some sort of hidden agenda on my part for the return of a particular form of containment. Far from it! What has happened has happened, once and for all. It would be vain and unreasonable not to accept that fact. It is not my aim to depart from what I consider to be a realistic vision of things. Indeed, let me be clear about this. I am in no way advocating for the clock to be put back or for any provisions that have been abandoned to be restored. How sensible should I be thought, if what is simple common sense on my part were imagined to imply fighting for contraception to be proscribed, for the monitoring of styles of married life, for limitation on numbers of divorces, or for the formal reinstatement of paternal authority unsupported by the social environment? It is one thing not to want to go back on what has been acquired; quite another to forsake fathers and mothers in their search for solutions to the problems they encounter, and abandon future generations to their lot. Are we supposed simply to resign ourselves to repairing damage that is seen as inevitable, when in so many other areas we are constantly developing arguments in favour of prevention?

If action needs to be taken, from what quarter is it to come? Do we need still more research into education than has already been done? Do we need more psychologists, psychoanalysts, child psychiatrists, speech therapists, psychomotricians, and other re-educators? Ought there to be more preventive consultations, and should they be compulsory for parents? Should everywhere nationwide have its own guidance centre or an establishment to train parents for their tasks? Or do all the establishments that children attend (day-nurseries, schools, junior academies, and the like) need to be provided with psychologists in order to supply additional assessments and syntheses during meetings with teachers and staff? Ought we to resolve to imitate the departments of health and road safety, and promote informative television programmes accompanied by hints on the right way to do things, and indeed strive to get high-quality messages across by every means conceivable? I assume we shall not be going so far as to force parents to obtain a licence to have children!

Well, what more could we invent? All the actions that I have just run through have been either begun or more or less tried already over a good few years. By public demand, interactive radio and television programmes on the subject of children have become ever more numerous. The same goes for all the literature available, whether in the form of books, audiovisual material, or magazines. All this cannot be proved to have had an impact. As for child guidance and educational psychology centres, not to mention the private sector centres that imitate their structure, they are so busy that some have been forced to introduce waiting lists. Psychologists now form a part of the world of early childhood, just as they do of the world of school. It is moreover essential to note, as I can testify from my forty years of practice, that the activities that have been invented and much expanded over the last few decades, while considered still inadequate by their users, have regularly been thought so over that time with the assent of officialdom.

Has all this effort enabled parents bringing children into the world to trust that they will eventually be able to dispense with it? Has it enabled them to be better prepared for the adventure on which they have embarked, and not to lose heart at the first difficulty they encounter? The appearance of the new pathologies, which are remarkably uncomfortable for paediatricians, do not suggest so. And no wonder. For what is happening is a concretization of the metaphor of Penelope's shroud, which, according to

Homer, she would weave all day and unravel each night. This went on for years, and it enabled her to await the return of her husband, Odysseus. Today's shrinks, of all sorts and conditions, seem stuck in the same pattern. They deploy all their art in order to try to help the children during the weekly or twice-weekly session. But as soon as the children go home, they are inevitably subjected once again to the same features within the parental environment that contributed to the emergence of their dis-ease. It has to be said, however, that the niche did not take long to be filled: the gap was plugged by family therapy, not without success it has to be said, though it is another indication of the ongoing enrichment of the panoplies of intervention. Be that as it may, all this proves that however well-intentioned or high-quality the inputs provided, activities geared to remedying consequences rather than attacking causes are unlikely to yield satisfactory end results. Now, children's symptoms do not emerge by chance. They are a voicing, a language, the only one that they can allow themselves vis-à-vis a parental world on which they depend and from which they need a minimum of security if not serenity. How can the parental world respond to them and reassure them when, albeit keen to do the best possible and be well-informed - just as it has learned to do by carefully reading the documentation accompanying the latest purchase of a washing-machine, computer, or digital camera - it ends up more at sea than it was before, having believed that it was possible to learn yet having to admit that what it has learned is not a great deal of help? For, faced with a child, reason often fails, and it is emotion that overwhelms and invades! You feel suddenly flattened by what has come out of nowhere, that you were never warned about, that is more dumbfounding than you would have believed and appears destined to exceed any competence you thought you had. It does not take parents long to lose their footing.

Maternal depression, accidents of paternity, feelings of loneliness, endless heart-searching, the more or less rapid breakdown of couple relationships - from all of this a confused picture is emerging, even if people do not want to stare it in the face, even if they angrily thrust away its obsessive hold or try to fight it. For they are well aware that if there is one thing parents cannot do with children, it is cheat them, pull the wool over their eyes. They are aware, too, as parents, that just as they cannot pull the wool over their children's eyes, so they cannot pull it over their own, either. All the same, they remain convinced that, when they had their children, they were performing the most important and most positive act of their existence. So, what has it brought them? The answer is: themselves! Themselves, with their own adventure, necessarily distorted: their own adventure, together with the pain it gave them because those placed over them, their own parents, were not up to the task. So, what are they to do? The same as their parents? How terrible! The opposite? Maybe. Differently? Yes! How so? One day, perhaps the next day, the children have symptoms. The parents begin by not wanting to see the symptoms, before going on to deny them; then they put them down to the children's age and hope that they will clear up on their own. Eventually, the worry becomes too much and the parents seek help, yet without managing to assuage the enormous guilt that goes with taking such a step. The offer of therapeutic assistance both gives them relief and rekindles hope. Except that therapeutic professionals often poorly understand, and may even deliberately exclude from consideration, all that has led to this point and which, whether they like it or not, ought to be investigated to everyone's benefit. However, the professionals have their own logic, and patiently weave their rows of cloth hoping that some of these, at least, will hold that evening against the attitude, the sigh, the gesture, the deadly word that will inevitably cause them to unravel.

And so we begin again. Next patient! We move from the refluxer who sometimes has damaged the oesophageal mucosa in the womb and is born vomiting blood - the so-called Mallory-Weiss syndrome - to the lisper who is brought along at four or five years old still attached to a feeding-bottle, use of which is quickly justified by the assertion that 'he can't do without it' and 'it's so practical to get him to drink the 300 ml recommended at breakfast'. From first to last there is always a question of language and communication - a non-linguistic language that is endlessly trying to say to whoever will listen what cannot be said in any other way, as if that were the only way to communicate something that encumbered, inhabited, and gnawed away like some sort of intolerable alien.

Note that I said 'to whoever will listen'. I did not say 'understand'. For these are not the same, and it is not always necessary to understand in order to help.

I remember one day seeing a mother and her ten-month-old baby girl. The child had a cadaverous look, as she had never been able to take down very much. She could scarcely swallow, either from a feeding-bottle or by taking the contents of a spoon into her mouth. Although from the account that the mother gave me of her child's state I was able to formulate a number of worrying diagnostic hypotheses, I learned that several hospitalizations in high-quality establishments had eliminated these one by one, and it had not been possible to make any organic diagnosis. All I could offer this mother was to see her for further sessions; it was clear that this was what she herself wanted, and she agreed straight away. I saw her once a week, with her baby girl for the first two or three appointments, then on her own thereafter over about three months. The extraordinary memory that I have of these sessions is that although I would listen to her for half-an-hour at a time, I never understood a word of what she was telling me. I never managed to link up, in any coherent way, the snatches of the story that she recounted or the conversations she reported with any scenario that might enable me to attach it, even remotely, to her daughter's symptoms. But perhaps I should not complain about this, for I learned that the ferocity of her daughter's anorexia abated after the third session. Why the third? No idea. I asked to re-examine the girl at the end of our work together, and she had doubled her weight!

It may be wondered why I have slipped this story in here. The first reason is to point out that there is an enormous amount that could be said on a purely technical and theoretical level, even if it is not my intention to go further down that road. The second and more important reason is that the story illustrates something that I have learned as a psychoanalytically experienced paediatrician, namely, that everyone comes across situations which they do not understand, but that this is not automatically a disqualification. Paediatricians, having been treated these last few decades to a whole discourse about the complex links between psyche and soma, have frequently withdrawn into the 'veterinary' side of their specialism. They have assumed that they have no competence in relation to the psyche, and they have referred on to psychological specialists - who, incidentally, declare that

that is indeed the only thing to do in such cases - the parents of patients with increasingly obstinate needs. While I applaud such probity, I regret the professional withdrawal which it has occasioned, since paediatricians are extraordinarily well-trusted and are the practitioners that most parents experiencing difficulties consult. For some years past they could have intervened to positive effect much more than they have done in the social disarray that our western societies have been experiencing. Without pretending to be something they were not or expanding into unofficial psychotherapies, they needed only to be more relaxed about letting their clients speak, regardless of whether they understood what their clients said or not, and about listening to, even if they could not 'hear', those who merely sought to speak. Listening professionals themselves stress the importance of 'hearing' over 'understanding', and assert that 'understanding' compromises 'hearing' insofar as 'hearing' does not touch or distort the message given, whereas 'understanding' involves - cf. the etymology of the synonym, 'comprehension' - taking hold of the message and processing it through one's own perception. Individuals always make the greatest progress when they are enabled to hear themselves reflected back by someone else assuming the role of a non-distorting receptacle of what they say, non-distorting precisely because the hearer sometimes waives the need to understand.

To provide this sort of service paediatricians would need it to become an integral part of their original training, and those already practising would require some sort of minimal briefing, if not more substantial in-service training, in order to respond to the new style of requests that their patients' parents have begun to present. As yet nothing has happened on that front. One still comes across paediatricians in their early thirties who have worked in the most prestigious paediatric departments and gone through their entire training without ever hearing about parents or parents' relationships with their children. They are brilliant finders of needles in haystacks, diagnostically speaking. But how common are such 'needles'? I am not saying that training of that meticulous sort is unnecessary or should be looked at again; simply that the turning it has taken illustrates once again the security reflexes and precautionary principle of our survivalist ideology. No wonder paediatrics as a special field is on the wane; health-service managers currently question what it provides children with that cannot be provided within the care provided at much lower cost by generalists. After all, general practitioners are well able to furnish such things as dietary prescriptions and vaccinations to children whom improved hygiene and preventive medicine have rendered far healthier physically than they were just two generations ago.

The lack of listening skill development among paediatricians is all the more regrettable as parents undoubtedly pay a great deal of attention to what medics, especially paediatricians, say. Indeed I myself am counting on that influence to put across the relevance of the solution that my analysis suggests needs to be offered to deal with children's current problems. It was moreover with that end in view that in the earlier chapters of this book, I dissected the essentials of the long adventure of the human species and the dynamics of interparental relations. Let us briefly recall what has been learned about those things.

The evolution of the species has endowed it with an authority that has been established very gradually, not by design but solely as a result of a series of adaptive reflexes. Human males, subject to the violence of their sexual drives, sought to resolve the interlinked problems of their self-centredness, their rivalry, and the risk of dying in the attempt to satisfy these drives. Having long muddled along in a fashion that is probably, even now, not totally adjusted, they endeavoured to settle their conflicts by decreeing a Law, the Law of the Species, based on exchanging their women. The women, whose own views had never been canvassed and who were for a long time subjugated - if indeed they are not still to some extent, even in lands that pay lip-service to sexual equality - never renounced their own intrinsic behavioural logic: driven by their hatred of death, they maintained a decisive relationship to their children, which tended to reassure them about both their status and the power it enabled them to wield. They always experienced huge difficulty in allowing their children to move away from them and, by a reflex movement, set about weaving round them a virtual uterus that was infinitely expandable, within which non-time prevailed together with the eradication of any idea of lack - the total opposite, in other words, of was supposed to be put in place by the Law of the Species.

Confronted, no doubt indirectly, by this situation, the males strove to reinforce the Law with all kinds of ancillary devices - culture, religion, systems of kinship, and provisions that placed containment around couples. The so-called traditional family thus conferred upon the paternal figure, without his necessarily willing it, a function that enabled children, without their necessarily being delighted by it, to leave the uterine world and simultaneously replace the uterine non-time with an assimilated consciousness of time. Such an awareness was harsh, because it compelled children to recognize and assume their own mortality, though it also hardened them and made them more prepared to integrate themselves into the social body and to set about organizing their lives around particular exchanges. It could be said, then, that evolution having first given to the species the 'gift of the father' (the father the gift), the father himself - though once again he did so neither deliberately nor even wittingly - gave his children the ingredient that was missing from their lives, the dimension of time. This 'gift of the father' (the father the giver) was the consciousness that the father had of time, the awareness that enabled him to experience that dimension.

The reality of this situation caused endless problems, as it brought into play two forms of behavioural logic so irreconcilable as practically to render men and women two subspecies of the same species. The equilibrium arrived at has, however, been destabilized by factors that have recently proved decisive, not least those linked to the development of an industrialized society with its economic consequences and associated changes in the predominant mental outlook. Alongside changes in the status of women in our western societies at least, the containing elements that used to operate around couples have vanished; contraception has been perfected, sexual mores have become freer, and there has been considerable weakening of the paternal dimension of parenthood; to have maintained it at its former level would have been impossible in view of all the modifications and measures that have been adopted.

Given the current situation, the approach I advocate consists in attempting, by other means than those exercised thus far, to restore to the protagonists, especially those of future generations, the major ingredient of which they have been deprived, i.e., the consciousness of time, purged of fear. At first sight this might seem a naive, even utopian objective, since it would mean re-establishing what was central to the endless struggles between mothers and fathers. In the form that I envisage, without the threat of dramatic incident or insurmountable difficulties, it will doubtless be met with scepticism, distrust, or perhaps simply surprised amusement. Easy when you know how - or just a trick? To such challenges I answer that what I suggest already exists, but that people have never realized its potential when employed to the extent that I envisage. Some may also wonder whether it is a procedure that has only preventive value or whether, provided it is properly adapted, it could serve in other circumstances, because it may be thought unlikely to work where things have already taken a worrying turn. In response to such reservations I offer below another clinical vignette from my own practice. As I set about telling it, I find myself wondering, with some amusement, at what moment in time to start, because time is so much of the essence of the story.

Anyone For Tennis?

He was magnificent, gorgeous, superb, radiant. Ludo seemed all that and more to me, as he came through my consulting-room door. For a fraction of a second he practically filled the opening. My eyes took in his every detail. Lord, he was beautiful! An athletic form in an elegant pearl-grey suit. Could this really be Ludo? I recognized his big blue eyes, but I'd never have foreseen beauty on that scale. The memory I had of him was of a fairly unattractive face, dominated, it is true, by enormous troubled and darting eyes, but including fat, floppy lips that were always open, revealing disproportionately large teeth, and a small, receding chin that seemed to me to translate a desperate weakness. All of that was gone. His face was clear, regular, and smiling; his firm, well-drawn mouth conferred on the whole a strong and uncommonly well-balanced expression.

He was hardly through the door before I rushed to greet him. We threw ourselves into each other's arms and hugged long and hard, as if to make up for all we'd been unable to say to each other down the long years that had passed since we last had sight of each other. I was the first to let go, out of regard for his wife, who, I realized, was standing behind him, still outside in the corridor, holding in her arms their little boy. Ludo's eyes were moist. Realizing my intention, he turned round to his wife and introduced her to me. She smiled, moved. She too was charming, and very beautiful.

Because of the length of my career, I have had the indescribable pleasure of receiving the babies of my former babies of both sexes. Some of them I may have treated over many years before they became parents in their turn. The relationships I have with them always differ from those I have with other clients. While the inevitable familiarity in no way detracts from the respect and deference usual in such professional exchanges, it has helped to provide my observations and personal researches with the sort of weight and depth that can come from such well-supplied longitudinal monitoring.

But the emotion with which I greeted Ludo was of a totally different order and intensity. I wasn't just pleased to find myself with one of 'my' children whom I hadn't seen for a long time; that was a pleasure that I had come to realize could happen with any of the former child patients who had become just a little bit mine also. No, when I saw Ludo, it was like being able at last to breathe a long pent up sigh of relief, as though I was being given confirmation of an unreasonable hope or a mad belief. This overwhelming emotion included, besides, a delighted submission to what had seemed incredible; it was like catching the subtle, hitherto unknown perfume of a resurrection.

Yes, that's it exactly! Ludo, as he stood there, compared to the memory I had gone on having of him, was as one risen from the dead. His journey - his fate? - had been a return to life. I had known his mother right at the start of my career, with her first child, a girl of several months, whom she left during the day with a childminder, a neighbour in the apartment block she lived in, as also sometimes at night. She was a single parent, having divorced her husband soon after she became pregnant. She ran a flower-shop on the other side of Paris. She explained to me that because of her circumstances she had grabbed at the offer of a social-housing apartment in our district, even if it meant that her affordable rent had to be set against hours of extra travelling. I saw her from time to time, though not so often as her daughter, whom I visited at the childminder's whenever the girl was sick. Our relations, though cordial, never went very deep. I scarcely managed to get any details about the little girl's father and the reasons for the divorce, which were ordinary enough: he had met somebody else. She must have been comfortable with me, however, as she recommended me to her brothers and sister, for their children, even though they all lived some distance away from my clinic.

I don't remember ever seeing her pregnant before she brought me her newborn baby boy, along with his father. It was the beginning of a nightmare that went on for some years, practically till the very last time I had seen Ludo. That was in spite of all the professional interventions that I had brought to bear upon the case whenever they seemed to be called for.

For a long time, the consultations were conducted in heavy silence. She scarcely unclenched her jaw, any more than did her husband - they were married, and she had changed her name - a man much older than herself, a bit thickset, with a cool, distrustful look. It was his second marriage, and he already had a big boy. A reconstituted family, in sum, of the sort that was just beginning to become increasingly common. I expected things to loosen up as we went on meeting. But Ludo was quickly affected by a skin problem specific to the first three months of life, Leiner-Moussous Disease, and this required constant, frequent refinement of painstaking treatment. This often brought them to see me, all three of them, for the father never missed a consultation. I thus experienced the most organicist consultation of my career. Whenever I armed myself with my most open expression and risked a kindly, 'And apart from that, is everything OK?' one or other of them would reply, 'Fine,' in a slightly weary voice that seemed to be saying to me, 'Don't ask.'

What a lot happened in those early years! The skin trouble soon gave way to extensive eczema, which required increasing doses of corticoid creams to at least calm down the ferocious itching. I wondered whether Ludo wasn't taking advantage of the situation. No sooner had he taken his clothes off and was sitting on the examining bench than he set about scratching the areas that were normally covered, challenging me with the big blue eyes whose long black lashes gave them a melancholy air. The start of his third year saw the emergence of asthma, with crises that were sufficiently frequent to justify a minimal maintenance of corticoid medication - we didn't have steroid inhalers in those days. His sleep was scarcely any better, and his rudimentary speech was further trammelled in its development by an ever-present dummy-teat, which he was allowed to keep because as soon as it was taken away he not only screamed and screamed, but was soon soaking in the floods of saliva that ran from his mouth. As for his general behaviour, it was simply deplorable, though all his whims and tyranny could not hold a candle to the fierce jealousy he had developed towards his big sister.

Then, one day, towards his third birthday, I learned from the couple of their divorce, which even so did not stop the father from being just as diligent about coming to consultations. I will not go into all the school-linked problems, which began as soon as Ludo started nursery school, with aggressive behaviour towards the other children, leading on to learning difficulties, for which I had sought psychomotor and orthophonic help - the dummy-teat did not disappear till after Ludo's sixth birthday - and then, finally, psychoanalysis. My regular attempts to get the couple to look at their own relationship always ran into a brick wall. It was as if the child's symptoms were essential to it.

I have to confess that I no longer remember why, one day, the father stopped coming with Ludo and his mother. I suppose it must have coincided with the new relationship he had started. Wearied, no doubt, by the long silence or resigned to it, it took me a few meetings to get used to the new configuration of our consultations. When, however, I finally invited Ludo's mother to give her side of this long, agonizing business, she hardly needed asking, and agreed to come back on her own to recount what hitherto had remained quite opaque to me.

She went right back to the beginning. One evening, tired after a long day in the shop, she had decided to take a taxi home. Several days later, she was surprised to find the same taxi waiting for her. She was amused by this, not suspecting at the time that the driver was going to use his diligent presence as a wooing technique. It was a technique that worked, for, after several weeks, she allowed him to come up one evening, having parked his taxi for the night opposite the block. It took only a few weeks for them to decide to get married - and only a few months more for them to begin the conflict that would eventually lead to their separation several years further on. She had taken the view that the fact that she had married her husband gave him no right to any say in the running of her business, while he saw things very differently. Was this just a pretext or the focal point of a disagreement that had other causes? In any event, the quarrel was well under way when she discovered she was pregnant. She was rather disappointed about the fact, and her husband was no more enthusiastic about the news than she was. As the arrival of the pregnancy did nothing to quell their growing dissension, the decision to go for a termination was in the air without anything definitive being said about it. Abortion at the time was still illegal in France, and was always a fraught business. She obtained information. She learned that she could have a termination properly conducted under safe conditions in Switzerland or England. She opted for England and, having made arrangements for her daughter and her flower-shop, caught a bus at a place and time indicated to take her and other candidates for the procedure to a clinic in London where it was normally carried out. The agency that organized these trips placed her overnight in a small hotel, and collected her the following morning to take her to the clinic. There she answered a long questionnaire, and she was given a number, with the instruction to wait her turn in a large hallway where dozens of women in her condition were waiting patiently. After less than half an hour she realized that she would be waiting the best part of the day before her turn would come. She lost herself in a book she had grabbed for the journey and tried to think about nothing. The hours dragged. She was hungry, having been allowed only a biscuit and a cup of tea at lunchtime. Suddenly she realized that there was only one woman in front of her and four after.

She was eventually called. She rose to go to the door where she had seen those before her go when, as she passed in front of the desk, the secretary handed her the telephone. Although her English was rudimentary, she gained the impression that there was a call for her. She imagined it must be a mistake; no one could be calling her, because no one knew where she was. She nonetheless took the handset. It was her husband; he shouted at her with no holds barred. 'I absolutely forbid you to do anything to my child! You hear, I forbid you! I've told the secretary that if they do anything, I'll take the clinic to court ...' She learned later that he had spent the night rushing around Paris looking for her, questioning her parents, other relations, and friends, until he found the one who had put her on to the London clinic. He'd have gone directly there in person, if he hadn't been scared of arriving too late.

Such were the circumstances in which she returned to Paris still pregnant and eventually gave birth to Ludo, as everyone called him, though she swore she would never allow the name that she had chosen, Ludovic, to be shortened. Did she know - could she know? - that Ludovicus meant 'the winner of the game'? He had played for his life and had carried off the victor's crown!

It was a highly charged, difficult, weighty history. I listened without missing a single detail. Without allowing me to make a precise link with Ludo's organic complaints, it helped me to understand the couple's long silences as well as the ever-distrustful presence of Ludo's father, attentive yet mute. She explained how Ludo's early upbringing, having gone down the road of a double dose of overprotectiveness, had created a tyrant around whom they had put no framework and whose energy they had allowed to discharge in all directions. As with Ludo, so in all normal cases a baby is like a sun, an immense ball of energy that radiates in all directions; but it is likely to suffer a serious lowering, if not exhaustion, of its energy reserves, if the parental environment does not channel it as narrowly as possible in order that the child may use it sustainably and profitably.

After hearing that story it was not so very difficult for me to persuade Ludo's mother to identify the successive failures of her

Fathers and Mothers

couple-relationships and to agree that they were worth examining. She left with the address of a psychoanalyst, with whom she did some fruitful longterm work.

Ludo, however, was not a great deal better. The psychoanalysis, the various therapeutic rehabilitations, and changes of school did not seem to make much difference. When he entered the sixth grade (around 11 years of age), he still read haltingly and had major spelling difficulties.

It was around then that I saw him for the last time before we would meet again all those years later. He was accompanied by his father and mother, who very quickly told me that they had come to ask my advice about a decision they were on the point of taking. They had long realized that Ludo, who was very sporty, excelled at tennis to the point where his teacher said he could have a real future in it. Having thought about it, they had seen a possible opening out of the dead-end in which they all found themselves. As Ludo wasn't an 'academic type' and would never make an intellectual, why not give him every chance to take a direction that he could one day make his own? They had carefully informed themselves about the options and had together agreed upon a solution: a prestigious tennis school in the States took boarders, whom they trained from the age that Ludo had just reached. The separation would certainly be as hard for them as it would for Ludo. But he, relieved to be finally rid of the torture of school and delighted at the chance to become a perfect player of the sport he adored, wasn't thinking of that and, without taking into account the momentousness of the decision, he was ready to go right away. I thought to myself that it was probably no accident that this child, given his history, should invest so heavily in the exploits of his body and end up opting for tennis, that sport in which the ball goes back and forth between the protagonists, just like, among other things, the guilt that had always held his two parents in its grip. I also discerned behind the extravagance involved in such a decision - for it was undoubtedly a financially costly option - both the extent of their guilt and the price they were prepared to pay to assuage it. Even so, the cost was more than financial, since they had agreed in advance to *confront the affective frustration they were going to experience in removing their child from their own problematic environment and in entrusting to others the next stage of his upbringing. Leaving aside the distance, the solution was not an original one. There have always been parents who, facing up to the fact that they have gone wrong, have 'boarded out' their children in one way or another and in various types of places. I not only subscribed to the intelligence of the solution they had found, I also predicted, in the light of the failure of the various therapeutic means tried, that the results would be good. I also gave them to understand that I personally considered it not a rejection but a genuine proof of love.*

And what possible question could I ask of this brand-new Ludo, whom I met as a new dad himself after all those years, other than what had happened in the meantime? 'How's the tennis going? Where are you with that?' 'Nowhere,' he replied, before adding, to my great surprise, 'I never want to hear the word again in my entire life, and I don't want to even think of a tennis racket, I can tell you!'

He then started to tell me the long story, blow by blow, of his American adventure, which had lasted several years. He described the life at school along with its rules, the teaching methods practised, and the iron discipline that was maintained. The failure of all the attempts by himself and his friends to dodge that discipline, and the suffering he had to endure, especially in the early days. Avoiding both smugness and pathos, he gave me a detailed account of the daily round, the timetables, the hierarchy of punishments meted out for bad behaviour, the periodic assessments, and so on. The sort of tale that would make most people's blood boil, and force us to show sincere sympathy for him, telling him how horrified we are by that sort of coercion, gratuitously brutal in appearance, and inescapably inhumane and stupid. Except that he himself said this to me, as he brought his story to an end: 'As for tennis, I never want to hear about that ever again. But I'm so grateful to my parents for sending me to that school. And I'm grateful, too, to my teachers and all the staff I had. I cried and I suffered. But it was that that turned me into a man. And if my own son ever turns into what I was, I won't hesitate for a second to send him over there.'

All we can do here is scratch the surface of this case. Yet even in mere outline it speaks volumes on many aspects of the way we live now. Its story is one to which I myself have been a witness over two generations. It concerns a young woman, already a mother, left on her own in no time at all, financially independent, living an existence whose features she has accepted. She of course has a history behind her, in which she herself is only a link (though I have no access to that information). She meets a man, who belongs to another contemporary category, with a home and a growing son behind him. They become expectant parents at what is doubtless the rockiest time in the relationship, a time when they are no longer consciously putting anything into it - another common situation and, as it happens, the repetition of a scenario already familiar to both these protagonists: her on her own with her first child, a daughter; him separated from a woman who has borne his first child. Confronted with the reality of their immediate situation, they envisage the elimination of the child. She takes action to accomplish what she believes to be the right thing to do under the circumstances. She wrestles with herself and the situation which prevailed in France before the 1975 law on abortion. He intervenes at the last possible moment. The pregnancy is preserved. But what are they going to do with this child whose elimination they had not hesitated to envisage? It is not that simple for people to process the experience they had been through, to block out the wish to effect a death. How is it that some imagine it to be easy? Human beings are not made that way. We are inheritors of what the evolution of our species has wired into us, a whole mechanism that punishes those who dare to brave, in reality or mere fantasy, the proscription on killing. I myself can testify - and am simply passing on information here - that I have never met a woman who, after going through an abortion, never mind the circumstances or justification, was not deeply and indelibly marked by the experience. As for Ludo's parents, their whole conduct was to revolve around what they inwardly registered as being their former ill conduct. His mother, racked by guilt, was to strive to satisfy her child's smallest needs, if not forestall them, fearing the reproaches of the man who, probably in order to relieve his own guilt, projected it onto her and kept her under constant watch, accompanying her to every consultation with me as if still fundamentally suspicious of the connivance that doctors might show towards mothers to the detriment of fathers and children. The longer this went on the heavier the atmosphere, and the stronger grew the pressure of the virtual womb that the boy's mother wove around him - with the father's approval insofar as he was ready to interpret such solicitousness as proof of a new and reassuring attitude on her part. In vain the child attempted to make himself more visible through the redness of his skin and to voice through his asthmatic crises his need for a change of atmosphere. Condemned to live in uterine non-time, he was excluded from any personal experience of time. He became the tyrant that I have described, who demanded everything, to be delivered straight away, as if the least experience of waiting, however short, contained in itself a threat of death. It was not even enough for his mother, ever fearful of her husband's reproachfulness, to be constantly present, but he hallucinated her by means of the dummy-teat that could not be taken away from him without triggering vehement protest. The saliva which soaked him as soon as his mouth was empty witnesses to a fixation of his deglutition at a very early stage, i.e., prior to three or four months. It is at this age that copious saliva may suggest that teeth are about to erupt, whereas it is simply the work of the salivary glands making use of an abundant production to modify the dynamics and coordination of the muscles associated with swallowing and enabling the child to take down other food than milk. It is thus a preparation of the separation from the mother's body. Was it, however, within Ludo's reach to do this, given his enclosure within a thick virtual uterus?

I have commented upon all this at some length, in order to emphasize how important it is for every mother to be able to give up keeping her child 'in' her and 'for' her. I have also stressed the fact that she should not be hesitant about inviting the child to leave her alone, and even force the child away if there is the least opposition. In so saying, I realize I may be criticized for attacking or culpabilizing mothers. My sole aim, however, is call upon them to be aware of their responsibility in this area, just as, if I were a driving instructor, it would be appropriate to remind them to keep to the correct side of the road and stop at red lights. If the burden of the initiative falls so often on mothers, it is because, having been the physical bearers of the children of both sexes, they are the centre of their children's universe and the object of demands that can become incessant; they are also, whether they like it or not, their children's most potentially gifted and efficient educators. Indeed the word 'education' extends beyond the merely scholastic, and is highly relevant to the authority and remit of mothers. The word derives from Latin - e or ex denoting 'out of' and *ducere* meaning 'to lead'. To 'educate' is therefore to 'lead out'. But where from? Where indeed if not from the uterine world, the world of the womb? Hence all education necessarily requires the adhesion of the mother to the project, for without her support it will become highly problematic, engendering, as in Ludo's case, a complex of difficulties that may actually elude any and all therapeutic specialists brought in.

It goes without saying, as I have already pointed out, that children - and boys more than girls - do not readily accept being turned away and their main aim is to stay riveted to their mothers, if not virtually in them. As it is not pleasant to be strongly set on a course with a built-in end to it, the child balks at having to come to terms with the situation. If it is the father who orders the end, the child goes on balking, and will have ferocious feelings towards him, to the effect that every rotten thing that happens is his fault; the child feels, as the mother's daughter or son, that such a bad decision would never have been taken by the loving mother he or she knows. Hence it is for *mothers* to intervene on a daily basis, impose embargoes, and pronounce all the 'noes' that the opinion-makers of recent times, some of them highly expert, have actually declared to be the *father's* exclusive prerogative. In order better to understand this, it is important not to lose sight of the fact that every demand on the part of a child is a demand made of the mother and that it has, more or less overtly, a sexual colouring. Although this may shock some, it is comprehensible in the light of the fact that every demand is a demand for the immediate satisfaction of a need, which in turn refers back to the needs expressed in the uterus - in other words, every demand refers back to the logic of the virtual womb. When the father says 'no', the child is convinced that his mother would certainly have said 'yes', and would have given him satisfaction. But when the mother says 'no', that 'no' carries an immensely powerful message, for it hints that although she is aware that she remains ever penetrable and, by virtue of that fact, is unable to hide from a attempt to penetrate her albeit in the metaphorical form of a demand, she says 'no' to that attempt, in whatever form it presents itself, in the name of the 'yes' that she says to the father alone. In other words, every 'no' proffered by the mother is always in the father's name. This is what enables the father to play to the full his symbolic third-party role, conferring on the mother the responsibility of activating his decisions and economizing on his direct interventions, these being reserved for important circumstances. I often say that a father is like a battery: it runs down, and can do so remarkably quickly if it is used all the time. It almost goes without saying that the maternal 'no' will be all the more effective if what it implicitly expresses corresponds to a certain reality, i.e., a real investment in the father by the mother. Similarly, the father's place will be all the surer if he takes care to remain the mother's lover, is thereby successful in pulling her over towards womanhood, and continues to service that status. Does this imply that a lone mother has no means to make herself heard? In order words, in Ludo's case for instance, does this mean that his mother, even had she tried, could not have successfully impressed her 'no' on him? By no means. The fact is that any message she might have given would not have been false, insofar as she had declared 'yes' to Ludo's father, leading to the boy's conception, and all her 'noes' harked back to that primary 'yes'. It is worth, in this connection, mentioning the relevance of the patronymic (father's) surname, long attributed to the child in order to recall this type of rule. There is a recent trend to dispense with this as an automatic arrangement, citing Spain and Portugal, where the child inherits the patronyms of both parents, the first being the only one passed on to the next generation. In reality there are historic reasons for this practice, dating back to the seven centuries of Arab occupation. The Arabs had harems and were duty-bound to give the forename Mohammed to at least one of their children. If, for example, one Ali had wives called Fatma, Zohra, and Khadidja, and each of them had a Mohammed, he could only distinguish between the boys by naming them Mohammed of Ali and Fatma, Mohammed of Ali and Zohra, and Mohammed of Ali and Khadidja. The practice created a rule for the naming of all children which continued after the Christian Reconquista.

Clearly, then, it is neither the impossibility nor inanity of the enterprise that should account for a mother's reluctance to say 'no'. It is rather that she would like to be able to take pleasure in saying 'yes' to her child, believing that, by thus satisfying the child in the name of the behavioural logic that directs her, she will be able to feel that she is a good mother, even if this is to lose sight of the fact that to seduce a child is equivalent to destroying him. It is very common for mothers to come to consultations about sleep and other problems that they are having with children whom they are raising as lone parents for whatever reason, and for them to indicate that the child shares their bed. When I tell them that this ought to stop, because the child should not occupy his or her father's place, they always reply in the same vein, i.e., that the father is not there, and the child would not understand the reason for being turfed out. In the event, they are able to bring this artifice of theirs to an end only when, after re-examining their own history, they can perceive fully that without these now absent fathers they would never have been mothers. It is not unusual at this point for them to confess their astonishment at the ease with which the child obeys them. In effect the child has obeyed because he has suddenly sensed, within the order given him, a grit and determination that he has never seen before and to which he is wonderfully sensitive; being directly connected to his mother, he has no need of words to recognize it for what it is. But without such determination there is no chance that the order will be carried out; what it signifies is that the mother is prepared to struggle and contend to have her view prevail, however much energy it may take! The mere exhibition of that determination, even apart from practical action being taken, re-establishes the generational hierarchy, and in its own fashion it endows the child with a touch of extra awareness of the existence and onward course of time, from whose sway no one is exempt.

Maternal reluctance is part of a general attitudinal category which, although questionable, has become normal, even routine among many modern parents who are concerned to treat children decently and democratically. They supply the children with a host of justifications; what happens, however, is that the justifications are productive of anxiety. For, if parents justify themselves to their children, they invert the generational order: by allowing the children to judge, they effectively place the children as judges over them. This is the exact opposite of what the children need. To combat their anxiety children normally say to themselves, in the light of what they have come to understand, that the upper generation always dies before the lower. The generational inversion established by the parents' justification thus produces a reverse effect and this strongly enhances pressure of anxiety on the children. In an equivalent counter-attitude, the parents often grant their children a totality of rights, while forgetting to impart to them the notion of duties. It is not unusual to hear such terms bandied about when, for example, having gone through a full range of long-winded and unavailing explanations, parents run out of arguments, and come out with the classic, 'You've no right....,' generally punctuating it with the equally classic 'OK?', which is a superb way of disclosing just how weak their determination is to see that their views prevail. Hence it is no surprise when the little tyrant pipes up, 'Yes, I do have a right!'. At this point the door opens upon a whole new negotiation, which the parents have lost in advance owing to the disparity in energy levels. For where energy is concerned, children always have more than enough, whereas parents will often already have exhausted much of theirs in a costly childhood of their own.

I have often shocked parents by inviting them to reflect on an aphorism that I deliberately couch in extreme terms so that it strikes their imagination - 'If you behave like democrats in raising your children, you are highly likely to end up with fascists: if you raise them in a more or less fascist way, you will certainly end up with democrats.' It is perfectly true. To launch into drawn-out justifications and appeals to reason for the least decision does not, as might be thought, create a hatred for authoritarianism, but rather the opposite: when the child grows up, he will remain so attached to his initial family unit that he will reject anything that differs from it. He will be truly intolerant of the least difference. On the other hand, if as a child he had to put up with the strictures of external authority, he will undoubtedly grow up to fight expressions of it. When the French Revolution attempted to give the most accurate definition of freedom, it came up with the following: 'The liberty of every person ends where the liberty of others begins.' By way of an insidious slippage toward demagoguery, the formula became one day: 'The liberty of every person begins where the liberty of others ends.' While the former establishes a social bond based upon otherness, the latter destroys it by fostering individualism, which promotes its perversion and causes neurosis.

That said, it is true that today's western societies find themselves in the happy position of having one institution without which there would be grounds for much greater cause for concern about the development of the generations to come: the school. School offers the most effective and appropriate means to limit the damage and give children a new framework. For this reason, it seems to me no bad thing at all that in France, as opposed to Britain and America, schooling starts so early. It does not simply provide instruction; it often supplies something otherwise missing to many children's upbringing in that it can check their inclination to tyranny and illusions of omnipotence by disabusing them of the conviction they may have had till then that they are little gods entitled to everything as a matter of course. School finally brings them - sometimes with considerable difficulty - into the real world, managing even to teach them of the existence of their fellows and opening for them horizons they never suspected. Obliged as they are nowadays to discharge this difficult yet laudable role, teachers would be totally justified in regretting that so much valuable time needs to be devoted to this type of task. Yet they often have to put up with interference from parents in action which they as teachers can clearly see is necessary and which they suspect will need to continue beyond the early years of schooling. Very often such parents, thinking that they are justified in reliving their own childhood through their children, have come to me and complained about the lack of comprehension shown by teachers, whom they would have preferred to share their own counter-educative attitudes!

It is no coincidence that the great Françoise Dolto[37] was sympathetic towards professional childcare and was an apologist for nurseries. It was an elliptical, often ill-understood way of saying that ways existed to shield children from mothers' natural propensity to overprotect and keep their children 'in' them too long - ways that did not cause distress to mothers, yet enabled their children to discover an environment of fellows who could give them a clearer awareness of what they were. It is for similar reasons that systems of *garderies* (short-term crèches) have developed, i.e., to enable children raised at home or by childminders to have the benefit of similar

---

[37] Famous French psychoanalyst and paediatrician (1908-88), whose aim was to be a 'doctor of child-rearing'; highly influential in the field of childcare in France from the 1960s until her death, she inaugurated the 'Maison verte' ('nurture centre') movement - trans.

experiences. When Françoise Dolto herself opened the first *Maison verte*, the aim of such nurture centres was no different: a low-key, subtly educative, psychoanalytically-led way of opening up to mothers and children alike those indispensable horizons that had seemed forbidding because falsely depicted in frightening terms. What is unfortunate - though it shows us the extent of what is at issue - is that all these measures and their associated institutions have been hijacked by the babyolatrous–maternolatrous current and turned into something intended to enhance the performance of babies and make their mothers better still! There may be nothing wrong with the intention as such, but it leads to confusion if it is not clearly stated what it actually means and how, practically speaking, it is to be realized. To take yet another motoring analogy: if you are driving down a steep hill complete with hairpin bends and are in first gear in order to slow you down, it will not help you if, as well as changing up into second gear on the straights, you press down on the accelerator - unless you want to leave the road at the next bend! It cannot be repeated often enough that to give explanations about the way certain things operate is not to culpabilize mothers and accuse them of being irresponsible. On the contrary, it is to give them a supplementary means to combat the patterns that affect, subject, and dominate them in spite of themselves. It is to arm their intelligence in order to free them to resist the parasitic drives that come to them from the remotest depths of their histories.

It is important to stress that all these interventionist systems and measures taken together are often of sovereign value. However, they can only benefit those children whose lives still offer openings, i.e., lives that are not too compromised. For example, they did not succeed in turning round the course of Ludo's affective development. One wonders what might have happened, had he attended a crèche, though like his sister he had a childminder, and this fact must partly have preserved him. But the atmosphere in which he lived during the day was no doubt inadequate to save him from that in which he found himself once again when he was back with his parents. It is hard to see how a school would have done any better.

If, having done a quick round-up of the various possibilities on offer, we ask ourselves whether there is one common factor informing their structure and direction, we see yet again that that ingredient is time. For it is the perception of the passing of time, about which I have already said so much, that provides such a counterpoint to the uterine non-time that is promoted by the immediate satisfaction of the merest need. It is the awareness of time in its directional dimension, its onward flow, that informs the capacity to say 'no' in the name of the father with whom the child was made. It is ever and always time that intervenes in the sort of child-rearing that rejects the laxness so often confused with democracy; for child-rearing that integrates time openly acknowledges the generational difference and does not maintain the child in the illusion of an equality of powers and prerogatives.

Now what did the adult Ludo tell me about what he had lived through? He told me that he had suffered. But he also told me of the indisputable benefit he had derived from the slow years of real re-education, years that had opened his eyes and enabled him to be born at last into the world around him as a desiring being, capable not just of saying that he never wanted to see another tennis racket, but also of forming a couple and of procreating with a serenity that his own father had never known. All this of course had nothing remotely to do with, for example, psychoanalytical work. But what I can testify, at the risk of seeming somewhat iconoclastic, is that I never saw in my long career any psychoanalytical work by any practitioner belonging to any psychoanalytical school produce an effect so spectacular and convincing.

What both amused and moved me the most in all that Ludo told me was his account of how he met his wife. He told me that he came across her at a young people's summer camp (*colonie de vacances*), where she was staying and he was a supervisor. He added very quickly, before I had said anything, 'But I didn't pick her up until after the camp had finished!' as if he was anxious to defend himself against any notion that he had infringed ethical rules and to say to me that there, too, he knew what he was about.

Ludo had returned to France for good from his American school at the age of 15. He had gone into the French third grade and aimed at studying to become an interpreter. As an adolescent he was no more of a problem to himself than he was to his parents - something that is sufficiently rare to be worth singling out and applauding as yet another benefit due to the indirect and probably behaviouristic-style 'therapy' that he was given by that remarkable school. We all know today what is meant by adolescent malaise

– or 'crisis' as some like to call it, suggesting that it is inevitable and must always be momentous. It is the period, dreaded by parents, when everything that was held over from the early years comes back in force and demands to be purged or resolved. Although parents of the last few generations have seen fit to move away from landmarks decreed obsolete (even though they had proved their worth in practice) and have been carried from one parenting fad to another, the upbringing they have tended to give their children has had many points of weakness and left in suspense a whole host of issues that go on begging responses.

It is not my intention to elaborate a great deal here on adolescence, now regularly viewed as tricky if not problematic, save to say that its character is not accidental but directly dependent upon the way in which things have happened in the very early years. The argument in favour of this view is so strong that it justifies both an emphasis on the importance of early education and on the firmness with which children should be handled even from their tenderest age. Yet another motoring analogy: you cannot drive staring at the bonnet; you need to look as far ahead as you can. It is enough for parents to hold such an attitude for their children to pick it up without any words being said. But insofar as that particular attitude has not always been held, what we regularly discover today is the intensity of fear that adolescents unwittingly experience. Indeed the fear they inhabit can be sufficiently intense as to set off fear in others, with their parents in the front line. This itself is of negative value, since parental fear feeds back greater fear to children, and a sort of vicious circle is set up of escalating fear that can even infect teachers and medical staff enlisted to help. That the access to adolescence is always accompanied by fear is a banality. When parents stand before their adolescent, it is for them like facing their newborn. They are suddenly afraid of a supposed fragility; they fear causing damage, causing harm through their own awkwardness, traumatizing[38] him or her, persuaded – wrongly – of the adolescent's genius and capacity to find the solutions to his or her malaise alone. Adolescents themselves sometimes try hard to ask for directives, a framework, a firmness of language that might tell

---

[38] Undoubtedly the technical term most frequently imported into popular parental parlance in contemporary France.

Fathers and Mothers

them what to do and what direction to take, at the risk of rejecting it all and setting their face against it. They scream, 'I'm not a baby!' Vain words that can nevertheless strike home with such unintended effect that the parents are confirmed in an attitude of wondering paralysis. The malaise then only deepens. Because this is such a common human pattern, rites of passage, now abandoned among us, were developed from time immemorial and in all latitudes. Yet it is not the abandonment of such rituals that accounts for the increased fear in today's adolescents. It is what comes back so intensely from the depths of their childhood, against which rites would probably be of little effect. And what comes back so strongly today, much more strongly than in times gone by, concerns the relationship to time and death. Adolescence has always been, more than any other stage in life, the age when individuals fear plunging ahead: they leave it till the last possible moment to abandon childhood, even when they have finally managed to turn the corner and enter what is known as adulthood. For to bow to that necessity is also to accept once and for all the directional logic of time, with death at the end. It is to turn the back once and for all upon the maternal discourse that has always subtly denied that dimension and may go on doing so.

A real-life and moving illustration of all this appears in Pierre Clastres's *Chronique des Indiens Guayaki*.[39] 'One day,' we read, 'the father decides that the time of childhood is over for his son.' There follows a description of the rite that then takes place, including the following passage, which seems to me highly significant:

> And for the first time ... the *kybuchu* [boys between seven and eight years old, the age regarded as adolescent] sing timidly; their still untrained mouths modulate the men's *prerä* [chant restricted to men]. Yonder the hunters make reply with their own chant encouraging that of the future *beta pou* [new initiates]. This goes on for quite some time; round about them are the silent night and glowing fires. Then, like a protest, like a complaint of regret and suffering, the voices of

---

[39] Paris, 1972. I am responsible for the definitions in square brackets in the long quotation. [There is an English translation by Paul Auster, entitled: *Chronicle of the Guayaki Indians*. London, 1998 -trans.]

the women are heard - the mothers of the young boys. They know that they are going to lose their children, that soon these will be men worthy of respect rather than their *memby* [little child]. Their *chenga ruvara* [chant restricted to women] expresses the last attempt to hold back time; it is also the first chant of their separation; it celebrates a break. The half-chanted, half-weeping refusal of the women to accept the inevitable is a challenge to the men: their *prerä* gets louder and stronger, aggressively masking, almost, the humble complaint of the women who hear their sons chanting like men. The youngsters understand the importance of the battle between the men and the women, and this encourages them to keep vigorously to their own role. Tonight they are no longer a part of the group. They no longer belong to the world of the women; they are no longer their mother's. But they are not yet men; they belong nowhere, and for that reason occupy the *enda ayiä* [the hut of initiation that the young men have built themselves]: a place of difference, a space of transition, a sacred frontier between a before and an after for those who are going to die and be reborn. The fires burn down; the voices die; everyone goes to sleep.

It is easy to understand how such rites of initiation achieve an intelligent metabolization of what is in process. It is even easier to see their global function, i.e., they subject postulants to the law that governs the species, and they remind adults present that the law concerns them no less also.

Our western societies have absolutely nothing along these lines to offer the adolescent. They encourage the sublimation of adolescent drives through the prestige attributed to learning or sporting activity. But such substitutes never tackle the basic problem. The result is that the problem continues, gnawing away and disregarding period, place, or social context. It is not so much that we have lost the notion of regulatory strategies to cope with this sort of phenomenon. Rather, we are dumbfounded by changes that crank up the difficulty, already enormous to begin with, to full power. Not to mention there are always those who gain from it. Hence the market has readily identified the opportunities, developing a vast panoply of articles intended to help if nothing else by inventing fashions, allegiances, addictions, and groups. For you do not trifle with the fear of death: every claim to combat it is worth a try.

It is of course quite possible to agree with this collection of arguments and still opt for a passive attitude that refuses in spite of everything to describe itself as fatalistic, preferring to present itself as realistic, and soliciting for itself esteem and sympathy for its apparent openness of spirit. The line it seems to follow is this: given that the former, traditional, patriarchal family models, as advocates of this approach choose to call them, did not offer their members one hundred per cent protection from the ravages of neurosis - what terrifying illusion is it that nurtures the notion that there could be an absence of neurosis, may I ask? - why deplore the possible ravages of the models that have been and will be invented, even if the damage they do is infinitely worse than what went before? This is the line one never ceases to hear from any number of journalists, sociologists, politicians, and even therapists of various sorts, who all campaign for the calm acceptance of all models without discrimination, as if implying that all, and nothing, is valid. They rule out any attempt to sort the various attitudes into some kind of hierarchy or advocate the least line of conduct whatever. The nostalgia for anarchy, which in this case assumes the mask of a respect for freedom, is reminiscent of the illusion of omnipotence wielded by sucklings. It is true that it is best to be like that, since the Zeitgeist is so intolerant of other opinions. And yet it would have you believe that the species, which probably has tens if not hundreds of thousands of years of potential development ahead of it, has attained the summit of its evolution with such a paltry discovery. I have personally lost count of the number of labels that have been attached to the line that I have continued to follow. But it is easier to be indifferent to what you observe in the aftermath than to something you actually witness taking place. The emotion an individual has when he sees the body of a murder victim bears no comparison to what he would feel if he witnessed the murder. In the former case, he knows that there is very little he can do, except press for an investigation which may or may not reveal the identity of the perpetrator. In the latter, he will be deeply distressed, being moved by the desire to intervene to save the victim from the attack and at the same time terrified by the violence shown by the aggressor, for people are always quite naturally frightened to draw fire to themselves. Even so, they have a choice between going on their way with as low a profile as possible, or of doing something, if only to shout out, even though they know it is likely no more to stop the murderer than summon the indifferent crowd. I have always chosen to shout out. I do so yet again, and it does not concern me that the reaction may be negative.

Part of the work of this book has been to show how, at some stage in life, albeit in a gender-differentiated fashion, the awareness that time is passing and the fear of death, which are as links in a chain, enter the life of the individual. Perhaps I have now said enough on that subject to be able to suggest one means in which these elements of consciousness may be better managed over the coming generations in order to lighten the load that human beings' experience of their new lot over the last two or three decades has placed upon them. The means I have to suggest would be extremely simple to put into effect. To the extent that it could moreover be easily integrated into publicly accepted ways of doing things, it ought not to create any problems. What, in sum, does it consist of, and how is it relevant?

What I have to suggest consists simply in a return to the feeding of infants at relatively fixed times and according to fixed quantities, and not, as now, on demand and with no restriction as to quantity. It will be said that this is a tiny detail, such a ridiculous detail that no one will think it important, still less see how it could be important. That is true. And yet it is precisely the sort of detail that may radically modify states of mind. Why? Because, very simply, it marks a change from a total absence of rules to a regime of rules, and from a state of anarchy to one of a small number of landmarks.

When I trained as a paediatrician, we had to absorb a whole raft of detailed information setting out strict rules on infant feeding. It was imperative to calculate the daily ration due to each child by adding 200 grammes to one tenth of the baby's weight, dividing this into six meals a day during the first two months of life, five meals a day during the following four months, and finally into four meals a day for the remainder of the first year. Breastfed babies followed exactly the same regime: the quantity given was checked by regular weighing before and after the feeds, which were all precisely timed - in fact, I hardly think we need to return to that degree of rigidity in regard to breastfeeding. Apart from this, parents were given complete latitude to do as they saw fit with their children. Those measures were not invented out of nothing. They were the result of much laboratory research calculating the precise alimentary needs of babies. Paediatricians were still working within a current that began in the nineteenth century, when their profession started, the object of which was first and foremost to reduce infant mortality. Some might mischievously interject here that it was still the period of the patriarchal family and of the 'order' that it had never ceased to impose - to which I should have to reply, 'Yes, and why not?', because what is at issue is precisely the gift of time that fathers have always unwittingly provided and that now needs restoring. It is worth mentioning in passing that babies raised in that way did not die like flies and, outside of the infectious diseases that have been eradicated by vaccination rather than any dietetic revolution, they were as beautiful and healthy as any born today. And - I ought to add - they were calmer. I remember working as an intern for months on end in charge of two wards totalling eighty cots in all. I was never subjected to ear-splitting crying from those infants, even though they were all fed at fixed hours.

Why did things change? The answer lies in a range of reasons linked to factors of various kinds. With the benefit of hindsight, let me risk citing the fact that the generation of medical professionals, and especially paediatricians, who had known war and privation alongside the positive effects of maternal concern and protection, had undoubtedly developed greater empathy for mothers. I would add that the circumstances of the time merely reinforced paediatricians' natural propensity insofar as people do not choose to become doctors in any field unless they have a strong maternal element in their makeup, and this is true of men as well as women. This increased empathy was, moreover, in tune with a profound change in the general outlook during those times and was doubtless fed by it - let us not forget that universal female suffrage in France similarly dates from the end of the war (1945). This basic new reality was probably enhanced, too, by various other factors of varying importance. Our natural laziness coupled with the absence of any explicit explanation for the regulated feeding I have just described - it was only to satisfy my own natural curiosity that, much later, I researched that background - encouraged us to dispense with rules that had been specific to our practice. Then there were two other small events which entered the picture, albeit of unequal importance.

The first of these was the translation into French of an American bestseller, which gained a similarly large readership in France. For a long time we called it simply, 'Spock'.[40] The author, an American paediatrician, was one day invited by a publisher friend to write a book for the general public. He himself admitted that he had somewhat boned up on Freud in order to write the upbringing part of his book, as he was not very familiar with that area. His adaptation of Freud led to the child's becoming an object of fascination and immediately promoted the ideology of the child as sovereign. Yet Spock himself had taken care to specify in the early editions of his book that once the child was three months old it was necessary to stop being flexible and to return to firmness. That part of the message was not heard and was quickly abandoned.

Meanwhile, for paediatric professionals in France the story was very similar. The year 1961 saw the translation into French of a paediatric textbook that every French paediatrician ought to be aware of, since it gets quoted all the time - the celebrated 'Nelson'.[41] It should be explained that when Nelson was published in French, the aura of the USA had never shone more brightly, and in France we had nothing so comprehensive or so reasonably priced. Among other things, Nelson, like Spock, recommended demand feeding. Circumstances thus conspired not merely to allow but to positively encourage the abandonment of earlier rules that now seemed out of date. At the same time, this was a development that certainly chimed with paediatricians. There were a number of reasons for this. In the first place, as I have already intimated, people's choice of profession is not a chance matter; nor do doctors once qualified choose their particular specialism idly. While paediatrics is undoubtedly fascinating at an speculative level, it is nonetheless a specialism that puts children at the very core of its exercise. It

---

[40] Dr Benjamin Spock, *Comment soigner et éduquer son enfant?* (Paris: Marabout, 1965). The original American edition dates from the end of the Second World War [*The Common Sense Book of Baby and Child Care* (New York, 1946); first UK edition, 1955—trans.]. It reappeared in many formats, including by Belfond in 1979 and Livre de Poche in 1982. It finally spawned a vast eponymous enterprise with a worldwide reach marketing both the book and products deriving from it.

[41] Waldo E. Nelson, *Traité de pédiatrie* (Paris: Maloine, 1961). [Translation by Noël Gofstein of Textbook of Pediatrics (7th ed., Philadephia, 1959)—trans.]

is well known that paediatricians are considered, by mothers especially but also more widely, as bordering on diviners or demi-gods. Do they not, after all, have substantial knowledge of that most precious and mysterious thing, the child? They must surely know and love children a great deal to devote their lives to treating them and above all else have no fear of them. What better ally can the parent have than the paediatrician? The paediatrician is the ideal 'parent', upon whom the parent can self-project, or otherwise depend, if prepared to follow blindly what that ideal 'parent' recommends. Yet something little known and even less voiced is the reality that all paediatricians have accounts of their own to settle with their own childhoods and with childhood in general. So much so that the paediatrician will be, all at the same time and in no particular order or hierarchy, the baby or child being treated, the child's father and, pre-eminently, the child's mother, if not the mother of both of the parents. The paediatrician will be all of those things after his or her own fashion, which will never exactly coincide with that of any paediatrician colleague. Hence it happens that one paediatrician will get on better, because of his or her particular style, than another with a particular group within a common client-base. Since most of the paediatrician's interlocutors will be mothers, it will not be surprising if he or she naturally, even unwittingly, slips into a marketing attitude that consists in being in sympathy with them and probably ratifying their ways of dealing. Add to this the fact that paediatricians are given no instruction in relationships and are never sensitized to the relational dimension of their practice, and it becomes easy to see how susceptible they may be to prevailing nostrums regarding which they do not have the same level of critical sense as achieved in other areas. Hence, for example, the fascination (reported earlier, in chapter 3) of 1960s paediatricians with African models that were imported as paradigms and recommended because regarded as natural and therefore healthy. I said earlier what I thought of that, commenting that once ripped from their symbolic context, such models lost all sense.

Historically, the next stage was marked by the events of May 1968 and the developments in French society that ensued, including the finishing blow dealt the father juridically and, in particular, the impetus given to the consumer society. Despite paediatric knowledge that babies are raised in different ways across the globe, the infant milk industry capitalized upon the changes in outlook that were making headway, and their marketing departments did well in exploiting the social context. Although the packaging in which infant milk was supplied continued to carry precise instructions about measuring doses according to age, the industry nonetheless did everything it could to promote demand feeding. The preparation of larger and more frequent bottles, on the pretext that what the baby did not want could be thrown away, necessarily entailed a rise in the volume of milk consumed.

Everything was now ripe for the increasing abandonment of mothers to their own propensities, as well as to the overwhelming sense of isolation and responsibility that went with it. But if now, ultimately, this way of proceeding is to be rejected, no doubt it will be asked whether the return to a more strict and regulated approach to feeding, supposing it is justified, will be physiologically tolerable for the infant.

Tolerable it most certainly will be, since it has been very widely used already without any of the sort of ill effects feared. Indeed it might well help in the avoidance of infantile obesity, as well as providing an ancillary form of treatment for gastro-oesophageal reflux, which is known to respond extremely well to reduced and split feeds.

But, it will be objected, the babies will cry if they are not full. Yes, they will, but not for long. They will certainly want a mouthful more at the end of the feed and will not hesitate to cry. But if they are not given in to, they will understand that their demands will not be satisfied, and will sooner or later stop crying. In other words, so long as they are habituated to their dose, they will end up accepting it. This fact is moreover an argument in favour of the practice. For the frustration that it causes the babies will provide a basis for their future rearing; there is no escaping the equation 'to rear = to frustrate', a truth that is always borne out and from the earliest age. Though a frustration of minor proportion, it nonetheless is an occasion of great benefit, inasmuch as the slight discomfiture it momentarily causes induces by small successive steps a surer perception of the extra-uterine the replacement of the non-time of the virtual womb, oversatisfaction, by the perception of time, whose rhythm ysical sensation.

Fathers and Mothers

If this approach is to be put into practice, it needs to be decided whether it should be from birth or after a certain age - in other words, should there be a return to the prudence of the early editions of Spock? It will also need to be decided whether feeds should be at fixed hours or whether a degree of tolerance is viable. My personal view would tend toward a tolerance of thirty minutes around the theoretical time during the first two months, with strictness as to quantities. Thereafter, I would suggest bringing down the tolerance to ten minutes, and being prepared to make the baby wait or wake the baby up as necessary. Again, I would urge firmness with regard to quantities. Once habits have been established, the move to diversified feeding should similarly obey precise rules; taking into account the contemporary view that it should not occur too early in order to obviate the development of allergies, this too will further accustom the child to temporal rhythms. A habit of sorts will thus have been given and taken. The necessary respect of time that will have slipped in between the mother and the child will restore the child to time, the sense of which is a vital need and something that the young have seriously lacked these last few decades. Children restored to time will develop less addicted to pleasure. They will be able to live temporal emptiness without feeling themselves invaded by fear of death. They will no longer be the sort of tyrants one sees every day. Though not lacking in personality, they will better accept boundaries and discipline. Because of all that, they will grow into calmer adolescents.

Meanwhile, it is mothers, surely, who will reap the most immediate benefits from a return to stricter ways. There is an analogy, here, with what happens when mothers first place their babies in a day-nursery. They go through, with their baby, what in France is called a 'week of adaptation'.[42] All infant-care professionals, not least nursery personnel, acknowledge, not without empathy, that this 'adaptation' is more problematic for the mothers than for the babies. As in the case of what I am proposing in regard to infant feeding, so in the field of day-nursery care mothers follow an externally

---

[42] A widespread practice in French day-nurseries, the semaine d'adaptation is an introductory week, during which the parent(s) are permitted to stay with their child within the nursery and can share time and exchange information about the child with the staff; the child is explicitly taken leave of by the parent(s) and left with the staff and the other children for longer period' as the week progresses - trans.

applied, socially widely-accepted prescription and are thereby relieved of crushingly burdensome responsibility in an area of everyday life. Aided by a simple and helpful ritual that gives them discreet and effective feedback, they can essentially 'adapt' and at the same time receive reassurance. Need they any more fear that they will be thought 'bad mothers' for placing their child in a nursery? People working with mothers know to what extent they report being tortured by such guilt-ridden fantasy; mothers often think that they need to compensate the quantity of time they spend at work by increasing the quality of the time spent with the child or else contribute a greater intensity of emotional investment. But they need to be reassured on that score. The smiles on their babies' faces as they greet them should give them adequate relief. Moreover, the babies have every reason to smile. Having quit the uterine world for the air-breathing world, they know that they can trust their mothers, something that they will be infinitely readier to do if they have not been condemned through excessive caution to stay welded to them.

There is more that could be said about how such an approach, whose introduction, from all points of view, could only be beneficial. Is it vital to show that it fits entirely with the Law of the Species, which no one seems to want to take the responsibility of putting into practice? Not really. Encouragement is better than imposition. The way that people automatically fasten their seat-belts when driving these days is demonstration enough that sustained encouragement can lead to voluntary adoption of a desirable practice. The community, in taking on wider responsibility and new functions, would in effect be carrying out the duty that pertained to the fathers whom it had wilfully dismissed. Mothers need no longer feel split between their own deep-down propensity and the need to take account of the possible reactions of a partner belonging to a subspecies ignorant of what motivated the subspecies to which she belonged. The eternal battle between the two subspecies could gradually calm down to everyone's benefit. Mothers might view their partners differently, and in turn their partners might safely opt for the sort of attitude they would like to have. Mothers could resume with their partners the contacts necessary for him to reinvest in the woman that is within each one them. More relaxed and more valued sexual activity within the couple would contribute to protect them both from all that, in relation to either of them, might suddenly come charging out of the furthest reaches of their past. For it is from there that the failure of the solution, if it is to fail, will come.

It would surprise me if this suggestion could win over the psychology professionals who would doubtless judge that it would change little and that they would still have just as many children to treat. But I do not think that is a correct assessment. For even if such a measure is unable - thankfully! - to block the transmission of the ravages of a history, the effect of that transmission will certainly be different. When a past history breaks upon a being who has been rendered anxious and fragile by external contingencies - upon one lost without landmarks in the desert of their own future, as also that of their child - its discharge is vast and ever-increasing. The child takes the full impact of it if enclosed within it. But when, on the other hand, time with its precise rhythms is allowed to work its magic, the child will end up being able to see, even if only confusedly, out of the uterine world, and that minimal distance will serve as protection. Meanwhile the mother, herself less burdened, no longer runs the same risk of stress that caused her to clash with her partner and possibly join with him in an outbidding exercise from which they can both, necessarily, only suffer.

Of course, it is possible to go on making fun of such a notion. It is possible to go on being sceptical. To refuse. But what would it cost to try it? There is nothing to lose from it, and everything to gain...